Intangible Capital

Dedication

To my recently expanded family:

My wife, Doris

My two sons, Russell and Jeffrey

And the exciting additions of my two new daughters-in-law,
Karina and Sonja

Intangible Capital

Its Contribution to Economic Growth, Well-being and Rationality

John F. Tomer

Professor of Economics, Manhattan College, New York

with a chapter by Bart Eikelenboom

Edward Elgar

Cheltenham, UK • Northampton, MA, USA

Published by
Edward Elgar Publishing Limited
The Lypiatts
15 Lansdown Road
Cheltenham
Glos GL50 2JA
UK

Edward Elgar Publishing, Inc.
William Pratt House
9 Dewey Court
Northampton
Massachusetts 01060
USA

A catalogue record for this book
is available from the British Library

Library of Congress Control Number: 2008927970

ISBN 978 1 84720 088 4

Printed and bound in Great Britain by MPG Books Ltd, Bodmin, Cornwall

Contents

Figures

Tables

Boxes

Acknowledgments

Although writing a book is a fairly solitary activity, it is important to note the support, helpfulness and appreciation of others who have made my research work more pleasant and manageable.

Dick Hattwick, former editor of the *Journal of Socio-Economics*, is especially noteworthy for the interest he has taken in the earlier phases of my research. As *Journal of Socio-Economics* editor, he was able to appreciate my article, 'Good habits and bad habits: a new age socio-economic model of preference formation,' and he decided to publish it. A slightly revised version of this article appears here as Chapter 10.

Morris Altman is my friend and fellow traveler; he is the current editor of the *Journal of Socio-Economics*. Morris has been tireless in promoting and developing the *Journal of Socio-Economics* and behavioral economics in general. Morris seems to have appreciated my research and has been instrumental in getting a number of my articles published in the *Journal of Socio-Economics*. A number of these articles appear here in slightly revised form as chapters.

The late Ken Koford, former editor of the *Eastern Economic Journal*, recognized the value of my article, 'Personal capital and emotional intelligence: increasingly important sources of economic growth.' He provided very valuable editorial assistance that led to revisions and ultimately to this article's publication in the *Eastern Economic Journal* in 2003. That article appears here in slightly revised form as Chapter 6.

John Davis has been interested in and supportive of my research for a long time. During his tenure as editor of the *Review of Social Economy*, he was very helpful in the process of publishing my article, 'Human well-being: a new approach based on overall and ordinary functionings' in his journal. Unfortunately, he was not able to prevail over two referees' objections in the case of another article.

Over the years, I have benefited from the support and interest in my research of Shoshana Grossbard, Gary Lynne, Shlomo Maital, Mark Pingle and many others in the Society for the Advancement of Behavioral Economics, the association in which I have most actively participated.

I am indebted to Manhattan College for granting me two year-long sabbatical leaves, one in 1999–2000 and the other in 2005–6, that enabled me to accomplish key parts of this book's research.

I appreciate the interest that the Rensselaer Polytechnic Institute Economics Department showed in my research and that they invited me to present several of my research papers at their seminars during each of my sabbaticals. They were generous in giving me permission to be a RPI Visiting Scholar enabling me, among other things, to have full access to their library during these sabbatical periods.

Tom Sadler is the coauthor of our article, 'Why we need a commitment approach to environmental policy,' also appearing here as Chapter 13. It was a pleasure to know Tom at Manhattan College and to interact with him on this research. It is regrettable that he is no longer at Manhattan College.

Last, but not least, is my beautiful, loving wife, Doris, who in addition to being supportive of my research has done much to create the kind of home environment that has enabled me to be productive in my research.

PART I

Intangible capital

Part I introduces and carefully defines intangible capital along with all its component types of capital.

1. Introduction

> In modern business practice, capital is distinguished into two . . . categories of assets, tangible and intangible.
>
> **Thorstein Veblen 1919: 352–3**

> In the early days at least, this [intangible assets] is far and away the most important and consequential category of the community's assets
>
> **ibid, 325–6**

INTRODUCTION

Unfortunately, the economics profession has not done very much to develop the early insights of Thorstein Veblen. True, practically all economists (and other social scientists) accept the view that investment in things like education and training creates a human type of capital which yields returns to the people in whom it is embodied. But when it comes to the noncognitive or more intangible forms of human capital, economists generally do not accept that these intangible forms of capital are relevant to their research.

The great recent interest of noneconomist social scientists in intangible capital, particularly social capital (SC), has, however, caused more than a few economists to pay attention. Nevertheless most mainstream economists who have bothered to consider SC remain skeptical of its importance. For example, while admitting the 'plausibility that social networks can affect economic performance,' Kenneth Arrow (2000: 3) doubts that the SC concept can be made 'operational for the purposes of analysis and policy.' Similarly, Robert Solow (2000: 6) thinks that SC writers 'are trying to get at something difficult, complicated, and important,' but he also believes they are trying 'to gain conviction from a bad analogy.' On the other hand, Joseph Stiglitz (2000: 59), while admitting that 'SC is a concept with a short and already confused history,' believes that 'SC is a very useful concept but an extremely complex one, in which different perspectives have much to contribute' (p. 67).

As has been widely noted, for SC (just one, albeit important, component of intangible capital (IC)), there are many different definitions and disciplinary perspectives. This proliferation of different types of capital in social science literatures has been interesting, at times exciting, but often frustrating and confusing. There is an obvious need for sorting through all these capital categories to determine what is valid, useful, and true to the meaning of capital as productive capacity. In clarifying the nature of IC and its component types of capital, this book seeks to understand IC as long lasting human capacity that is at once consistent with the core concept of capital in economics, but at variance with the narrow interpretation of capital generally taken by mainstream economists. On the other hand, some noneconomists may find the concept of IC used here too narrow or too economic for their purposes. This is understandable. Nevertheless, a prime purpose of this book is to indicate the importance of IC by demonstrating how utilizing the IC concept can provide new understanding of a range of problems and issues that have at least a partially economic nature. In its emphasis on the economic or socio-economic aspect of IC, this book arguably ignores some interesting and fruitful noneconomic applications. This is not to say that these are unimportant or incorrect; they are just not the focus of this book.

As later chapters will spell out in detail, IC refers to the many things that are in humans or in their relationships, things that enable people to perform well in their work situations, and thus be productive and successful. It also refers to things that enable people to be rational and experience well-being. IC certainly includes things like standard education and training which provide knowledge and know-how, generally things with a high cognitive component. This is the well recognized and widely accepted part of IC. Another part relates to the noncognitive qualities of people. Some people perform better at work because they are more motivated, more persistent, more empathetic, manage their emotions better, manage their social relationships better, are more patient, more focused on goals, are more tough mindedly competitive, and so on. Some groups of workers produce more because they have developed relationships with each other that channel their energies and communications in positive, constructive ways. Workers' social networks and the organizational structures that control them insure that communications occur easily and are well directed. The quality of these relationships may contribute to cooperative, coordinated efforts that lower the cost of getting things accomplished. In sum, when workers are equipped with the requisite knowledge and training, when they have developed the necessary personal qualities, and when they have developed appropriate organizational relationships, assuming they have been inspired and focused by strong leaders, these workers have the capacity for superior performance. In the absence of these IC qualities, these workers' productive capacity and performance are likely to be severely limited. An important purpose of this book is to provide a framework for thinking about the whole range of these long lasting human qualities, and thereby to enable clear economic thinking about these phenomena.

The IC topic is part of behavioral economics; it is a part, thus far, relatively lacking in appreciation. Hopefully, by bringing our analytical tools and interdisciplinary perspectives to bear on IC, it will be possible to bring the human factor related to productivity more fully into economic analysis than has heretofore been the case. Also, greater understanding of the intangible human factor should add to our appreciation of what determines human well-being and what contributes to truly rational human behavior.

There are many good reasons to be skeptical about the value of the IC concept. First, most of us have a clear understanding of how machines can raise productivity, either by saving labor or by enabling production that humans could not otherwise do. It is much less clear how human qualities and relationships can contribute to productivity. Thus, one of the purposes of this book is to indicate how the IC components enable greater productivity and can be either a substitute for or complement to tangible capital. Another reason to be skeptical about IC is that by its very nature it is difficult to observe and measure. Relatedly, it is difficult to incorporate into economic theory, which often finds mathematical expression. If it cannot be quantified and put into an equation, does it exist? Economists who adopt a strongly positivistic orientation may answer no.

Further, there are other traditions in economics that reinforce the neglect of the intangible human factor. Traditionally, productive wealth is thought of as tangible, something that is owned and traded. The owners of productive wealth are known as capitalists who buy the services of labor. Most people think in terms of production by means of capital and labor, two distinct and opposed entities. When the capital term is extended to the intangible human aspects, it inevitably blurs these traditional associations. But that's not necessarily a bad thing. The breakdown of these traditional patterns and distinctions is one reason why it would be good to recognize and utilize the IC concept. Juxtaposing capital and labor, even investment and consumption, as has been done in the past, is becoming ever more counterproductive to understanding the economic world of today.

It is interesting to note that there is evidence that intangible human factors of all kinds are becoming relatively more important contributors to output compared to tangible factors. Notably, intangible factors seem to be increasingly important in advanced industrial economies. At the same time, there is also reason to believe that IC is critical to less developed countries' efforts to achieve sustained economic development. Lack of critical intangible human competencies, not lack of tangible resources, arguably is the biggest roadblock to these countries' efforts to close the gap between themselves and their more developed brethren.

PLAN OF THE BOOK

Chapter 2 is devoted to carefully defining IC and its component capital types. The purpose of this chapter is to develop a comprehensive and unifying conception of IC. This chapter indicates how the IC definition is consistent with and integrated with definitions of tangible capital, human capital and social capital among others. Particularly important here are a number of the more intangible components of IC such as noncognitive human capital, personal capital, moral capital, and cultural capital.

Chapter 3 deals with the contribution that IC makes to economic growth. The first half explains how investment in the major components of IC (human capital in individuals, social capital and organizational capital) contributes to productivity growth and makes possible economic growth. The second half of the chapter reviews pertinent empirical findings on IC's contribution to economic growth. The main findings of nine studies of the effect of SC on economic growth and performance are summarized. In essence these researchers find that SC variables have a highly significant (economically and statistically) effect on economic growth and performance, which is independent of and strong relative to the effect of the standard human capital variables. Also findings relevant to the contribution of noncognitive human capital to economic growth are reviewed. The findings indicate that noncognitive skills/traits are an important and neglected determinant of earnings.

Chapter 4 concerns organizational capital's contribution to the economic performance of the innovative businesses that invest in it. More specifically, the chapter explains how businesses which adopt high performance work systems, involving clusters of innovative human resource practices, are able to achieve superior economic performance. In doing this, the chapter draws on two largely separate literatures, the human resource management literature and economic theory, notably X-efficiency theory. A key part of the explanation relates to the advantages that an involvement-oriented organization has over a control-oriented organization.

Chapter 5 is an empirical study by Bart Eikelenboom of Nyenrode University in the Netherlands. Eikelenboom's study is unique and notable in that it utilizes data relating to the organizational capital or capabilities of business units in Netherlands-based multinational corporations and their economic performance. He finds a significant, positive relationship between their organizational capital and their economic performance. This finding constitutes important support for the notion that investment in intangible capital is important for the performance of business organizations, and thus presumably for a nation's economic growth.

Chapter 6 concerns personal capital, a noncognitive type of human capital. It carefully defines and explains the nature of personal capital, especially its most important component, emotional intelligence. The chapter utilizes Daniel Goleman's conception of emotional intelligence and explains why a variety of human emotional competencies are crucially important for individual and company success. Based on the chapter's arguments, evidence from Goleman's studies, and other findings provided in Chapter 3, there is strong support for the view that investment in personal capital provides an explanation for the part of economic growth unexplained by the growth in the more tangible factors. In other words, personal capital is an important source of the economy's performance, quite separate from the influence of standard, cognitive-types of human capital.

Chapter 7 involves an application of the intangible capital concept to understanding the problematic aspects of the late-twentieth-century Eastern European transition from socialism to capitalism. The essence of the transition has generally been conceived of as the substitution of the organizational structures and the legal, financial and political relationships of capitalism for those of socialism, that is, a substitution of capitalism's hard features for socialism's. But this conception of socio-economic systems leaves out the important soft aspects such as social capital and personal capital. These important soft factors such as attitudes, behavioral orientations, values and beliefs must mesh with the hard elements of a socio-economic system, otherwise the system's performance will be impaired. Unfortunately, the transition processes in most of these countries followed the neo-liberal radical reform strategy in which the hard features were changed very quickly without attention to the soft features. The result tended to be a severe shock which greatly retarded the transition process. If the architects of change had been informed by a transition model that included the soft, intangible capital factors, it is likely that the transitions would have been less problematic and would have achieved greater economic success. The socio-economic model developed in this chapter, first explains the differing degrees of transition success among Eastern Europe nations and second, suggests alternatives to neo-liberal transition strategy.

Human well-being is ultimately about living a good life. Chapter 8 concerns the key elements in a person's life that determine how well off he or she is. Contrary to the welfarist approach's emphasis on material factors, the analysis of this chapter indicates why certain intangible factors in a person's life are essential to well-being. The welfarist approach does well in accounting for the tangible means to a good life, but it misses much that is important. Even Sen's valuable functionings approach that considers people's intrinsically important doings and beings does not capture all of the higher, broader aspect of life. The approach developed in this chapter modifies Sen's functionings approach and considers a person's higher human functionings as well as his or her ordinary, lower functionings. At the heart of this approach is the idea that raising a society's level of well-being requires a variety of kinds of intangible capital formation, particularly investment in personal capital and social capital.

Chapter 9 develops a socio-economic model of addictive behavior that explains why, contrary to the mainstream economic model of Gary Becker and others, addiction is not an example of rational economic behavior. Addiction is a harmful habit that involves dependence (often on a commodity), compulsive consumption and craving, and usually severe withdrawal symptoms. The model is designed to explain the behavior of addicts or would-be addicts and understand why their decision making is often not rational in the sense of weighing expected benefits and costs in a careful, unbiased way. According to the model, addictions develop in people who have 'significant imbalances' and who encounter situations where addictive goods are available, affordable, and attractive. The five external and internal influences that explain an individual's degree of imbalance and the factors that modify the strength of the imbalance are:

1. the individual's personal capital;
2. the individual's social capital;
3. the individual's consumption capital;
4. the societal and community influences on the individual; and
5. the stressfulness of the individual's current life situation.

In essence, individuals with a degree of imbalance above a certain threshold are likely to have a biased perception of what the addictive good offers, tending to overvalue the expected benefits and undervalue the expected costs.

Chapter 10 develops a model of preference formation, a model explaining how a person's preferences for consumer goods change over time and may change for the better or worse. At the heart of the model are four types of preferences (corresponding to four selves): actual preferences, metapreferences, true preferences and unrestrained preferences. An individual's initial actual preferences reflecting their investment in consumption capital are likely to change to the extent that they differ either from one's metapreferences or one's unrestrained preferences. Temptations from the latter could lead to a deterioration of actual preferences. Or the intrapsychic stress that occurs when metapreferences are significantly out of synch with actual preferences could lead to improved actual preferences. A person's actual preferences improve when they change toward true preferences, the unique set of preferences that represent what is really and truly the best for that person. Other factors in the model include first, an individual's predispositions reflecting their endowment of personal capital, and second, the external influences on preference formation reflecting systematic societal or cultural influences. Probably the most novel, and presumably most controversial element in the model, is the idea that everyone has a true self with true preferences and that one's well-being is inversely related to the gap between one's actual and true preferences.

Chapter 11 builds on the concepts introduced in Chapter 10 and develops a normative conception of rationality, true rationality, that is arguably more appropriate than the conception used by most economists. This alternative concept of rationality integrates the familiar instrumental rationality (applying reason to choose in order to maximize one's satisfactions given one's preferences) with rationality of ends (applying reason to select the ends that are really best). If true preferences represent what is really right and best for a person, not only in the short-term but in the long-term, not only materially and psychologically but morally and spiritually, then the ultimate of rationality, true rationality, means choosing in line with true preferences. Our analysis of true rationality implies that with respect to certain goods there is a likelihood that people will fail to make decisions that fully reflect what is really in their best interests. People may, for example, consume far too little of goods that are really good for them. In this case, there is an argument for government provision of merit goods to rectify this situation. If one aspires to behave in a truly rational manner, this implies that one must transform one's actual preferences in the direction of one's true preferences, in the process overcoming one's neurotic behavior and gaining maturity, emotional balance, and wisdom. In other words, a person would have to make a significant investment in intangible capital, notably personal capital.

Chapters 2 through 11 have either explained about the nature of IC or explained about its contribution to economic growth, well-being, or rationality. Chapter 12 builds on these explanations and develops their implications for government policy. In a number of cases considered earlier, there has been good reason to believe that a particular kind of IC is both critically important for economic growth (or possibly well-being or rationality) and experiencing some kind of blocked growth or development. Further, due to the blockage, the economy is not likely to be realizing its potential. Clearly in such a situation, it makes sense for the government to facilitate a process by which the critical IC formation takes place. The government actions that make the most sense resemble a kind of industrial policy in which the government is performing a 'coaching' role, helping economic entities improve their behavior and performance through IC formation. The governmental coach typically helps individuals or firms develop the pertinent intangible human capacities by nurturing, facilitating, prodding and otherwise encouraging them. Because the contributions of the more intangible forms of IC are relatively less understood and accepted, it is anticipated that persuading people concerning these government policy implications will not be as easy as it is in the case of standard human capital.

Chapter 13 is an example of applied economic research relating to the government's environmental policy; it is also related to investment in IC. This chapter (coauthored by Thomas Sadler) proposes a new class of environmental policies based on a 'commitment approach' (CA) rather than conventional 'control-oriented' policies which rely on the use of regulatory financial incentives to induce improvements in businesses' environmental behavior. While control-oriented policies were designed for firms presumed to behave like the firms of neoclassical economic theory, policies based on a CA are designed for the increasingly prevalent high performance organizations which are capable not only of innovative behavior but of making principled commitments, taking responsibility and acting in a trustworthy manner. A CA policy is a nonregulatory approach in which firms are self-regulated. The CA is only for firms that are able first to make a commitment to high environmental performance and second to develop the capabilities to meet these commitments. Part of the relevant capabilities are intangible human capacities (IC) necessary for carrying out these firms' business and environmental commitments. The environmental protection agency that administers the CA would be charged with selecting the particular 'high commitment' firms that would be subject to the policy. The potential of the CA is great. The high commitment, high performance organizations which are selected for a CA can be expected to make high environmental performance choices that directly benefit themselves as well as their communities and societies. The initiative and responsibility for dealing with environmental problems would be with the firms, not the government agency, albeit the agency's facilitative role may be important.

The IC concept has implications for economics as a discipline. Chapter 14 is concerned with one aspect of this, namely the concept of human nature in the different schools of economic thought. This chapter compares economic man, the concept of man at the heart of mainstream economics, with a variety of heterodox men (the conceptions of man found in the writings of different heterodox economists) each of whom is more human than economic man but still not fully human. The backdrop for this comparison is Ken Wilber's (1996) comprehensive view of human nature and the predictable stages of human development he identifies. These different concepts of human nature (economic man and the heterodox men) can be interpreted as humans who have reached different stages of human development, and thus, differ in the extent of their IC (especially personal capital) formation. Economic man, for example, reflects a relatively low stage of human development. Humanistic economic man, on the other hand, arguably reflects the highest level of human development of any of the heterodox men. Employing a fully human concept of man as part of the discipline of economics would be ideal, even if it is understood that humans rarely realize all of their human potential. This is because a broader conception of man makes it easier to conceive of human growth, along with its various types of IC formation, as an inherent part of economic growth and development.

Intangible capital, as the next chapter will make clear, is a variety of intangible human capacities that are critically important for the economy because they are a key source of productivity, well-being, and true rationality. Hopefully, the reader of this book will gain a much greater appreciation not only of the nature of and contribution of these intangible qualities but of their implications for government policy.

REFERENCES

Arrow, Kenneth J. (2000), 'Observations on social capital,' in Partha Dasgupta and Ismail Serageldin, (eds) *Social Capital: A Multifaceted Perspective*, Washington, DC: World Bank.

Solow, Robert M. (2000), 'Notes on social capital and economic performance,' in Partha Dasgupta and Ismail Serageldin (eds) *Social Capital: A Multifaceted Perspective*, Washington, DC: World Bank.

Stiglitz, Joseph E. (2000), 'Formal and informal institutions,' in Partha Dasgupta and Ismail Serageldin (eds) *Social Capital: A Multifaceted Perspective*, Washington, DC: World Bank.

Veblen, Thorstein (1919), *The Place of Science in Modern Civilization and Other Essays*, New York: Viking Press.

Wilber, Ken (1996), *A Brief History of Everything*, Boston, MA: Shambhala.

2. Intangible capital: a comprehensive and unifying view

INTRODUCTION

In any scientific study, it is important to define carefully the important terms. With respect to intangible capital (IC), this is doubly important because of the confusion that has been generated by many different definitions and usages of key terms in the different social science literatures. As has been widely noted, for social capital (SC) (just one, albeit important, component of IC), there are many different definitions and disciplinary perspectives. Baron and Hannan (1994: 1122–4) lament that there has emerged 'a plethora of capitals,' and sociologists 'have begun referring to virtually every feature of social life as a form of capital.' It is quite apparent that not all the IC concepts are equally valid; moreover, there are many confusing and overlapping categories. Obviously, there is a need for clarification and integration. What exactly are the legitimate types of IC? What types are not? And how does it all fit together?

The purpose of Chapter 2 is to develop a comprehensive and unifying conception of IC. Because one of the sources of confusion in the IC and SC literatures is the variety of disciplinary perspectives, this chapter will attempt to lessen that confusion by focusing solely on a definition of IC that would be useful in a study of IC as an explanation of economic growth. This narrowing of focus makes the topic more relevant for economists, but hopefully still of interest to many noneconomists.

TOWARD A BROAD CONCEPTION OF INTANGIBLE CAPITAL

To fully understand intangible capital as a source of economic growth, we need a conception of intangible capital (IC) that is consistent with our conception of the other types of capital, physical, human, social, and so on. What is desired is a broad definition of IC, but not one so broad that it includes intangibles that lack a 'capital' nature. Because this chapter is oriented toward economics, noneconomic applications of IC have not been an important consideration in defining IC. For instance, some applications of social capital (for example, explaining crime, social solidarity, ethical behavior, divorce and social conflict), which sociologists have made, have not been given much consideration here. This is not to say that these noneconomic subjects are unimportant; it is just that they are not the focus of this study because they are not central to economists' concerns. Let's start by carefully defining capital and then human capital. With this in hand, we will have a solid basis for defining IC and its important component types of capital.

Capital

When economists use the term capital, they are likely to be envisioning physical (or tangible) capital, the material resources that contribute to a firm's productive capacity and enable it to realize a flow of future income. As everyone knows, capital in this sense is plant, equipment, tools, vehicles, computers, and more. As the term capital has been extended more and more to less tangible resources, it has become necessary to define capital more abstractly in order to determine whether or not a particular nonphysical resource can legitimately be considered capital. Accordingly, I have previously defined capital as 'lasting productive capacity that is produced and, subsequently, used by economic entities to achieve their purposes' (Tomer 1999a). Ostrom (2000: 174–5) has emphasized that the process of investment, whereby new capital is created, is usually a self-conscious process made in the expectation that productive capacity will be raised, leading in all likelihood to greater future income. Of course, as Ostrom points out, the intended increase in productive possibilities is not always realized. Further, investment in capital, even physical capital, could have a 'dark side' such as when the investment in a deficient nuclear power plant winds up leaking so much radioactive material that the project has net negative benefits to society (p. 175). It should also be emphasized that capital resources are long lasting; they typically endure for much more than one period of time. And it is important to note that bringing capital into existence involves an opportunity cost; there is a sacrifice of what could otherwise have been created with the resources expended. Some have claimed that alienability, the ability to transfer ownership from one party to another, is an essential feature of capital. However, as the term capital has been extended to forms which are embodied in humans, it has become more and more clear that alienability is not an essential aspect of capital. Note also that there are types of physical capital with very limited alienability. In sum, capital is that which is produced by humans, is long lasting, represents productive capacity, involves a cost, and might be invested in on the basis of a self-conscious calculation relating to the future.

Human Capital

Although quite a few well known economists in the history of economic thought (including Adam Smith, Walras and Irving Fisher) have recognized the capital nature of people skills (Kiker 1966: 481), current economic research on human capital owes much to the scholarship of T.W. Schultz, Gary Becker and Jacob Mincer. According to Becker (1964: 1), human capital (HC) refers to the 'resources in people,' typically the skills and knowledge that enable people possessing more of these resources to realize higher monetary and psychic income. Investment in this HC typically takes the form of schooling and on-the-job training. Becker and others recognize that activities such as investment in medical care, migration and search also produce HC, but the lion's share of economic research has focused on education and training. Schultz (1963: 3 as quoted in Sison (2003: 10)) has emphasized that education involves bringing out a person's potential, developing a 'person morally and mentally,' and enabling a person to acquire a vocational or professional discipline. In general, human capital refers to mental, social, and physical attributes that are produced, are embodied in humans, are not alienable, and contribute to a person's productive capacity, enabling the possessor to earn higher income as a consequence.

While economists by and large accept the idea of HC, the standard HC concept that they accept is a fairly limited version of HC. Standard HC refers largely to skills and knowledge, particularly the types acquired using cognitive mental capacities and involving explicit technological knowledge. This kind of HC is relatively tangible because the process of acquiring these abilities is generally observable as is the case, for example, with instruction taking place in a classroom or on the factory floor. Note also that another category of standard HC skills is physical or largely physical in nature (for example, welding, carpentry, brick laying). Standard HC skills, whether involving physical or cognitive-related abilities, are on the tangible side of the HC tangible-to-intangible spectrum. On the other end of the spectrum are the human skills that are largely nonphysical and unrelated to cognitive mental functioning. Human competencies closely related to good mental health (as opposed to physical health) are generally located on the intangible end of the spectrum. To the extent that these latter skills enable a person to be productive, they have a 'capital' nature, the same as more tangible skills. The more intangible HC capacities, however, have not been recognized as part of HC, at least not by the economic mainstream. HC in the broad sense used here also includes HC that is embodied in human relationships (social capital), not just HC embodied in individuals (see below for more on social capital). It should be noted that in a sense all HC is intangible; it is intangible compared to physical capital. But within HC, some types are obviously more intangible. This chapter focuses on the latter and makes the case that economists need to pay much more attention to these than has been the case thus far.

Intangible Capital

Intangible capital as defined here includes all the elements of HC in the broad sense indicated above plus a little more (to be explained later). It is, obviously, a much broader category than standard HC. All of intangible capital (IC) is embodied in or possessed by humans; it is embodied either in particular individuals, in groups, or in the relationships among individuals or groups. The features that comprise IC provide long lasting productive capacity for the economy. In other words, an intangible feature can not be considered to be IC if it is something ephemeral, something likely to change in a day or week. On the other hand, it is possible that certain normally enduring and productive intangibles (which are part of IC) might quickly disappear or appear in the presence of unusual and powerful events. An important consideration in defining IC, and its component types of capital, is that IC should be considered instrumental for achieving economic growth and that it should be distinctly different from the other main factors of production. A related consideration is that the concept should be forged in such a way as to foster appropriate policy measures designed to create more and better IC in order to accelerate economic growth.

Intangible capital is used here as an umbrella concept that includes in whole or in part quite a few different types of capital that are embodied in humans. In particular, IC includes standard HC, social capital, the more intangible types of HC such as personal capital, some parts of intellectual capital, and a number of overlapping categories such as organizational capital, moral capital, ethnic capital, cultural capital, customer capital, and so on. No doubt the most prominent, maybe the most important, of these IC components is social capital (SC). In defining HC and SC and the other main IC components below, IC, the umbrella concept, is in effect being defined.

Social Capital

Social capital has been defined in many different ways, reflecting the different uses made of it by different researchers. Since the interest here is in developing a comprehensive and unifying concept of SC (and thus IC), what is desired is to find the common thread in all or most of these definitions, and thereby, to arrive at a common conception of SC. Let's start by presenting a general definition of SC and then exploring how and to what extent some of the different definitions might be included within it and be consistent with it.

Social capital refers to enduring features of the social landscape that provide productive capacity by enabling important recurrent social activities. Some of these social features might have been created in the distant past or might have been created for reasons unrelated to their economic function. Other SC features might have been created, changed, or augmented via more recent purposeful efforts involving a sacrifice of resources. SC in its pure form is embodied in social relationships, but it may be at least partly embodied in individuals. It can exist within formal organizations, between or among organizations, or entirely outside organization boundaries. SC excludes the formalized features and larger structures of the social and political environment, notably political regimes and basic governmental operations such as court systems and law enforcement. This is because SC, as a type of HC, has to do with the quality of human social functioning, albeit in the context of society's larger formalized structures. Although there is good reason to believe that SC generally makes a net positive contribution to the economy's productive capacity, any particular SC might make a net negative contribution. An example of the latter is the SC of organized crime families. In the case of SC that individuals use to get access to resources or jobs in instances where a zero-sum game is involved, the value of the SC is presumably zero. This is because one person's acquisition of a resource comes at the expense of another, thereby leaving a zero net societal gain.

The SC definitions used by different researchers have three common elements that are useful for comparing them to each other and to the broad definition above. First is the specific form of the social feature constituting SC; second is the intermediate purpose of the SC; and third is its ultimate purpose. For example, a researcher might decide to define SC as social networks (form) that coordinate economic activity (intermediate purpose) in order to foster economic growth (ultimate purpose). James Coleman (1988, 1990) has defined SC as social-structural resources that typically take the form of obligations and expectations, information channels, social norms and effective sanctions, authority relations, family and friendship bonds, and intentional organization (forms) all of which facilitate the actions of persons or collective entities (intermediate purpose). An important focus of Coleman's SC research was explaining schools' educational performance (ultimate performance); his research was not focused on economic growth as an ultimate purpose. In *Making Democracy Work*, Robert Putnam (1993: 167) defined SC as 'features of social organization such as trust, norms and networks,' especially 'norms of reciprocity and networks of civic engagement' (forms), 'that can improve the efficiency of society by facilitating coordinated action' (intermediate purpose). Putnam (pp. 174–5) emphasized the importance of dense horizontal networks within groups and networks of civic engagement across groups that enable wider cooperation (intermediate purpose). He found that Italian regions with more of these civic qualities had relatively more effective public institutions and had greater economic growth (ultimate purposes) (p. 176).

In Bourdieu's (1986: 248–9) view, SC is what individuals possess when they are able to create 'durable networks of more or less institutionalized relationships of mutual acquaintance and recognition [that is connections]' (form) that enables them to gain access to resources or opportunities (intermediate or ultimate purpose). According to Fukuyama (1995: 90), SC is 'an unwritten set of ethical rules or norms that serve as the basis of social trust' (form). Such 'trust can dramatically reduce . . . transaction costs – costs of negotiation, enforcement, and the like – and make possible efficient forms of economic organization that otherwise would be encumbered by extensive rules, contracts, litigation, and bureaucracy' thereby enabling efficient cooperation (intermediate purpose) and fostering economic growth (implicit ultimate purpose). SC, following Ostrom (2000: 176–7), is 'shared knowledge, understandings, norms, rules, and expectations about patterns of interactions that groups of individuals bring to a recurrent activity' (forms). These forms of SC enable the coordination of activities and the overcoming of perverse short-run temptations (intermediate purposes) enabling greater productivity and presumably greater economic growth (ultimate purpose).[1] For Zeleny (1995: 280), the forms of SC include 'the enabling infrastructure of institutions, civic communities, cultural and national cohesion, collective and family values, trust, traditions, respect and sense of belonging' (forms) that enables 'HC to manifest itself effectively,' enables people to work toward common goals, and enables the dismantling of old institutions without conflict and violence (intermediate purposes). These, in turn are expected to produce high national economic performance and wealth (ultimate purpose). According to Serageldin and Grootaert (2000: 44–5), SC consists of institutional arrangements and organizational designs (forms) that 'enhance efficiency, facilitate the exchange of information, promote cooperation between government and industry,' reduce conflicts, and enable decision-making and policy formulation (intermediate purposes) in order to contribute to economic growth (ultimate purpose). Finally, Klaus Nielsen (2002: 3) defines SC as a 'set of norms and social relations embedded in the social structure' (forms) that a 'single subject . . . or a collective subject . . . can make use of at any given moment to achieve desired goals' (intermediate or ultimate purpose).

The two paragraphs above are highly indicative of how the specifics (that is the forms and intermediate purposes) of different SC definitions are often very different even though the definitions have a strong common thread. It follows that if one desires a useful general purpose SC definition, it is probably unwise to define SC as any very specific form, or even as any very specific intermediate purpose, even if for a particular research project it might make sense to do so. In a particular study, a narrow definition can serve to provide focus, limiting the scope of inquiry, but for the purposes of general understanding it is more important to have a SC definition that facilitates broad thinking about the nature of SC. It should be noted that a particular SC form, for example, horizontal social networks, might in one society foster economic growth, while in another society, or the same society in another era, might thwart economic growth. The social forms that function well in Russian socialism probably will not function well in US capitalism, and those that work in nineteenth-century capitalism might not work in the twenty-first-century version. Also, different types of business organization (say, companies with different products and technologies) probably function better with different types of SC. Further, creative managers in different, but similar, organizations may develop quite different SC mechanisms for achieving the same purposes. For these reasons, it makes sense to define SC in a broad, general manner as above without reference to specific forms and intermediate purposes. Otherwise, the use of a very specific definition is likely to serve as a set of blinders, narrowing scholars' view of all that SC might involve. The broad definition can serve to define SC as a general concept within which more specific SC definitions (used in narrowly focused research) can be subsumed. Specific forms and intermediate purposes of SC can then be considered as examples of SC rather than as elements that define and limit what SC is.

Any particular social feature will function better or worse as SC depending on a number of contingencies (Adler and Kwon, 2002: 26, 32–4). First, in some cases, 'it is the specific content of the shared norms that determines whether they function as a source of SC' (p. 26). Second, strong or weak network ties may be a more valuable form of SC depending on various organizational factors. Another important contingency is how well SC networks fit with company goals (p. 32). And, finally, 'norms and beliefs in the surrounding environment influence the value of a given stock of SC' (p. 33; see pp. 32–4 for other types of contingencies).

SC, which is part of IC, has some elements that are relatively tangible and others that are highly intangible. One classification that helps understand this is the three SC dimensions: structural, relational and cognitive (Nahapiet and Ghoshal, 1998). The first, structural SC, is on the tangible side and includes such relatively observable things as the number of ties and the configuration of social networks. The two other dimensions are on the intangible side. 'The cognitive dimension includes shared codes, language, and narratives. The relational dimensions includes trust, norms, obligations, and identification' (Adler and Kwon, 2000: 97).

As indicated earlier, SC in its pure form is embodied in social relationships, formal or informal, that is, the connections between people and groups. In this pure form, it is the relationship that makes for higher productive capacity. But in many cases, investment in the social networks or structure cannot by itself enable the realization of the full productivity potential without some kind of adaptation and learning on the part of the individuals involved. Thus, to realize this potential, a kind of hybrid investment in social-human capital must also occur (see Tomer, 1987: 24–7). Individuals who have made this kind of investment in hybrid social capital will have embodied the attitudes, appreciations, and knowledge that enables them to function well in the context of the newly created relationships. Hybrid SC is a type of HC in individuals.

An important distinction in the SC literature is between external and internal SC. External SC is a 'resource facilitating action by a focal actor, a resource that inheres in the social network tying the focal actor to other actors,' thereby aiding the focal actor in achieving his/her ends (Adler and Kwon, 2000: 90). Much of the sociological literature on SC deals with external SC. Internal SC refers to the social relationships within collective actors (groups, organizations, communities, regions, nations, and so on) (pp. 92–3). An important, and somewhat overlooked, form of internal SC is organizational capital or organizational social capital (Tomer, 1987 and 1999b; Eikelenboom, 2005; Gittell, 2000; Waddock, 2001; Westlund and Nilsson, 2005). A type of organizational capital investment of growing importance is that involved when businesses devote resources to creating bundles of innovative human resource practices (or High Performance Work Systems) (Tomer, 2001; Blair and Wallman, 2001: 14–15; Gant *et al.*, 2002).

Personal Capital

Personal capital (PC), like standard HC, is a type of HC that is embodied in individuals, but it is very different from standard HC in that it consists of human capacities that are largely noncognitive and nonphysical. Personal capital

> relates to an individual's basic personal qualities and reflects the quality of an individual's psychological, physical, and spiritual functioning . . . Further, it mirrors one's internal biochemical balance, physical health and conditioning, psychological strengths and weaknesses, and purpose in life. A person's stock of personal capital is partly a product of one's genetic inheritance, partly a result of the life-shaping events that one has encountered, and partly an outcome of one's efforts to mature and to grow in nonintellectual ways. It is in part produced intentionally. (Tomer, 2003: 456)

A very important component of PC is emotional intelligence (EI) which Daniel Goleman has done much to define, apply and popularize (see for example, Goleman, 1998; Goleman *et al.*, 2002). In Goleman's (Goleman *et al.*, 2002: 38–9, 253–6) view, there are two broad categories of EI competencies, personal competence (consisting of self-awareness and self-management) and social competence (consisting of social awareness and relationship management), and there are 18 specific competencies. Different kinds of jobs, organizations, and industries require different kinds of EI. Individuals who have the kinds of emotional competence demanded by their work situations can be expected to be successful in their job performance (see many examples in Goleman, 1998 and Goleman *et al.*, 2002). Employees who spend time and effort to raise these key competencies are making valuable investments in PC (Tomer, 2003: 457). Goldsmith *et al.*, (1997) use a concept similar to PC, psychological capital, to refer to work-related psychological qualities such as 'a person's perception of self, attitudes toward work, ethical orientation, and general outlook on life' (p. 815). Psychological capital, while similar, is a narrower concept than PC. PC relates not only to a person's emotional/psychological functioning but to a person's social and spiritual functioning.

Noncognitive Human Capital

James Heckman's research on the noncognitive aspects of human capital is closely related to PC. According to Carneiro and Heckman (2003: 204–5), 'noncognitive skills are a form of human capital and can be produced.' Heckman and his coauthors challenge the conventional view that there is only one kind of HC skill, that is, cognitive HC or intelligence, that is related to socio-economic success (p. 141). The neglect of noncognitive skills, notably personal qualities such as motivation, persistence and self-esteem, in HC analyses is certainly due in good part to the lack of reliable ways to measure them (p. 138). But recent research by Heckman and others has demonstrated that noncognitive abilities matter as much or more than cognitive abilities for success both on the job and in school (Heckman *et al.*, 2006: 27; see also Heckman and Rubinstein, 2001). Heckman *et al.* (2006: 4) find that parents play a key role in producing (or not producing) the noncognitive skills of their children and that for children with noncognitive deficits, early child hood interventions 'have been successful in alleviating some of the initial disadvantages.' Therefore, Carneiro and Heckman (2003: 93) conclude that 'current analyses of skill formation focus too much on cognitive ability and too little on noncognitive ability.' Note that what Heckman *et al.* refer to as noncognitive skills or noncognitive HC has a reasonably close correspondence to the PC component of HC. The difference between the two is that Heckman's category is largely defined by what it is not, that is, it is not cognitive. Whereas PC, although largely noncognitive, is defined in a more positive way, that is, PC is defined in terms of the specific human qualities or categories of qualities that it contains.

Intellectual Capital

Intellectual capital is similar to SC in the sense that there are many different definitions and much confusion concerning its nature (see Andriessen, 2004: 60–64 for a brief overview of these definitional differences). Intellectual capital (ItlC) is defined here as knowledge which is useful for producing goods and services and which is owned by a social collectivity (such as a business organization) or its individual participants (this is similar to the definition used by Nahapiet and Ghoshal (1998: 245)). Unlike the ItlC definitions used by many managerial writers (for example, Stewart, 1997), knowledge embodied in humans (either individuals or organizations) or embodied in tangible capital is not included in this definition. Thus, ItlC here is purely disembodied knowledge or knowledge assets. ItlC includes intellectual property, knowledge protected by legal rights (copyrights, patents and trademarks); trade secrets (unprotected know-how) (Lev, 2001: 24); generally any explicit, documented technology or organizational procedures and practices; and personal intellectual capital. Of these, only the latter is included in intangible capital.

Personal intellectual capital (PIC) is firm-specific knowledge possessed by individuals, say in an organization. Typically, this knowledge is in the form of notes kept in files, computers, personal digital assistants, and so on. It is knowledge that the individuals use regularly, have a significant command of, but may need to refer to on a regular basis to do their jobs correctly and successfully. It might include notes on procedures, technology, management/organization and so on. These are generally recorded in an informal, idiosyncratic way, and therefore, are not very useable and accessible by others. Thus, this PIC would, if the owner of it left the organization, be of little value to others. PIC is in sharp contrast to knowledge in the form of explicit technological knowledge and procedural manuals of the organization that provide much documented valuable knowledge that would be very useful even if the present organization participants were to leave. PIC, although not embodied in humans, may be considered to be embodied in an organization (and possessed by individuals). PIC is a supplement and complement to the knowledge that is embodied in individuals. In some cases, PIC may be possessed collectively by a group of people who all use it.

As indicated earlier, IC includes PIC but not the other forms of ItlC. Recall that the rest of IC is HC that is embodied in humans. So IC is what is either possessed by humans or is embodied in humans. In other words, IC is entirely something that would be lost if all the individuals were to leave. While certain types of knowledge assets (such as intellectual property) are definitely intangible and may be part of an organization's property, they are not part of IC as they are separate from the humans in the organization.

Other Types of Intangible Capital

Other types of IC have been identified and written about. Some of these are just different names for types of IC already considered; others are subcategories of types considered; and still others are categories that overlap several types considered earlier. It does not seem necessary to delve into all of these. However, let's consider a few of the most noteworthy types. The first is moral capital. According to Sison (2003: 31–5), moral capital (MC) refers to the human capacity for being and behaving virtuously. An individual invests in MC by taking the time to cultivate right or virtuous habits, thereby becoming habitually moral in conduct (Ratnapala, 2006: 99). A person well-endowed with MC 'would never readily sacrifice his moral excellence as a condition to gain health, knowledge, social connections, or profit' (Sison, 2003: 31). 'MC is what makes a person good as a human being' (p. 31). According to Ratnapala (2006: 98), this moral disposition is a kind of capital because it facilitates 'production and exchange by enhancing the security of person and property and by promoting the keeping of contracts.' MC is a type of HC embodied in individuals, more specifically, it is a type of PC (the EI competency related to displaying honesty and integrity (Goleman *et al.*, 2002: 39)). Conceivably, it might also be a type of HC embodied in relationships (that is, SC) to the extent the social relationships reflect moral considerations.

Another noteworthy type of IC is patience capital. *Patience capital* is the product of investment efforts designed to reduce a person's excessive discounting of future utility (see Becker and Mulligan (1997: 730)). According to Doepke and Zilibotti (2005: 2), it is useful to view investment in patience as a form of human capital investment. In particular, they regard patience capital 'as a component of a broader set of noncognitive skills determining how well people can focus on long-term tasks, behave in social interactions, and exert self-restraint' (p. 4). In other words, they regard patience capital to be part of the noncognitive HC that Heckman has studied. Presumably, patience capital is also an element of emotional intelligence (in PC), but Goleman's books on EI do not explicitly mention this element. When an investment is made in patience, the individual acquires a lower discount rate, arguably a desirable outcome, because the individual will then assign a higher weight to anticipated utility far in the future and, accordingly, will not assign an excessively high weight to immediate or near-term utility. There is research evidence that favorable family nurture and upbringing develops patience in children and that programs targeting disadvantaged children can help them overcome patience deficits and become more future-oriented (pp. 4–5).

Bourdieu (see, for example, 1986: 243–8) is notable for being an early developer of the concept of cultural capital, a form of HC embodied in individuals. Bourdieu's perspective on cultural capital provides an alternative view to that of neoclassical HC theory which emphasizes that HC decisions are made by rational, self-interested individuals in response to economic incentives (Lin, 2001: 14–17). According to Bourdieu, citizen workers are subjected by society to education and socialization in order that they will internalize the symbols, values and meanings of the dominant culture (or dominant class). As a result, these citizens acquire their society's durable cultural traits (for example, a Protestant ethic, frugality, entrepreneurial orientation, and so on) (Olson, 1996: 15–16). These acquired dispositions are personal cultural capital (a marketable type of HC), something that new immigrants who come from very different societies lack in comparison to natives even if they do have an equivalent level of schooling and demographic and socio-economic status (see also Clague and Grossbard-Shechtman, 2001: 8–11).

Besides what is included in IC, it is important to note what is not. Not included is what Hall and Jones (1999: 95) label 'social infrastructure', that is,

> the institutions and government policies that provide the incentives for individuals and firms in an economy. Those incentives can encourage productive activities such as the accumulation of skills or the development of new goods and production techniques, or those incentives can encourage predatory behavior such as rent-seeking, corruption, and theft.

Olson (1996), similarly, has analyzed the structure of incentives arising from governmental economic policies and a nation's legal systems. In theory, the social infrastructure variable analyzed by these economists is entirely separate from the IC variable. Unlike IC, the social infrastructure factor is not something embodied in humans (either individuals or relationships). However, because both these variables are intangible and qualitative in nature and seem to have some similar effects on labor productivity, it is likely that the attempt to sort out the separate economic effects of each will not be entirely successful.

Intangible Capital Summary

Figure 2.1 provides a useful way to summarize the preceding discussion in order to obtain an overview of all that IC comprises. IC is HC in the

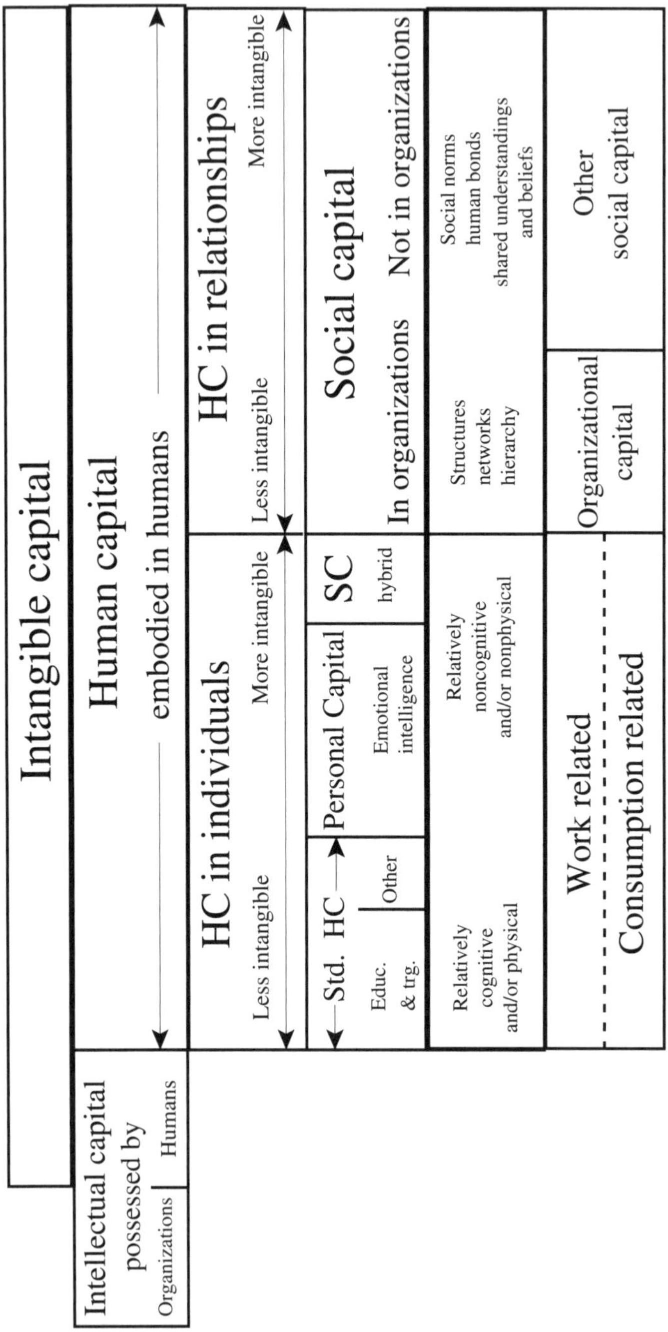

Figure 2.1 Types of intangible capital

broadest sense with the addition of some ItlC possessed by individuals. It is embodied both in individuals and in relationships and has varying degrees of intangibility. It is all of what makes human effort more productive than merely totally unskilled labor. It is, thus, what would be lost if the existing labor force died and was replaced by totally unskilled laborers (using the word skill in the broadest possible sense). IC, like all capital, has a lasting, quasi-permanent nature. Presumably, therefore, managerial instructions, directives, and rules would not qualify as IC to the extent that they can be changed easily, without much resistance, or without a difficult process of pattern or habit breaking.

NOTE

1. Ostrom and Ahn (2003: xiv) have emphasized that SC enables individuals and groups to solve collective action problems where there is a conflict between the short-term self-regarding choices of individuals and the choices that would benefit the whole group.

REFERENCES

Adler, Paul S. and Kwon, Seok-Woo (2000), 'Social capital: the good, the bad, and the ugly,' in Eric L. Lesser (ed.) *Knowledge and Social Capital: Foundations and Applications*, Boston, MA: Butterworth Heinemann, pp. 89–115.

Adler, Paul S. and Kwon, Seok-Woo (2002), 'Social capital: prospects for a new concept,' *Academy of Management Review*, **27**(1), 17–40.

Andriessen, Daniel (2004), *Making Sense of Intellectual Capital: Designing a Method for the Valuation of Intangibles*, Amsterdam: Elsevier.

Arrow, Kenneth J. (2000), 'Observations on social capital,' in Partha Dasgupta and Ismail Serageldin, (eds) *Social Capital: A Multifaceted Perspective*, Washington, DC: World Bank.

Baron, James N. and Michael T. Hannan (1994), 'The impact of economics on contemporary sociology,' Journal of Economic Literature, **32**(3), 1111–46.

Becker, Gary S. (1964), *Human Capital: A Theoretical and Empirical Analysis with Special Reference to Education*, New York: National Bureau of Economic Research.

Becker, Gary S. and Casey B. Mulligan (1997), 'The endogenous determination of time preference,' *Quarterly Journal of Economics*, **112**(3), 729–58.

Blair, Margaret M. and Steven M.H. Wallman (2001), *Unseen Wealth: Report of the Brookings Task Force on Intangibles*, Washington, DC: Brookings Institution.

Bourdieu, Pierre (1986), 'The Forms of Capital,' in John G. Richardson (ed.) *Handbook of Theory and Research for the Sociology of Education*, New York: Greenwood Press, pp. 241–58.

Bowles, Samuel, Herbert Gintis and Melissa Osborne (2001), 'The determinants of earnings: a behavioral approach,' *Journal of Economic Literature*, **39**(4), 1137–76.

Carneiro, Pedro and James J. Heckman (2003), 'Human capital policy,' in James J. Heckman and Alan B. Krueger *Inequality in America: What Role for Human Capital Policies?* Cambridge, MA: MIT Press, pp. 77–239.

Clague, Christopher and Shoshana Grossbard-Shechtman (2001), 'Preface on economic development and cultural institutions,' *Annals of the American Academy of Political and Social Science*, **573**(8), 8–15.
Coleman, James S. (1988), 'Social capital in the creation of human capital,' *American Journal of Sociology*, **94**(Supplement), 95–120.
Coleman, James S. (1990), *Foundations of Social Theory*, Cambridge, MA: Belknap Press, 300–21.
Collier, Paul (1998), 'Social capital and poverty,' Social Capital Working Paper Series #4, December, Washington, DC: World Bank.
Dasgupta, Partha (2000), 'Economic progress and the idea of social capital,' in Partha Dasgupta and Ismail Serageldin, (eds) *Social Capital: A Multifaceted Perspective*, Washington, DC: World Bank.
Dasgupta, Partha and Ismail Serageldin, (eds) (2000), *Social Capital: A Multifaceted Perspective*, Washington, DC: World Bank.
Doepke, Matthias and Fabrizio Zilbotti (2005), 'Patience capital and the demise of the aristocracy,' Center for Economic Policy Research Discussion Paper 5106, June, London.
Duncan, Greg and Rachel Dunifon (1998b), '"Soft-skills" and long-run labor market success,' *Research in Labor Economics*, **17**, 123–49.
Dunifon, Rachel and Greg Duncan. (1998a), 'Long-run effects of motivation on labor-market success,' *Social Psychology Quarterly*, **61**(1), 33–48.
Dunifon, Rachel, Greg Duncan and Jeanne Brooks-Gunn (2001), 'As ye sweep, so shall ye reap,' *American Economic Review*, **91**(2), 150–4.
Easterly, William and Ross Levine (1997), 'African growth tragedy: policies and ethnic divisions,' *Quarterly Journal of Economics*, **112**(4), 1203–50.
Eikelenboom, Bart (2005), *Organizational Capabilities and Bottom Line Performance: The Relationship between Organizational Architecture and Strategic Performance of Business Units in Dutch Headquartered Multinationals*. Delft: Eburon.
Filer, Randall (1981), 'The influence of affective human capital on the wage equation,' *Research in Labor Economics*, **4**, 367–416.
Fukuyama, Francis (1995), 'Social capital and the global economy,' *Foreign Affairs*, **74**(5), 89–103.
Fukuyama, Francis (2001), 'Social capital, civil society and development,' *Third World Quarterly*, **22**(1), 7–20.
Gant, Jon, Casey Ichniowski and Kathryn Shaw (2002), 'Social capital and organizational change in high-involvement and traditional work organizations,' *Journal of Economics and Management Strategy*, **11**(2), 289–328.
Gittell, Jody H. (2000), 'Organizing work to support relational co-ordination,' *International Journal of Human Resource Management*, **11**(3), 517–39.
Goldsmith, Art. H., J.R. Veum and William Darity (1997), 'The impact of psychological and human capital on wages,' *Economic Inquiry*, **October**, 815–29.
Goleman, Daniel (1998), *Working with Emotional Intelligence*, New York: Bantam Books.
Goleman, Daniel, Richard Boyatzis and Annie McKee (2002), *Primal Leadership: Learning to Lead with Emotional Intelligence*, Boston, MA: Harvard Business School Press.
Granovetter, Mark (2005), 'The impact of social structure on economic outcomes,' *Journal of Economic Perspectives*, **19**(1), 33–50.

Groves, Melissa Osborne (2005), 'How important is your personality? Labor market returns to personality for women in the US and UK,' *Journal of Economic Psychology*, **26**(6), 827–41.
Hall, Robert E. and Charles I. Jones (1999), 'Why do some countries produce so much more output per worker than others?,' *Quarterly Journal of Economics*, **114**(1), 83–116.
Heckman, James J. and Yona Rubinstein (2001), 'The importance of noncognitive skills: lessons from the GED testing program,' *American Economic Review*, **91**(2), 145–9.
Heckman, James J., Jora Stixrud and Sergio Urzua (2006), 'The effects of cognitive and noncognitive abilities on labor market outcomes and social behavior,' National Bureau of Economic Research Working Paper 12006, January, Cambridge, MA.
Helliwell, John F. and Robert D. Putnam (1995), 'Economic growth and social capital in Italy,' *Eastern Economic Journal*, **21**(3), 295–307.
Keefer, Philip and Stephen Knack (1997), 'Why don't poor countries catch up? A cross-national test of an institutional explanation,' *Economic Inquiry*, **35**(3), 590–602.
Kiker, B.F. (1966), 'The historical roots of the concept of human capital', *Journal of Political Economy*, **74**(5), 481–99.
Knack, Stephen (1999), 'Social capital, growth and poverty: a survey of cross-country evidence,' Social Capital Initiative Working Paper No. 7, World Bank.
Knack, Stephen and Philip Keefer (1997), 'Does social capital have an economic payoff? a cross-country investigation,' *Quarterly Journal of Economics*, **112**(4), 1251–88.
Krishna, Anirudh (2002), *Active Social Capital: Tracing the Roots of Development and Democracy*, New York: Columbia University Press.
La Porta, Rafael, Florencio Lopez-de-Silanes, Andrei Shleifer and Robert W. Vishny (1997), 'Trust in large organizations,' *American Economic Review*, **87**(2), 333–8.
Lev, Baruch (2001), *Intangibles: Management, Measurement, and Reporting*, Washington, DC: Brookings Institution Press.
Lin, Nan (2001), *Social Capital: A Theory of Social Structure and Action*, Cambridge: Cambridge University Press.
Nahapiet, Janine and Sumantra Ghoshal (1998), 'Social capital, intellectual capital, and the organizational advantage,' *Academy of Management Review*, **23**(2), 242–66.
Narayan, Deepa and Lant Pritchett (2000), 'Social capital: evidence and implications,' in Partha Dasgupta and Ismail Serageldin (eds) *Social Capital: A Multifaceted Perspective*, Washington, DC: World Bank.
Nielsen, Klaus (2002), 'Social capital and innovation policy,' (Unpublished manuscript), Roskilde University, Denmark.
Olson, Mancur (1996), 'Big bills left on the sidewalk: why some nations are rich, and others poor,' *Journal of Economic Perspectives*, **10**(2), 3–24.
Ostrom, Elinor (2000), 'Social capital: a fad or a fundamental concept?,' in Partha Dasgupta and Ismail Serageldin (eds) *Social Capital: A Multifaceted Perspective*, Washington, DC: The World Bank, pp. 172–214.
Ostrom, Elinor and T.K. Ahn (2003), 'Introduction,' in Elinor Ostrom and T.K. Ahn *Foundations of Social Capital*, Cheltenham, UK and Northampton, MA, USA: Edward Elgar.
Putnam, Robert D. (1993), *Making Democracy Work: Civic Traditions in Modern Italy*, Princeton, NJ: Princeton University Press.

Ratnapala, Suri (2006), 'Moral capital and commercial society,' in Robert Higgs and Carl P. Close (eds) *The Challenge of Liberty: Classical Liberalism Today*, Oakland, CA: Independent Institute.
Rupasingha, Anil, Stephan J. Goetz and David Freshwater (2000), 'Social capital and economic growth: a county-level analysis,' *Journal of Agricultural and Applied Economics*, **32**(3), 565–72.
Rupasingha, Anil, Stephan J. Goetz and David Freshwater (2002), 'Social and institutional factors as determinants of economic growth: evidence from the United States counties,' *Papers in Regional Science*, **81**(2), 139–55.
Schultz, Theodore W. (1963), *The Economic Value of Education*, New York: Columbia University Press.
Serageldin, Ismail and Christiaan Grootaert (2000), in Partha Dasgupta and Ismail Serageldin (eds) *Social Capital: A Multifaceted Perspective*, Washington, DC: The World Bank, pp. 40–58.
Sison, Alejo Jose G. (2003), *The Moral Capital of Leaders: Why Virtue Matters*, Cheltenham UK and Northampton, MA, USA: Edward Elgar.
Solow, Robert M. (2000), 'Notes on social capital and economic performance,' in Partha Dasgupta and Ismail Serageldin (eds) *Social Capital: A Multifaceted Perspective*, Washington, DC: World Bank.
Stewart, Thomas A. (1997), *Intellectual Capital: The New Wealth of Organizations*, New York: Doubleday.
Stiglitz, Joseph E. (2000), 'Formal and informal institutions,' in Partha Dasgupta and Ismail Serageldin (eds) *Social Capital: A Multifaceted Perspective*, Washington, DC: World Bank.
Tomer, John F. (1987), *Organizational Capital: The Path to Higher Productivity and Well-Being*, New York: Praeger.
Tomer, John F. (1999a), 'Social and organizational capital,' in Philip Anthony O'Hara (ed.) *Encyclopedia of Political Economy*, Vol. 2, London: Routledge, pp. 1049–51.
Tomer, John F. (1999b), *The Human Firm: A Socio-Economic Analysis of its Behavior and Potential in a New Economic Age*, New York: Routledge.
Tomer, John F. (2001), 'Understanding high-performance work systems: the joint contribution of economics and human resource management,' *Journal of Socio-Economics*, **30**(1), 63–73.
Tomer, John F. (2003), 'Personal capital and emotional intelligence: an increasingly important intangible source of economic growth,' *Eastern Economic Journal*, **29**(3), 453–70.
Tomer, John F. (2006), 'Organizational capital and personal capital: the role of intangible capital formation in the economy,' in Morris Altman (ed.) *Handbook of Contemporary Behavioral Economics; Foundations and Developments*, Armonk, NY: M.E. Sharpe, pp. 257–74.
Torsvik, Gaute (2000), 'Social capital and economic development: a plea for the mechanisms,' *Rationality and Society*, **12**(4), 451–76.
Veblen, Thorstein (1919), *The Place of Science in Modern Civilization and Other Essays*, New York: Viking Press.
Waddock, Sandra (2001), 'How companies build social capital,' *Reflections: The Society for Organizational Learning Journal*, **3**(1), 18–24.
Westlund, Hans and Elin Nilsson (2005), 'Measuring enterprises' investments in social capital: a pilot study,' *Regional Studies*, **39**(8), 1079–94.

Whiteley, Paul F. (2000), 'Economic growth and social capital,' *Political Studies*, **48**, 443–66.
Woolcock, Michael and Deepa Narayan (2003), 'Social capital: implications for development theory, research, and policy,' in Ostrom, Elinor and Ahn, T.K. *Foundations of Social Capital*, Cheltenham, UK and Northampton, MA, USA: Edward Elgar, pp. 416–40.
Zak, Paul J. and Stephen Knack (2001), 'Trust and growth,' *Economic Journal*, **111**, 295–321.
Zeleny, Milan (1995), 'Human and social capital – prerequisites for sustained prosperity,' *Human Systems Management*, **14**, 279–82.

PART II

Intangible capital, economic growth and change

The five chapters of Part II are concerned with the contribution of intangible capital to economic growth and change. Chapter 3 reviews and summarizes the important empirical literature on the contribution of several types of intangible capital to economic growth. Chapter 4 is concerned with the contribution of organizational capital to businesses which have adopted High Performance Work Systems. Chapter 5, written by Bart Eikelenboom, provides important empirical evidence on the contribution of investments in organizational capital to the economic performance of Netherlands-based multinational firms. Chapter 6 develops the concept of personal capital, especially personal capital related to emotional intelligence, and explains why it makes sense to think of it as an increasingly important source of economic growth. Finally, Chapter 7 concerns the dramatic economic transition in Eastern Europe in the years after 1989. This chapter explains why intangible capital is a crucial but overlooked factor in understanding these transitional economies' progress or lack thereof.

3. The contribution of intangible capital to economic growth: an overview

INTRODUCTION

This chapter examines intangible capital as a determinant of economic growth; it links IC to the important theoretical and empirical literature on this subject.

INTANGIBLE CAPITAL AS A SOURCE OF ECONOMIC GROWTH

Is IC an important source of economic growth in the sense that standard factors of production such as physical capital and labor are? If so, we ought to be able to investigate this proposition using empirical methods such as economic growth accounting in which we determine what fraction of the annual average economic growth percentage is accounted for by the annual growth in IC (Dasgupta, 2000: 390–394). To do this, the first step is a theoretical one, that is, specifying the form of the production function for the economy and how IC fits into this relationship. This raises a couple of questions. Does the IC input act independently of physical capital and the pure labor input in determining output? Or is IC best specified as a shift factor whose changes can cause changes in output per input for given quantities of the standard factors (see Dasgupta, 2000: 390–398 for a good discussion of these kinds of considerations with respect to SC; also see Serageldin and Grootaert, 2000: 53–4 and Collier, 1998: 5–12). Unfortunately, as Dasgupta (2000: 396) has suggested, the kind of data that would enable one to give good answers to these specification questions is not known to exist.

IDEAL MEASUREMENT OF INTANGIBLE CAPITAL

Ideally, we would like to find good measures of all the IC components, measures that closely correspond to the definitions in the earlier sections of this chapter. These measures would then need to be aggregated to form one or several IC series usable in a growth accounting exercise. With respect to the SC component of IC, the types of SC that we desire to measure are those for which the intermediate purpose makes a contribution to the ultimate purpose of fostering economic growth. For example, following Putnam (1993), the desired SC measure is of 'norms of reciprocity and networks of civic engagement,' both of which arguably facilitate coordinated action and wide cooperation, thereby contributing to economic growth. Following Fukuyama (1995), the desired SC measure is of the rules and norms that are the basis of the trust which dramatically reduces transaction costs, thereby making possible greater economic growth. Ideally, the comprehensive SC measure used would be one that takes into account all the types of SC that make a legitimate contribution to economic growth. To find the IC aggregate, the aggregate SC would then have to be added to the other HC aggregate (the part in individuals, including cognitive, noncognitive, physical and nonphysical HC) that similarly makes a legitimate contribution to economic growth. Finally, add to that a measure of the intellectual capital possessed by humans in order to produce the ideal IC measure. Because the best specification of the production function may not be knowable, and because the ideal IC aggregate measure is unlikely ever to be constructed, it is probably necessary to settle for empirical evidence that is far from ideal, evidence that is just a part of the larger story concerning the IC contribution to economic growth.

HOW INTANGIBLE CAPITAL AFFECTS ECONOMIC GROWTH

Human Capital (in Individuals)

Recall that included in the part of HC that is in individuals, there is, first, standard HC, much of it due to education and training, and, second, the relatively noncognitive type including personal capital and the social capital hybrid. With respect to the standard part of HC, investment in this HC raises productivity as a result of the increased resources (notably improved skills and knowledge) in laborers (Becker, 1964). The higher productivity of the existing labor force in turn makes possible a greater national economic output. With respect to noncognitive HC, it turns out that even though it is quite different from standard HC and of uncertain nature, its effect on productivity and national output is essentially the same. According to Heckman and Rubinstein (2001: 148), noncognitive traits are valued in the marketplace and directly determine wages and personal achievement (see also Heckman *et al.*, 2006: 25–7). Although Heckman does not attempt to define precisely what specific skills are included in the noncognitive skills category, he and his coauthors have mentioned such qualities as self-discipline, persistence, reliability, dependability, stability, consistency, self-esteem, optimism, future orientation, sociability and self-control. As indicated earlier, the evidence from Heckman's studies is that these noncognitive skills are as important as cognitive skills in determining labor market and social outcomes, thereby contributing to productivity and national output (see, for example, Carneiro and Heckman, 2003: 137–48 and Heckman *et al.*, 2006: 2–3).

Personal capital, as indicated earlier, is an important part of the noncognitive HC in individuals, and its nature is more precisely identified than Heckman's noncognitive skill category. This is especially true for its emotional intelligence component, and this makes possible more specific statements about how investment in PC can raise productivity. For instance, Goleman (1998; Goleman *et al.*, 2002) provides many specific examples of successful economic outcomes when businesses are able to match employees who have acquired particular emotional competencies with jobs that require those noncognitive skills. Let's consider two. First, Goleman (1998: 259) finds that the emotional competencies critical to success as a strategic planner are: astute political awareness, the ability to make arguments with emotional impact, and high levels of interpersonal influence. Second, for retail buyers in department store chains, the key competency is a negotiating style involving problem solving and compromise, not one involving the making of aggressive threats and demands (p. 181). Moreover, as Goleman (p. 243) points out, people who are in the process of acquiring these kinds of emotional competency, that is those who are investing in their PC, are acquiring and/or strengthening neural connections in their brains. These are lasting changes. The result is higher productivity because these people who have more of the appropriate competencies are able to do more quantitatively and qualitatively than if they had a smaller endowment of PC. This higher productivity makes possible greater national output (Tomer, 2003).

It is important to emphasize that Heckman defines this relatively intangible type of human capital by what it is not, that is, it is not cognitive. On the other hand, the term, personal capital, especially the part related to emotional intelligence, is defined by listing its important component competencies. Personal capital is, thus, defined by what it is, that is, by the nature of these emotional intelligence components. From the standpoint of understanding this intangible human capital, the personal capital approach has an advantage because it is explicit about the human skills involved. However, the personal capital approach has the disadvantage of limiting our conception of this intangible capital to just the listed competencies and categories of competencies. Perhaps the best approach would be to define this intangible human capital as broadly as possible but provide sufficient specific examples in order that the human capacities involved can be clearly understood.

Social Capital

Due to their SC, people who are interacting with others are able to get things done more effectively and efficiently than in its absence. If they get things done more effectively, it implies that without their SC, these things either would not have gotten accomplished or fewer of them would have gotten done. If they get things done more efficiently, it implies that with SC, it takes less resources, that is, less cost, to get these things done. Regardless of whether SC adds to effectiveness or efficiency, productivity is increased as the ratio of output to input rises making possible greater national output. Where SC researchers differ among themselves is on how the different types of SC function in order to increase effectiveness and efficiency. Let's consider the basic explanations of a number of these SC writers.

According to James Coleman (1988: S98), SC, which consists of a variety of social structural entities, contributes to effectiveness insofar as it makes 'possible the achievement of certain ends that in its absence would not be possible.' His example of the role of orthodox Jews in the wholesale diamond market is instructive. It is their very close, strong ties of family, community and religion that enable a very high degree of trust among these diamond merchants, thereby enabling trade to occur with ease. 'In the absence of these ties, elaborate and expensive bonding and insurance devices would be necessary – or else the transactions could not take place' (p. S99). Thus, not only effectiveness but efficiency is provided by this type of SC.

In Robert Putnam's (1993: 166–76) view, social or generalized trust arises from norms of reciprocity and networks of civic engagement, and this trust facilitates coordinated actions and spontaneous cooperation. In situations where people are inclined to be opportunistic in the sense of taking advantage of situations for their own benefit, transaction costs will be higher as people will attempt to protect themselves from losses at the hands of opportunists by taking costly actions to forge contractual agreements, to enforce these, and to monitor performance. Therefore, where SC in the form of strong, generalized norms of reciprocity exists, it will tend to restrain opportunism, thereby encouraging trust, leading to lower transaction costs and fostering coordinated, cooperative actions. This makes possible effectiveness and efficiency, contributing to national output.

According to Francis Fukuyama (1995, 2001), SC is an informal norm that serves as a basis for generalized trust and thereby promotes cooperation. In contrast to Putnam, Fukuyama (2001: 7) emphasizes that a wide range of norms constitute SC, from the basic norm of reciprocity to complex and elaborately articulated doctrines such as Christianity and Confucianism. Similar to Putnam, Fukuyama states that 'the economic function of SC is to reduce transaction costs,' but, as Fukuyama emphasizes, transaction costs are not just associated with trade and contracts, they are associated much more with formal coordination mechanisms like hierarchies, bureaucratic rules, and the like (p. 10). In his view, coordination and cooperation is certainly possible without SC, but it would 'entail additional transaction costs of monitoring, negotiating, litigating, and enforcing formal agreements' (p. 10). It follows that high-trust societies with abundant SC 'make possible certain efficient forms of economic organization that otherwise would be encumbered by extensive rules, contracts, litigation, and bureaucracy' (Fukuyama, 1995: 90). Fukuyama points to the US, Japan, and Germany as high-trust societies that as a consequence have been able to develop economically successful large-scale corporations that contribute greatly to the high output and growth of their economies.

Gaute Torsvik (2000) has explained in greater detail than other writers why SC, in the form of dense, inclusive, strong, and vital horizontal associations, leads to trust which in turn contributes to output through its reduction of transaction costs. According to Torsvik (pp. 461–9), SC affects trust in two ways: first making reciprocity mechanisms work more effectively and second producing more prosocial or altruistic motivation. The essence is that SC in the form of tight interwoven social networks: (a) increases the probability of detecting opportunism as well as increases the likely amount of punishment of opportunism; and (b) increases altruistic concern due to the strong nurturing of community as well as due to the strong sense of group identity among community members (pp. 466–9).

Elinor Ostrom's perspective on the role of SC in the economy emphasizes collective action dilemmas. The latter 'concern settings in which there is a group of individuals, a common interest among them, and potential conflict between the common interest and each individual's interest' (Ostrom and Ahn, 2003: xiv). If all or many individuals succumb to the temptation to follow their short-term selfish interests, they will all be worse off as their common purposes will be sacrificed. If the individuals can develop or evolve SC in the form of 'norms and rules that define how this activity will be carried out repeatedly over time and how commitments will be monitored and sanctions imposed for nonperformance,' the collective action dilemma should be resolved (Ostrom, 2000: 176). If the dilemma is successfully resolved by this investment in SC, it will produce trusting behavior, and there will be no need to resort to government bureaucracy or other formal mechanisms. Consequently, the project (for example, farm irrigation system) or organized activity should achieve its potential economic benefits in an efficient manner.

Narayan and Pritchett (2000: 282) provide explanations of several other important economic functions of SC. First, a country with greater SC (and the social connections implied) is likely to suffer less from ethnic fragmentation which has been associated with lower spending on productive public goods. This lower spending is because high ethnic fragmentation has been observed to contribute to intractable distributional conflict that makes it very difficult for the groups involved to agree on common public spending. Relatedly, there is reason to believe that SC contributes to the efficiency of governments' provision of public goods. This is because greater SC can facilitate the performance of government through greater monitoring of government agents (p. 282), a point also made by Putnam (1993). Second, in the case of common pool resources, strong SC among local groups, leading to cooperation, can 'play a large role in avoiding the negative consequences of the excessive exploitation or undermaintenance of assets that would result from purely individualistic behavior under open access' (p. 283; see also Ostrom, 2000).

Third, strong SC connections can circumvent market failures that might otherwise block the diffusion of innovations (Narayan and Pritchett, 2000: 283). Studies suggest that a variety of strong social connections are associated with early adoption of innovations. Fourth, good SC can help to overcome barriers to the flow of information. For example, 'SC could lead to a better flow of information between creditors and borrowers and hence may involve less adverse selection and moral hazard in the market for credit' (pp. 283–4). More generally, as Granovetter (2005: 33) points out, 'Much information is subtle, nuanced and difficult to verify, so actors do not believe impersonal sources and instead rely on people they know.' Fifth, SC can serve as social insurance, substituting to a degree for formal insurance. The social relationships involved may provide informal insurance, in effect a social safety net, thereby allowing households or businesses to pursue opportunities involving higher returns but also higher risks (p. 284). In sum, to the extent that SC serves these different functions, it contributes economically and adds to national output.

Taking Advantage of SC

As indicated above, there are many reasons why SC should be considered an important resource for economic growth. However, to gain full advantage of its SC, a society or community must do more than simply possess this resource. First, Anirudh Krishna's (2002) research in the villages of India suggests that with respect to economic development, communities can only obtain the full potential benefit from their SC when they use capable agents who can negotiate and represent their communities' interests to external parties such as higher level governmental organizations. In general, even the most valuable SC requires for full effect the help of agents who can focus the SC potential on appropriate, common ends. Second, the synergy view provides an important perspective on what works best to foster economic development (Woolcock and Narayan, 2003: 235–6). The essence is that SC resources can contribute most effectively to economic development when government actions foster and complement, in synergistic fashion, those of citizen groups and networks.

Organizational Capital

As indicated earlier, organizational capital (OC) is the SC in organizations and is sometimes referred to as organizational social capital. Because, as Harvey Leibenstein noted, a firm's actual output is typically much less than its potential output, that is, internal inefficiency (or X-inefficiency) is the usual state of affairs, investment in OC typically raises organizational productivity, thereby making possible higher national output (Tomer, 2006: 259–65). There are many ways that OC investments can raise organizational productive capacity. Broadly, investment in OC can raise the organization's capability for: (a) rational organizational decision making; (b) socially responsible behavior; (c) entrepreneurial behavior; and (d) organizational learning (p. 259). Investment in OC can improve organizational cooperation by helping to attenuate opportunism and building trust (p. 260). Investment in developing a firm's joining-up process can remedy employees' low effort choices owing to inadequate organizational citizenship (p. 261). Higher worker effort is also the likely outcome of OC investments that improve the implicit psychological contract between employees and the organization (p. 262). If a firm decides to adopt the bundle of human resource practices known as HPWS, the investment in OC can transform the organization from a control-oriented one to an involvement-oriented one in which workers experience deep owner motivation (high internal motivation), not just agent motivation (where motivation comes from external rewards and penalties) (p. 263). The above is far from an exhaustive list of the ways that organizational investment can raise productivity and contribute to economic growth

EMPIRICAL FINDINGS ON INTANGIBLE CAPITAL'S CONTRIBUTION TO ECONOMIC GROWTH

The contributions of standard HC to economic growth have received plenty of attention elsewhere. Therefore, the empirical findings on IC's contribution to economic growth summarized here focus only on the more intangible of the IC types, namely SC and noncognitive HC.

The Contribution of SC

Starting from the perspective that SC is an important source of economic growth, a source separate and distinct from standard HC, a variety of researchers have estimated regression equations in which economic growth (or another aspect of economic performance) is the dependent variable and an SC variable(s) is a prominent independent variable. Typically, these are cross-section analyses that attempt to demonstrate how differences among geographic areas in important factors explain (or not) differences in the areas' long-run economic growth rates. Since the specified regression equations used by these researchers have much in common, let's consider a generalized version (Equation 3.1):

$$\mathrm{Gr} = \beta_0 + \beta_1\, Y + \beta_2\, Ed + \beta_3\, SC + \beta_4\, P + \beta_5\, Ec + \beta_6\, G + \beta_7\, X \qquad (3.1)$$

where Gr is the long-run economic growth rate (typically average annual rate of growth of GDP per capita); *Y* is initial income per capita; *Ed* is educational attainment (typically years of schooling attained by adults); *SC* is the social capital variable; *P* is a variable reflecting the political and stability conditions in the area; *Ec* is a variable reflecting pertinent economic and/or financial conditions in the area; the *G* variable relates to certain governmental factors in the area; and *X* stands for a variety of other control variables. Most of the researchers include *Y*, *Ed* and *SC* as independent variables in their equations, but they differ with respect to their use of *P*, *Ec*, *G*, and the other control variables.

Table 3.1 summarizes the empirical findings from nine articles reporting regression results related to the effect of SC on economic growth and performance. Almost uniformly the SC variable(s) has a highly significant (economically and statistically) effect on economic growth and performance. The effect of SC on economic growth is also strong relative to the

Table 3.1 Summary of empirical findings regarding the effect of social capital on economic growth and performance

Author(s) and date	Geographical areas	Social capital variable(s)	Dependent variable	Main finding
Easterly and Levine (1997)	96 nations	ETHNIC. Ethnolinguistic Fractionalization or Diversity	Average annual growth in per capita GDP for three decades	ETHNIC associated directly and indirectly with lower growth
Helliwell and Putnam (1995)	20 regions in Italy	CIVIC: composite of four indicators on breadth and depth of community and political behavior	Log per capita GDP 1990 – log per capita GDP 1950	CIVIC has strong, significant relationship to growth
Knack and Keefer (1997)	29 nations (mostly developed, market economies)	TRUST: Generalized trust (response to survey question) CIVIC: Strength of civic norms (responses to survey questions) GROUPS: Average number of memberships in listed types of groups	Average annual growth in per capita income 1980–92	TRUST and CIVIC: Strong and significant relationship to growth GROUPS: Not significant relationship to growth
Narayan and Pritchett (2000)	84 villages in Tanzania	Village SC: Reflects average memberships in groups, character of groups, trust/perception of groups	Income per person; probability of adopting improved agricultural practices	Village SC has highly significant relationship with both dependent variables
La Porta *et al.* (1997)	40 nations	TRUST: Generalized trust (response to survey question)	Average annual growth in per capita GDP 1970–93	TRUST has not strong, but significant, relationship to growth

Table 3.1 (continued)

Author(s) and date	Geographical areas	Social capital variable(s)	Dependent variable	Main finding
Rupasingha *et al.* (2000)	3040 US counties	Per capita number of listed types of groups in county (GROUPS); crime index (CRIME); public's charitable giving (CHARITY); participation of voters in federal elections 1988 and 1992 (VOTING)	Per capita growth of personal income 1990–6	GROUPS has a significant positive effect on growth; CRIME has a significant negative effect; CHARITY has little or no effect; VOTING has a nonlinear effect
Rupasingha *et al.* (2002)	3040 US counties	GROUP1: Per capita number of listed types of Putnam groups in county: GROUP2: Per capita number of listed types of Olson groups in county; Ethnic fractionalization, Income inequality	Per capita growth of personal income 1990–7	GROUP1, GROUP2, and ethnic diversity have a significant positive effect on growth; income inequality has a significant negative effect on growth
Whiteley (2000)	34 nations	Log SC Index: Index derived from factor analysis of survey responses to three questions regarding trust (generalized, family, and fellow nationals)	Log of average per capita GDP growth 1970–92	SC Index has a highly significant positive effect on growth
Zak and Knack (2001)	41 nations	TRUST: Generalized trust (response to survey question)	Average annual per capita GDP growth 1970–93	TRUST and related institutional factors have a significant positive effect on growth

effect of the HC variable (educational attainment). While this provides a kind of strong general support for the economic importance of SC, it should be noted that these empirical results do not provide careful tests of specific hypotheses about how SC contributes to economic growth. This is not the fault of the authors. In general, the ideal data on SC does not exist, and the authors were making the best of the imperfect SC data available. For a more detailed survey of the empirical literature related to SC and economic growth, see Knack (1999).

In connection to SC and economic growth, it is important to note the effect on economic growth of institutions and governmental policies. These institutional and governmental factors are not included in the definition of SC (or IC) used here, but some researchers lump them together. According to Olson (1996: 6), it is the quality of both institutions and governmental economic policies that determine whether countries reach their economic potential. In his view, poorer countries suffer from the lack of an adequate structure of incentives, incentives that derive from the 'legal systems that enforce contracts and protect property rights and . . . [the] political structures, constitutional provisions, and the extent of special-interest lobbying and cartels.' Similarly, Hall and Jones (1999) point out that an appropriate 'social infrastructure' is needed to prevent or suppress diversion by private and government agents, the kind of diversion that is associated with predatory behavior and that lowers the returns to private productive behavior. Based on their empirical analysis, Hall and Jones (p. 114) conclude that 'differences in social infrastructure across countries cause large differences in capital accumulation, educational attainment, and productivity, and therefore large differences in income across countries.' In a similar vein, Keefer and Knack (1997) investigated whether deficient institutions act as an impediment to poorer nations seeking to catch up economically to richer ones. Among the institutional deficiencies that they focused on were the lack of rule of law, the pervasiveness of corruption, and the risk of expropriation and contract repudiation (p. 590). The statistical evidence they provide strongly supports the proposition that 'institutions are powerful determinants of the ability of countries to benefit from the catch-up effect' (p. 601).

The Contribution of Noncognitive Human Capital

As yet, no researchers have investigated empirically the effect of noncognitive HC (including PC) on economic growth in a way similar to the research on SC summarized above. However, there is an accumulation of evidence suggesting the importance of noncognitive HCs' effect on economic growth.

First, let's consider the findings from a group of studies explaining earnings differences among individuals. In general, these studies have found that certain noncognitive personal traits are strongly associated with differences in earnings among workers. Filer's (1981) study explores the extent to which variations in affective skills (or personality traits) as well as cognitive skills (both human capital variables) explain worker wage differences. Ten personality traits were used to explain workers' monthly salaries from their primary job (p. 383). Filer (pp. 404, 407) finds that adding affective skills to the standard wage equation, which controls for many socio-economic and demographic considerations, 'adds significant explanatory power' without reducing the significance of the other variables in the equation. The most important affective skill was drive, followed by ascendance (desire to 'be on top').

Duncan and Dunifon's (1998a, b) studies focus on the long run effects of worker motivation on wages. They explore the relationship between a number of social psychological traits observed in men aged 21 to 29 and their labor market attainments 15 to 25 years later. In one analysis (1998a), they focus on two motivational measures, challenge versus affiliation and sense of personal control. Controlling for many factors, they find that the two motivational variables are highly significant predictors of these men's wages in later periods and that the explanatory power was about as strong as that for years of completed schooling (pp. 40–2). In their other analysis (1998b), they use four motivational measures or 'soft skills,' challenge versus affiliation, personal efficacy, fear of failure, and trust/hostility. They find that individuals with an orientation to achievement and self-efficacy earned considerably higher wages 20 to 25 years later (p. 146). The motivational measures 'added nearly as much to the explanation of long-run earnings differentials as did years of completed schooling.'

In a similar subsequent study, Dunifon and Duncan joined with Jeanne Brooks-Gunn (2001) to examine another key noncognitive personal characteristic, organization and efficiency, as operationalized by data on the cleanliness of a worker's dwelling. The authors 'argue that keeping a clean and organized home reflects an overall ability and desire to maintain a sense of order in a wide range of life activities' (p. 150). The authors find a highly significant (economically and statistically) relationship between the cleanliness/organization variable and workers' wages 25 years later. They also find a highly significant relationship between cleanliness/organization and the wages of these workers' children 25 years later. The authors conclude that 'these results suggest that models predicting labor-market success and educational attainment would be strengthened by the addition of a wider range of so-called "noncognitive" factors' (p. 154).

In a more recent study, Osborne Groves (2005) used two large, nationally representative data sets to explore the role of personality or psychological factors in explaining wage differences. She finds that three variables, 'locus of control, aggressiveness, and withdrawal, have statistically significant influences on women's wages, controlling for standard human capital variables' (p. 839). External locus of control, aggression, and withdrawal are all associated with lower wages. The size of the 'coefficient on locus of control is similar to estimates for many standard human capital variables' (p. 839). Also, compared to the withdrawal variable, aggression is the dominant factor influencing the wages for women.

A study by James Heckman and his coauthors (2006) provides important evidence that noncognitive skills are at least as important as cognitive skills in determining labor market and social outcomes. Their findings indicate that noncognitive abilities play a major role in explaining teenage and young adult behaviors such as crime and pregnancy and are an important direct determinant of wages in most educational labor markets. These 'findings challenge a pervasive view in the literatures in economics and psychology that cognitive ability, as measured by test scores, plays a dominant role in explaining personal achievement' (p. 27).

If the studies cited above are right that noncognitive skills/traits, 'seemingly irrelevant personal characteristics' (Bowles *et al.*, 2001: 1138), are important, and neglected, determinants of earnings, it is not unreasonable to infer that investment in these noncognitive human capital factors ought to raise individual productivity, and thus be important in explaining economic growth. It is important to note that the noncognitive skills/traits considered in these studies do not come close to encompassing all the relevant elements of noncognitive HC skills and traits, or even all of the elements of emotional intelligence, but they do include some of the more important noncognitive elements. Thus, these empirical studies are interesting and provide general support for the thesis that investment in noncognitive HC is an important determinant of economic growth.

Due to space limitations, findings from other studies, especially those related to the effect of investment in organizational capital on economic growth, are not provided here.

CONCLUSION

Economists need to have a broad conception of the nature of capital, that is, capital as productive capacity regardless of its tangibility. This chapter presents arguments and evidence indicating that intangible capital (and all its components) is extremely important to understanding economic growth. Using a comprehensive conception of intangible capital helps understand that human skills, capacities, and relationships are fundamental to the economic achievement that makes economic growth possible. With regard to formulating policies on economic growth, this suggests that economists need to learn to put the human element, especially intangible human skills and relationships, at the forefront.

REFERENCES

Becker, Gary S. (1964), *Human Capital: A Theoretical and Empirical Analysis with Special Reference to Education*, New York: National Bureau of Economic Research.

Bowles, Samuel, Herbert Gintis and Melissa Osborne (2001), 'The determinants of earnings: a behavioral approach,' *Journal of Economic Literature*, **39**(4), 1137–76.

Carneiro, Pedro and Heckman, James J. (2003), 'Human capital policy,' in Heckman, James J. and Krueger, Alan B. *Inequality in America: What Role for Human Capital Policies?* Cambridge, MA: MIT Press, pp. 77–239.

Coleman, James S. (1988), 'Social capital in the creation of human capital,' *American Journal of Sociology*, **94**(Supplement), 95–120.

Collier, Paul (1998), 'Social capital and poverty,' Social Capital Working Paper Series No. 4, December, Washington, DC: World Bank.

Dasgupta, Partha (2000), 'Economic progress and the idea of social capital,' in Partha Dasgupta, and Ismail Serageldin (eds). *Social Capital: A Multifaceted Perspective*, Washington, DC: World Bank.

Duncan, Greg and Rachel Dunifon (1998a), 'Long-run effects of motivation on labor-market success,' *Social Psychology Quarterly*, **61**(1), 33–48.

Duncan, Greg and Dunifon, Rachel (1998b), ' "Soft-skills" and long-run labor market success,' *Research in Labor Economics*, **17**, 123–49.

Dunifon, Rachel, Greg Duncan and Jeanne Brooks-Gunn (2001), 'As ye sweep, so shall ye reap,' *American Economic Review*, **91**(2), 150–4.

Easterly, William and Ross Levine (1997), 'African growth tragedy: policies and ethnic divisions,' *Quarterly Journal of Economics*, **112**(4), 1203–50.

Filer, Randall (1981), 'The influence of affective human capital on the wage equation,' *Research in Labor Economics*, **4**, 367–416.

Fukuyama, Francis (1995), 'Social capital and the global economy,' *Foreign Affairs*, **74**(5), 89–103.

Fukuyama, Francis (2001), 'Social capital, civil society and development,' *Third World Quarterly*, **22**(1), 7–20.

Goleman, Daniel (1998), *Working with Emotional Intelligence*, New York: Bantam Books.

Goleman, Daniel, Richard Boyatzis and Annie McKee (2002), *Primal Leadership: Learning to Lead with Emotional Intelligence*, Boston, MA: Harvard Business School Press.

Granovetter, Mark (2005), 'The impact of social structure on economic outcomes,' *Journal of Economic Perspectives*, **19**(1), 33–50.

Groves, Melissa Osborne (2005), 'How important is your personality? Labor market returns to personality for women in the US and UK,' *Journal of Economic Psychology*, **26**(6), 827–41.

Hall, Robert E. and Charles I. Jones (1999), 'Why do some countries produce so much more output per worker than others?,' *Quarterly Journal of Economics*, **114**(1), 83–116.

Heckman, James J. and Yona Rubinstein (2001), 'The importance of noncognitive skills: lessons from the GED testing program,' *American Economic Review*, **91**(2), 145–9.

Heckman, James J., Jora Stixrud and Sergio Urzua (2006), 'The effects of cognitive and noncognitive abilities on labor market outcomes and social behavior,' National Bureau of Economic Research Working Paper 12006, January, Cambridge, MA.

Helliwell, John F. and Robert D. Putnam (1995), 'Economic growth and social capital in Italy,' *Eastern Economic Journal*, **21**(3), 295–307.

Keefer, Philip and Stephen Knack (1997), 'Why don't poor countries catch up? A cross-national test of an institutional explanation,' *Economic Inquiry*, **35**(3), 590–602.

Knack, Stephen (1999), 'Social capital, growth and poverty: a survey of cross-country evidence,' Social Capital Initiative Working Paper No. 7, World Bank.

Knack, Stephen and Philip Keefer (1997), 'Does social capital have an economic payoff? A cross-country investigation,' *Quarterly Journal of Economics*, **112**(4), 1251–88.

Krishna, Anirudh (2002), *Active Social Capital: Tracing the Roots of Development and Democracy*, New York: Columbia University Press.

La Porta, Rafael, Florencio Lopez-de-Silanes, Andrei Shleifer and Robert W. Vishny (1997), 'Trust in large organizations,' *American Economic Review*, **87**(2), 333–8.

Narayan, Deepa and Lant Pritchett (2000), 'Social capital: evidence and implications,' in Partha Dasgupta and Ismail Serageldin (eds) *Social Capital: A Multifaceted Perspective*, Washington, DC: World Bank.

Olson, Mancur (1996), 'Big bills left on the sidewalk: why some nations are rich, and others poor,' *Journal of Economic Perspectives*, **10**(2), 3–24.

Ostrom, Elinor (2000), 'Social capital: a fad or a fundamental concept?,' in Partha Dasgupta and Ismail Serageldin (eds) *Social Capital: A Multifaceted Perspective*, Washington, DC: The World Bank, pp. 172–214.

Ostrom, Elinor and Ahn, T. K. (2003), 'Introduction,' in Elinor Ostrom and T. K. Ahn *Foundations of Social Capital,* Cheltenham, UK Northampton, MA, USA: Edward Elgar.

Putnam, Robert D. (1993), *Making Democracy Work: Civic Traditions in Modern Italy*, Princeton, NJ: Princeton University Press.

Rupasingha, Anil, Stephan J. Goetz and David Freshwater (2000), 'Social capital and economic growth: a county-level analysis,' *Journal of Agricultural and Applied Economics*, **32**(3), 565–72.

Rupasingha, Anil, Stephan J. Goetz and David Freshwater (2002), 'Social and institutional factors as determinants of economic growth: evidence from the United States counties,' *Papers in Regional Science*, **81**(2), 139–55.

Serageldin, Ismail and Christiaan Grootaert (2000), in Partha Dasgupta and Ismail Serageldin (eds) *Social Capital: A Multifaceted Perspective*, Washington, DC: The World Bank, 40–58.

Tomer, John F. (2003), 'Personal capital and emotional intelligence: an increasingly important intangible source of economic growth,' *Eastern Economic Journal*, **29**(3), pp. 453–70.

Tomer, John F. (2006) 'Organizational capital and personal capital: the role of intangible capital formation in the economy,' in Morris Altman (ed.) *Handbook of Contemporary Behavioral Economics; Foundations and Developments*, Armonk, NY: M.E. Sharpe, pp. 257–74.

Torsvik, Gaute (2000), 'Social capital and economic development: a plea for the mechanisms,' *Rationality and Society*, **12**(4), 451–76.
Whiteley, Paul F. (2000), 'Economic growth and social capital,' *Political Studies*, **48**, 443–66.
Woolcock, Michael and Deepa Narayan (2003), 'Social capital: implications for development theory, research, and policy,' in Elinor Ostrom and T.K. Ahn *Foundations of Social Capital*, Cheltenham, UK Northampton, MA, USA: Edward Elgar, pp. 416–40.
Zak, Paul J. and Stephen Knack (2001), 'Trust and growth,' *Economic Journal*, **111**, 295–321.

4. Understanding high performance work systems: the contribution of organizational capital

INTRODUCTION

High performance work systems (HPWS) are organizations that utilize a fundamentally different approach to managing from the traditional hierarchical approach associated with mass production/scientific management. At the heart of this emerging approach is a radically different employer-employee relationship. Leading organizational behavior specialists believe that HPWS has the greatest potential to provide sustained competitive advantage to companies adopting it. Thus, human resource managers and scholars as well as economists ought to be very interested in it. While much has been written about HPWS in the human resource management (HRM) literature, economists' attention to it has been practically nil despite the fact that organizational economics is a significant area within economics.

The primary purpose of this chapter is to improve our understanding of the superior economic performance of HPWS and the nature of this important investment in organizational capital. The secondary purpose is to compare the respective contributions of the HRM and economics disciplines to this understanding. The HRM/organizational behavior literature contains important explanations regarding the economic performance of HPWS. In contrast, there is hardly any economic literature explicitly focused on HPWS. However, as indicated below, economic theory, particularly x-efficiency theory, can be adapted to this purpose. The explanations that make the most sense of the economic performance of HPWS are interdisciplinary ones that integrate economics with organizational behavior.

The plan of the chapter is as follows. The next section describes the characteristic features of HPWS and cites evidence regarding its economic performance. The following section examines HPWS from the standpoints of mainstream organizational economics and mainstream HRM. The fourth section brings to bear behavioral economic and organizational behavior perspectives with respect to understanding the performance of HPWS and attempts to integrate these. In addition, this section focuses on the essential reasons for HPWS' superiority and why, despite this, HPWS' diffusion has been slow. The final section provides conclusions.

HIGH PERFORMANCE WORK SYSTEMS

Characteristic Features

High Performance Work Systems, sometimes known as high involvement or high commitment organizations, are organizations that use a distinctive managerial approach that enables high performance through people. Although different HRM authors have emphasized slightly different features and management practices in describing HPWS, the essential characteristics are the seven key dimensions identified by Jeffrey Pfeffer in *The Human Equation* (1998, Chapter 3). These are:

1. Employment security.
2. Selective hiring of new personnel.
3. Self-managed teams and decentralization of decision making as the basic principles of organizational design.
4. Comparatively high compensation contingent on organizational performance.
5. Extensive training.
6. Reduced status distinctions and barriers, including dress, language, office arrangements, and wage differences across levels.
7. Extensive sharing of financial and performance information throughout the organization.

The main idea of HPWS is to create an organization based on employee involvement, commitment and empowerment, not employee control. The particular set of managerial practices will vary from company to company. 'The small business unit that controls its own fate and involves everyone in the business is the best image for the involvement-oriented approach' (Lawler, 1992: 29). In these high involvement organizations, employees 'feel responsible for and involved in its success' (p. 3); they 'know more, do more, contribute more' (p. 5). They have the power, information, knowledge, and rewards to perform at the highest level (Lawler *et al.*, 1995). Among the successful companies making use of this approach are Norwest, Men's Wearhouse, ServiceMaster, Southwest Airlines, USAA, Procter and Gamble, Wal-Mart and Virgin Atlantic Airways (Pfeffer, 1998: 293–6).

HPWS is not the same as Total Quality Management (TQM) but these two approaches can be used along with each other.

> Although the TQM approach stresses employee involvement, the type of involvement it stresses is limited to allowing employees to make suggestions and control certain elements of the production process and the quality-control process. It does not suggest that organizations be restructured and redesigned to emphasize employees having the information, knowledge, power, rewards that will give them a business experience. Instead employees are given information, knowledge, and power to improve certain elements of the organization's work processes. (Lawler, 1992: 326)

HPWS organizations use an approach that is fundamentally different from the traditional hierarchical or bureaucratic approach, otherwise known as the control-oriented approach (Lawler, 1992: 25).

> The fundamental difference between the control-oriented approach and the involvement-oriented approach concerns how work is organized and managed at the lowest level in an organization. Companies using the control-oriented approach assume that work should be simplified, standardized, and specialized and that supervision and pay incentives should be used to motivate individuals to perform their tasks well. In essence, the thinking and controlling part of work is separated from the doing of the work. (p. 28)

Workers at the lowest levels, especially those employed in the context of mass production/scientific management, are agents, unthinking agents, of owner/manager principals.

Involvement-oriented organizations, on the other hand:

> should be structured so that individuals at the lowest level in the organization not only perform work but also are responsible for improving work methods and procedures, solving problems on the job, and coordinating their work with that of others. Employees also can and should be expected to operate without a controlling supervisor. (Lawler, 1992: 30)

In HPWS, workers are to a large degree self-controlled and self-managed (p. 28). With the help of leaders who develop a clear vision, mission and goals, HPWS workers are expected to respond in nonprogrammed ways to changing circumstances. HPWS is participative management to the *n*th degree. Workers in HPWS have shed the mentality of agents; they have become owners in their outlook.

Performance Superiority

There are many empirical studies that have investigated whether firms utilizing particular HPWS managerial practices achieve a higher level of performance than traditionally managed firms. However, comparatively few studies have focused on a group of HPWS practices and have examined in a rigorous fashion the extent to which these are associated with higher operating and financial performance. It is beyond the scope of this chapter to provide a complete, careful review of these studies. Nevertheless, it is important to summarize some of their important results and to indicate whether they support the hypothesis of HPWS performance superiority.

First, consider the studies reviewed by Pfeffer (1998; Chapter 2), the most important of which is by Mark Huselid. Using survey data from 968 firms in many industries, Huselid (1995) has found evidence consistent with the hypothesis that companies' use of systems of high performance work practices: (a) diminishes their employee turnover and (b) increases their productivity (sales per employee) and corporate financial performance (stock market value to book value). He concludes that

> The magnitude of the returns for investment in High Performance Work Practices is substantial. A one standard deviation increase in such practices is associated with a . . . 7.05 percent decrease in turnover and, on a per employee basis, $27 044 more in sales and $18 641 and $3814 more in market value and profits, respectively. (p. 667)

Several single industry studies reviewed by Pfeffer (1998) are noteworthy. First, studies of the auto industry by researchers at MIT have compared auto plants with lean or flexible production methods to those with traditional mass production methods (pp. 38–41). They found that flexible production methods that emphasize the use of teams and employee involvement are associated with higher quality and productivity than mass production. Second, a major study of the steel industry rated the human resource policies of companies on a scale of one to four, one being progressive and four being the traditional Tayloristic approach (pp. 44–6). This study found that firms with more progressive management systems operated their lines a significantly higher proportion of the time and had significantly lower costs. Third, a study of 15 semiconductor fabrication plants used an index of participation with four elements: power, information, knowledge and reward (pp. 51–3). The researchers found a clear linear relationship between this participation index and three performance indicators, defect density, line yield and cycle time. Finally, a study of the oil refining industry found that a multi-skilled, trained, and committed workforce pays off in reduced maintenance expense and higher refinery utilization (pp. 53–4).

John Paul MacDuffie (1995) studied the relationship between 'bundles' of interrelated and internally consistent human resource practices (not individual practices) and productivity and quality in 62 auto assembly plants throughout the world using questionnaires and site visits. Some plants used HR bundles associated with mass production involving a narrow division of labor and low commitment policies. Other plants used HR bundles associated with flexible productions systems involving a multiskilling orientation (greater use of teams, suggestions, job rotation and workers performing quality tasks) and high commitment policies. Some plants were in-between. MacDuffie (pp. 217–18) found strong, statistically significant evidence supporting the hypothesis that innovative bundles of HR practices are positively related to both productivity and quality.

The conclusions of Ichniowski *et al.* (1997) for steel production lines are similar. They studied 36 homogeneous steel finishing lines owned by 17 companies to determine whether clusters of complementary HRM practices are related to productivity. They identified four systems of HRM practices: (1) System 4 is the traditional system with no innovative practices; (2) System 3 is System 4 with the addition of worker involvement in teams and enhanced labor-management communication practices; (3) System 2 adds extensive skill training and high worker involvement in teams; and (4) System 1 incorporates innovative practices in all HRM policy areas (pp. 296–8). Productivity was measured by the percentage of uptime (time not involving delays). The evidence from their careful regression analyses, which controls for all relevant differences in the production lines, indicates that systems of innovative HRM practices have a statistically significant large and positive association with workers' productivity, while changes in individual HRM practices have little or no effect (p. 311).

In a similar study, Ichniowski and Shaw (1999) examined evidence on the performance difference between Japanese and US steel manufacturing companies. The Japanese companies utilized HRM systems featuring problem-solving teams, employment security, flexible job assignments, training, careful employee selection, and high levels of labor-management communication. The US companies, as above, had four levels of HRM systems, from traditional to innovative. The regression analyses indicated that the Japanese steel companies performed better in both productivity and product quality than the US companies. However, the US companies that utilized innovative HRM systems equaled the productivity and came close to the quality performance of the Japanese companies (pp. 713–17).

Other studies and reviews of studies have come to the same general conclusion as the ones cited above. For example, Kling's (1995: 32) review article concludes that

> Taken together, the studies reviewed show that specific practices such as training, alternative pay systems, and employee involvement often are correlated with higher productivity. These and other practices are associated with even greater productivity improvements when implemented together in systems.

Based on survey data obtained from firms listed among the 1000 largest service and industrial companies, Lawler *et al.* (1995: 74) found that:

> Companies that use employee involvement practices overwhelmingly believe that they receive significant benefits from them. The use of a wide variety of specific power-sharing, reward, information-sharing, and training practices is linked to specific positive impacts.

It is on the basis of these types of findings that Pfeffer (1998: 32) concludes that 'substantial gains, on the order of 40 percent or so in most of the studies reviewed, can be obtained by implementing high performance management practices.'

MAINSTREAM ECONOMICS AND HUMAN RESOURCE MANAGEMENT

Mainstream Organizational Economics

Does mainstream organizational economics help us understand the superiority of HPWS? The answer is basically no. This is because the analyses of mainstream organizational economics are designed to explain behavior in control-oriented organizations where there is a clear principal-agent relationship (see, for example, Milgrom and Roberts, 1992: Chapters 7 and 12). The basic problem addressed in organizational economics' theory of incentives is 'to induce the agent to provide "effort" of various sorts' (p. 39). Thus, much of the relevant organizational economics, or personnel economics, involves how to devise incentives to get the employee/agent to exert a particular type and amount of effort that the employee experiences as onerous or at least does not want to exert. Because the employer/principal wants this effort exerted, or at least wants its fruits, the employer must give rewards (usually pecuniary) to the employees in order to direct their efforts away from what they naturally would do. Personnel economics provides a comprehensive analysis of the advantages and disadvantages of different methods of compensation including both individual and group incentives (see Lazear, 1995). An important aspect of personnel economics is developing an understanding of the effect on employee behavior of the entire structure of economic incentives. Mainstream organizational economics largely ignores the social and psychological, not to mention the spiritual, aspects of organization. It should be noted that mainstream organizational economics may be useful for understanding organizations that are hybrids in the sense of combining control-oriented organization with involvement-oriented organization.

Mainstream Human Resource Management

Traditional human resource management, sometimes known as personnel management, is concerned with a variety of personnel related duties in control-oriented organizations. For example, it is concerned with employee recruitment, selection, training, development, performance appraisal, compensation and labor relations (see, for example, Bateman and Snell, 1996: Chapter 12). Traditional HR managers have been especially concerned with getting the right person for the job, a person with appropriate training, experience, motivation and attitude/orientation. These traditional tasks take for granted the basic employer–employee relationship, the principal–agent relationship. Thus, mainstream HRM has not been concerned with transforming the approach to management (as is the case with HPWS) in order to gain competitive advantage. Concern with the latter is only recently becoming an important issue for HR managers.

BEYOND THE MAINSTREAM: DEVELOPING AN UNDERSTANDING OF HPWS

Behavioral Economics

To add to our understanding of the superiority of HPWS, it is important to start with x-efficiency theory, an important branch of behavioral economics. Some of the perspectives of x-efficiency theory (see, for example, Leibenstein, 1976) are very useful even though this theory is not explicitly oriented to understanding HPWS. One such perspective is that employees have discretion with respect to their efforts and employees typically exert significantly less effort than they could. Morris Altman in *Human Agency and Material Welfare* (1997) uses x-efficiency theory in a way that is suggestive of and anticipates important HPWS insights. For example, Altman recognizes that investment of time and energy is required to develop a more cooperative system of labor relations that elicits higher worker effort, and thus, higher x-efficiency (internal efficiency) (p. 44). Altman, however, does not spell out the nature of such cooperative systems nor why, except for his reference to cooperation and trust, we would expect high x-efficiency from them.

Organizational Behavior

Among the important insights developed by organizational behavior specialists is that:

> Innovative human resource practices are likely to contribute to improved economic performance only when three conditions are met: when employees possess knowledge and skills that managers lack; when employees are motivated to apply this skill and knowledge through discretionary effort; and when the firm's business or production strategy can only be achieved when employees contribute such discretionary effort. (MacDuffie, 1995: 199)

With regard to HPWS, many organizational experts have found that employees do in fact work harder, smarter, more creatively, and more cooperatively than employees in traditional organizations. Why is this so? The most important reasons are as follows. Because of these workers' higher involvement and commitment and their greater control over and say in their work, they work harder (Pfeffer, 1998: 33). They also work harder because of contingent compensation that rewards these efforts and because of 'peer pressure activated in self-managing teams' (p. 60). Because of HPWS' emphasis on developing workers' skills and competence, these workers' efforts are also better directed, that is, smarter. They also work smarter 'because of the training and job rotation practices that enhance the opportunity to learn' (p. 60). Because of HPWS' emphasis on teamwork, trusting relationships, and innovation, workers' efforts are more cooperative and creative. Because HPWS place greater responsibility on workers at the operational level, it 'saves on administrative overhead [layers of management are eliminated] as well as other costs associated with having an alienated work force in an adversarial relationship with management' (p. 33). In particular, HPWS reduces employment disputes, and thus, saves on the direct and indirect costs of employment litigation. According to Huselid (1995: 638), because of HPWS organizational structures such as cross-functional teams, job rotation and quality circles, workers' cooperative efforts are increased. For these and other reasons, HPWS workers' efforts are expected to be higher and more effective than for those working in a control-oriented organization. It should also be noted that, according to Lawler (1992: 41), there is likely to be less labor turnover in HPWS simply because of the attractiveness of this type of work environment.

Integrating Organizational Behavior with Behavioral Economics

That HPWS workers exert higher effort than those in control-oriented organizations is consistent with a body of theory that explains the relationship between worker participation and worker effort (Tomer, 1987). This theory draws upon fundamental organizational behavior insights and integrates these with x-efficiency theory. The most important psychological insight comes from Chris Argyris (1960) who explained why the demands of hierarchical organizations on healthy, mature individuals cause low motivation. According to Argyris, workers in traditional control-oriented organizations will experience frustration, psychological failure, short time perspective, internal conflict, an orientation to a part of the organization rather than to the whole, and counterproductive informal activities because they have little opportunity to be in control of work situations and to exercise their abilities (pp. 14–17). Conversely, it is only when an organization enables a member to satisfy their higher needs, notably the need for self-actualization, that an individual will get beyond the above difficulties and will have available high psychological energy for organizational purposes.

The basic model of worker motivation (Tomer, 1987: Chapter 5) builds upon Leibenstein's effort determination model in which workers choose the level of effort that maximizes their utility. This model adds a number of important factors missing from Leibenstein's factors suggested by Argyris' psychological insight. In particular, it adds four dimensions of the individual's work environment: first the match between an individual and the characteristics of both the job and the organization; second, the existing structure and supervision of the job; third the existence of clear, meaningful goals for jobs and the organization; and finally the nature and enforcement of the implicit contract between employer and employee (p. 49). The essence of the model is that when the work environment enables workers to have considerable control over how work is done, to acquire valued skills, and generally to experience significant 'ownership' of the workplace, workers will be able to satisfy their higher needs, and because of their high motivation, will choose high effort. This is clearly the case with HPWS.

A slightly more complex version of the above model (Tomer, 1987: Chapter 7) utilizes an implicit psychological contract spectrum with several important dimensions. For example, at the left end along one dimension, the employee is an agent of the firm's principals; on the opposite end, the employee has become a part of the work community, shares its goals, and participates in its decision making. At the left end of another dimension, the employee is controlled explicitly through a written contract and directive supervision, and on the right end, experiences implicit control through the internalization of goals and values. Another dimension is employee tenure from short-term (left) to lifetime employment (right). These moves from left to right on the spectrum are, according to this theory, associated with improvements in internal efficiency. Because HPWS is located on the far right of these several dimensions of the implicit psychological contract spectrum, it would be expected to have high internal efficiency stemming from high employee motivation and effort.

Two Kinds of Motivation

The essential reason for the superiority of HPWS over a control-oriented organization involves the distinction between two types of motivation, agent motivation and deep ownership motivation. These in turn involve a distinction between two types of employer–employee relationships. As explained below, understanding agent motivation is not a problem for economists but understanding deep ownership motivation is a major challenge for economists.

Agent motivation is what moves the employee as agent to do what the employer as principal wants. It involves the use of rewards and penalties, or external control, by the principal. Because of the prospect of the reward, generally involving the satisfaction of lower human needs away from work, the employee is willing to do other than what he really wants to do. This kind of motivation is very familiar to economists.

Deep owner motivation is the motivation experienced by employees who are not an agent of anybody and who are 'owners' of the organization in much more than the financial/legal sense. Employees motivated in this way experience high psychological energy when their organizations provide them with the opportunity for self-actualization (recall Argyris). Deep owner motivation arises when the employee is connected with or bonded with the organization in a deep and meaningful way, sharing a common destiny, mission, core values and spirit. Such employees are highly involved and committed to the organization; they experience genuine enthusiasm, empowerment and inspiration. Organization members are not simply making a calculative commitment; they are making an affective commitment charged with emotion (Ashforth and Humphrey, 1995: 110). This motivation is not external but it is not entirely internal; it is a product of the relationship of the member to the organization, a relationship which is entirely different from the principal–agent relationship. This kind of motivation is difficult for economists to understand: (a) because it does not involve external control, simple responsiveness to standard rewards and penalties; and (b) because it involves a conception of higher human need, a humanistic psychology, that does not fit well with the rudimentary psychology that economics incorporates.

Organizational Relationships as Capital

Deep ownership motivation, strictly speaking, is not something that is in an individual, and it is not something that is external to the individual like a structure of incentives. Deep ownership motivation derives from a particular type of employer–employee relationship that has been developed in the organization. Because of this relationship, the organization has a performance capability that is greater than it would be without it. Because of this relationship, the organization has a productive capacity greater than what could be attributed to the sum of all the other assets/resources utilized by the enterprise. This capacity or capability clearly has an asset-like or capital-like quality which has been recognized by a number of organizational behavior and economics writers.

My previous writings have developed the concept of organizational capital (see Tomer 1987, 1999). Organizational capital is a kind of human capital in which the productive capacity is not simply embodied in individuals but is embodied in the organizational relationships that have been developed in the organization. Because it is embodied in social relationships, organizational capital may also be considered a kind of social capital. When a business transforms its organization by installing the managerial practices and organizational features known as HPWS, it is making a very significant investment in organizational capital. Presumably a good part of the payoff to that investment is the improved performance deriving from the enhanced deep owner motivation.

Note that Ichniowski and Shaw (2003) refer to the 'connective capital' of the workers, presumably a kind of organizational capital. They 'define connective capital as a worker's access to the knowledge and skills of co-workers and model it as a key ingredient in effective problem solving' (p. 167). Generally, substantial investment in connective capital is indicated where HRM systems are innovative and workers interact with many others in problem solving.

Brian Becker and his coauthors (1997: 39) have recognized explicitly the usefulness of the organizational capital concept in connection with the organizational capabilities associated with HPWS. Becker *et al.* argue that implementing HPWS raises employee motivation, improves employee skills, and improves job design and work structures (p. 40). These, in turn, lead to improved operating performance which generates higher profits and growth, ultimately raising the market value of the firm (a sequence supported by the empirical studies cited earlier). In other words, investment in this kind of organizational capital functions very much like any other important capital asset. And according to a number of studies, intangible assets such as organizational capital account for up to 85 percent of a corporation's value (Becker *et al.*, 2001: ix). Unfortunately, organizational capital and other types of intangible capital are the assets that are 'least understood, least prone to measurement and, hence, least susceptible to management' (p. ix).

To understand better the nature of the intangible investment involved in changing an HRM system, Gant *et al.* (2002: 290) ask us to consider the difference in performance in two otherwise comparable establishments which differ in their HRM systems. The performance difference, they explain, came about due to the investment in social capital that produced differences in the 'structure of interactions and information transfer' making the innovative HRM system more productive than the traditional system.

Despite the evidence on the performance superiority of HPWS, it would, be a mistake to think that HPWS can be installed easily by simply imitating the best practices at other companies. Making successful organizational investments in HPWS creates intangible, unique, firm-specific organizational capabilities that are not easily replicated (Becker *et al.*, 1997: p. 41; Collis and Montgomery, 1995: 120). Investment in HPWS can produce a sustainable source of competitive advantage, according to leading HRM professionals, when the different managerial practices are combined into an internally coherent system involving alignment with existing organizational features (internal fit) and alignment with operating and strategic objectives (external fit) (Becker and Gerhart, 1996: 781; Becker *et al.*, 1997: 41). Moreover, based on their review of many studies Becker and Gerhart (1996: 784) conclude that these different component practices are complementary resources that do not produce superior performance in isolation; they only do so in combination. Thus, it is only when firms go beyond adopting best practices imitatively and create a well-integrated system that they can achieve a lasting competitive advantage and realize superior returns on their investment in organizational capital (p. 788).

Slow Diffusion

In spite of the prospects for high economic returns, diffusion of HPWS has neither been quick nor extensive in the US and the United Kingdom (Pfeffer, 1998: pp. 32, 61–2; see also Appelbaum and Batt, 1993: 41–55).

> In fact, some firms are moving away from the use of high commitment management – changes in practice are too often short-lived. Even when implemented, changes in management approach are often introduced in a truncated and partial manner. (Pfeffer, 1998: 32)

The most important reason for this is that installing HPWS is not a simple matter of acquiring and plugging in a best practice technology or method. Not only is there difficulty involved but opting for HPWS commits an organization to a profound change, one that involves a transformation of the relationship between employer and employee.

> Each of these changes [in managerial practices] challenges existing ways of doing things – particularly if the existing way emphasizes a Tayloristic, control-oriented approach. It is almost impossible to successfully implement high performance or high commitment work practices in the absence of mutual trust and respect. But trust is missing in many employment relationships. (Pfeffer, 1998: 62)

Other barriers to the spread of HPWS include: (a) high initial training costs; (b) the difficulties involved in satisfying short-term oriented investors; (c) managerial inertia and resistance due to their conservative instincts and values and due to their uncertainty about what is required; (d) the existing relationship and contracts with labor unions; and (e) other institutional barriers such as US labor law (Appelbaum and Batt, 1993: 48–59). According to Appelbaum and Batt (p. 42), the institutional framework of the US is geared to outmoded managerial approaches associated with mass production and does not provide adequate support for the emergence of HPWS. Moreover, many US firms are adapting to competitive pressures by attempting to make minor alterations in mass production so it is more flexible but consistent with the use of low skill, low wage workers (p. 45). The existence of and temptation of this low wage path is another obstacle to the diffusion of HPWS.

CONCLUSIONS

High performance work systems are a form of organization in which workers are not agents of principals, are not controlled by structures of incentives, but have become owners or principals in their outlook. Workers in this type of organizational relationship may be able to satisfy their need for self-actualization and experience deep owner motivation. Because these workers are identified with, committed to, and fully participating in the organization, their efforts are expected to be much higher and more effective than those of workers in control-oriented organizations who experience agent motivation. To understand the productivity of HPWS, and organizational excellence generally, economists need to go beyond the familiar agent motivation and incorporate into their theoretical frameworks the conception of deep ownership motivation. Also, note that to realize the full potential of HPWS requires going beyond imitation of other companies' best managerial practices; it requires installation of an internally coherent system. The payoffs to such an investment in organizational capital can be great but because it often involves such a profound change from past practice many managers are understandably reluctant to make more than hesitant steps toward it.

REFERENCES

Altman, Morris (1997), *Human Agency and Material Welfare: Revisions in Microeconomics and their Implications for Public Policy*, Boston, MA: Kluwer Academic.

Appelbaum, Eileen and Rosemary Batt (1993), *High Performance Work Systems: American Models of Workplace Transformation*, Washington, DC: Economic Policy Institute.

Argyris. Chris (1960), *Understanding Organizational Behavior*, New York: John Wiley.

Ashforth, Blake E. and Ronald H. Humphrey (1995), 'Emotion in the workplace: a reappraisal,' *Human Relations*, **48**(2), 97–125.

Bateman, Thomas S. and Scott A. Snell (1996). *Management: Building Competitive Advantage*, 3rd Edn, Chicago, IL: Irwin.

Becker, Brian and Barry Gerhart (1996), 'The impact of human resource management on organizational performance: progress and prospects,' *Academy of Management Journal*, **39**(4), 779–801.

Becker, Brian E., Mark A. Huselid, Peter S. Pickus and Michael F. Spratt (1997), 'HR as a source of shareholder value: research and recommendations,' *Human Resource Management*, **36**(1), 39–47.

Becker, Brian E., Mark A. Huselid and Dave Ulrich (2001), *The HR Scorecard: Linking People, Strategy, and Performance*, Boston, MA: Harvard Business School.

Collis, David J. and Cynthia A. Montgomery (1995), 'Competing on resources: strategy in the 1990s,' *Harvard Business Review*, **73**(4), 118–28.

Gant, Jon, Casey Ichniowski and Kathryn Shaw (2002), 'Social capital and organizational change in high-involvement and traditional work organizations,' *Journal of Economics and Management Strategy*, **11**(2), 289–328.

Huselid, Mark A. (1995), 'The impact of human resource management practices on turnover, productivity, and corporate financial performance,' *Academy of Management Journal*, **48**(3), 635–72.

Ichniowski, Casey and Kathryn Shaw (1999), 'The effects of human resource management on economic performance: an international comparison of US and Japanese plants,' *Management Science*, **45**(5), 704–23.

Ichniowski, Casey and Kathryn Shaw (2003), 'Beyond incentive pay: insiders' estimates of the value of complementary human resource management practices,' *Journal of Economic Perspectives*, **17**(1), 155–80.

Ichniowski, Casey, Kathryn Shaw and Giovanna Prennushi (1997), 'The effects of human resource management practices on productivity: a study of steel finishing lines,' *American Economic Review*, **87**(3), 291–313.

Kling, Jeffrey (1995), 'High performance work systems and firm performance,' *Monthly Labor Review*, **118**, 29–36.

Lawler, Edward E. (1992), *The Ultimate Advantage: Creating the High Involvement Organization*, San Francisco, CA: Jossey-Bass.

Lawler, Edward E., Susan A. Mohrman and Gerald E. Ledford (1995), *Creating High Performance Organizations: Practices and Results of Employee Involvement and Total Quality Management in Fortune 1000 Companies*, San Francisco, CA: Jossey-Bass.

Lazear, Edward P. (1995), *Personnel Economics*, Cambridge, MA: MIT Press.

Leibenstein, Harvey (1976), *Beyond Economic Man: A New Foundation for Microeconomics*, Cambridge, MA: Harvard University Press.

MacDuffie, John Paul (1995), 'Human resource bundles and manufacturing performance: organizational logic and flexible production systems in the world auto industry,' *Industrial and Labor Relations*, **48**(2), 197–221.
Milgrom, Paul and Roberts, John (1992), *Economics, Organization and Management*, Englewood Cliffs, NJ: Prentice Hall.
Pfeffer, Jeffrey (1998), *The Human Equation: Building Profits by Putting People First*, Boston, MA: Harvard Business School Press.
Tomer, John F. (1987), *Organizational Capital: The Path to Higher Productivity and Well-being*, New York: Praeger.
Tomer, John F. (1999), *The Human Firm: A Socio-Economic Analysis of its Behavior and Potential in a New Economic Age*, New York: Routledge.

5. The impact of organizational capital on economic performance: evidence from Netherlands-based multinational corporations

Bart Eikelenboom*

INTRODUCTION

An organization (or, more specifically in this chapter, a corporation) can be looked upon as a bundle of resources or capital.[1] This perspective derives from the resource-based view (RBV) within the domain of strategic management. There are multiple classifications of an organization's resources or capital. First is the distinction between the tangible and intangible assets of the corporation. Another distinction that has emerged in the RBV is the division between resources and capabilities (Makadok, 2001). A resource is an observable (but not necessarily tangible) asset that can be valued and traded – such as a brand, a patent, a parcel of land or a license. A capability on the other hand, is not observable (and hence necessarily intangible) and hard to value (Hoopes *et al.*, 2003). A third classification stems from Barney and Hesterly (1999) who distinguish several categories of a corporation's capital:

- *Physical capital*: This is the physical manifestations of the technology used in a firm, a firm's plant and equipment.
- *Human capital*: These are resources or capabilities linked to individuals associated with a firm.
- *Organizational capital*: This refers to the *relationships* among organization members (Tomer, 1987).
- *Financial capital*: This refers to the debt and equity financing available to firms.

The first category is tangible; the second, human capital, is intangible and embodied in individuals. The standard human capital part of the latter includes the knowledge and skills that contribute to employees' productive capacity (Becker, 1964). Another part of human capital is more intangible and includes noncognitive and nonphysical capacities important for individual job performance. The third category, organizational capital, is intangible and is embodied in employees' relationships. Note that the fourth category, financial capital, is not capital in the same sense as the other types because it is not produced productive capacity.

The economics profession has largely focused on the physical capital and standard human capital of the corporation because these are the tangible or at least not very intangible elements of capital. Partly because of the great recent interest of noneconomist social scientists in intangible capital, particularly social capital, some economists have become greatly interested in the intangible aspects of the corporation (for example Andriessen, 2003). Interestingly, one reason for this was that around the year 2000 there had been a growing difference between the stock market value of many corporations and the sum of the book value of their tangible assets. This suggested to some observers that the difference, a measure of the value of corporations' intangible assets, was becoming a more important and growing factor in the economy. The subsequent drop in stock market values in 2001 and after no doubt has caused some reconsideration of this view.

This chapter limits its focus to one category of intangible capital, namely organizational capital. Organizational capital is not observable, is firm-specific, and is aimed at enhancing the productivity of the other resources that the firm possesses (Makadok, 2001; Hoopes *et al.*, 2003). It can indeed be characterized as 'the most intangible of the company's resources' (Tomer, 1987).

Organizational capital may be viewed as the organizational context or environment in which organization members work. From a strategic management viewpoint, organizational capital may leverage the efforts of the organization members to the degree that it structures, coordinates, motivates, facilitates and enables individuals and groups to interact more effectively with customers and each other, thereby adding to the firm's productivity (Nadler and Tushman, 1997). If organizational capital produces these favorable results, it produces value, and it will be captured in the 'bottom line' performance of the corporation. The purpose of this chapter is to investigate empirically how the organizational capital in the business units of five Netherlands-based multinational corporations affects their economic performance.

The plan of the chapter is as follows. The next section assesses the 'hard-to-assess' variables related to organizational capital and economic performance. Following that, the empirical research setting is described. Finally the results are displayed and analyzed, and conclusions are drawn.

The empirical research task involves inherent complexity. This is because the relationship between the intangible, company-internal organizational capital and economic performance is anything but simple. On the one hand, organizational capital has been characterized as 'perhaps the least understood of the intangible assets' (Kaplan and Norton, 2004a). The intangible nature of organizational capital requires extensive conceptualization and dimensionalization before it can be measured. Conceptualization is turning the term (organizational capital) into a potentially measurable concept. Dimensionalization involves the next step, subdividing the concept into dimensions that can be measured. On the other hand, while economic performance is certainly a measurable concept, the measures tend to be 'noisy' (Ghoshal and Bartlett 1994), and performance data on business units within multibusiness corporations is often not available (Dess and Robinson 1984).

ASSESSING THE KEY VARIABLES

Operationalizing Organizational Capital

Organizational capital has been operationalized using the concept of organizational architecture (Eikelenboom, 2005). The concept of organizational architecture inextricably combines the company's 'hardware' – its business configuration and organization structure – and its 'software' – the motivations, values and commitments of the company's employees – all of which have an impact on the behavior of individual organization members (Nadler *et al.*, 1992; Bartlett and Ghoshal, 1995).

The term organizational architecture stems from the ancient Greek notion of 'tecture', which denotes ordinary construction or building. In addition, archi-tecture meant 'something higher than construction or building'. This something higher applies to the three-dimensional design, including space, materials and light providing both opportunities for and constraints on physical movement. Therefore, physical architecture has been defined as 'the art of shaping space to human needs and aspirations' (Janson, 1991). Similarly, organizational architecture has been defined as 'the art of shaping organizational space to meet human needs and aspirations' (Nadler *et al.*, 1992). Organizational architecture does not focus solely on formal structure, rather it has been described as the '*modus operandi*' of the firm that would include 'hard' organizational elements such as structure and systems, as well as 'soft' elements such as the informal organization, work practices, and management processes (Nadler *et al.*, 1992).

For the dimensionalization and assessment of organizational architecture, a comprehensive, internet-based, research and reporting platform was used, namely the *MeyerMonitor*, developed by MeyerMonitor in the Netherlands. This survey instrument captures respondents' answers quantitatively with the help of specific algorithms. Also, it provides very extensive operationalizations, encompassing 186 organizational performance indicators in 39 categories. Furthermore, the instrument has undergone extensive psychometric analyses such as smallest space analysis, hierarchical cluster analysis, multidimensional scaling and expert reviews.

Additional validity and reliability analyses have been conducted on the MeyerMonitor instrument (Eikelenboom, 2005). Factor analysis has resulted in five core underlying factors. The underlying dimensions are: quality and culture, personal empowerment and development, quality of management, benefits and rewards, and image. They have been found to reflect organizational architecture dimensions that were found in the literature. With Cronbach's alphas ranging from 0.76 to 0.93, relatively high reliability was demonstrated.

With the help of the MeyerMonitor instrument, respondents are able to score how their business unit is doing on all categories of organizational architecture. See the example in Figure 5.1.

The example in Figure 5.1 shows how quantitative data were obtained by having respondents score their perceived organizational context on a particular dimension, rating it on a scale from minus ten to ten (current). Also, the weight of their score was measured by asking the respondent to score the importance of the particular dimension (desired) on a scale from minus ten to ten.

Organizational architecture data were obtained from over 1500 individuals representing 41 business units in five large, Dutch headquartered, multinationals, all active in over 20 countries, with up to 1 billion euro sales and employing over 2000 employees. Based on the expected homogeneity within business units of multi-business corporations, which is far greater than the homogeneity on the level of the whole multinational, the business unit was determined to be a valid level of analysis for organizational architecture assessment. The MeyerMonitor instructions to individual organization members pointed out explicitly that their responses should relate to their own business unit only. This facilitates the problem of aggregating individual responses to the business unit level (see Van Muijen, 1994).

Assessment of Performance

Although performance is supposedly more straightforward to operationalize and measure than organizational architecture, it has been measured and

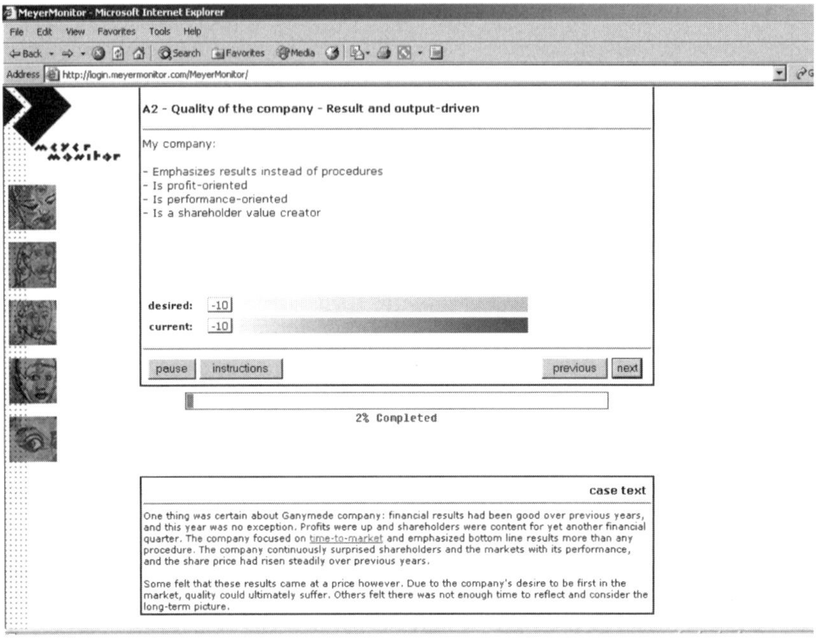

Figure 5.1 Example of web-based MeyerMonitor screen

operationalized in a wide range of ways. We have conceptualized the dependent variable 'performance' as 'strategic performance.' Strategic performance contains the short-term performance indicators that are based on the narrow conceptualization of 'financial performance,' which contrasts with broader concepts such as 'operational performance' and 'organizational effectiveness' (Venkatraman and Ramanujam, 1986). Therefore, strategic performance contains 'operating profits' and, 'gross profit margin' (Govindarajan and Gupta, 1985). Since it is expected that the influence of organizational architecture on strategic performance might take some time to materialize (compare: Van Eenennaam, 2001), performance indicators with a more long-term character such as sales growth and market share (Govindarajan and Gupta, 1985) are also included (Murray *et al.*, 1995). Figure 5.2 depicts these four performance elements.

Since performance data on business units in multinationals is not available for research, the subjective (survey) method of data gathering is considered a valid alternative (Dess and Robinson, 1984). The four strategic performance indicators have been tested in a pilot study for correlation with objective performance data as received from the accounting department in one of the participating multinationals. Encouraging correlations were

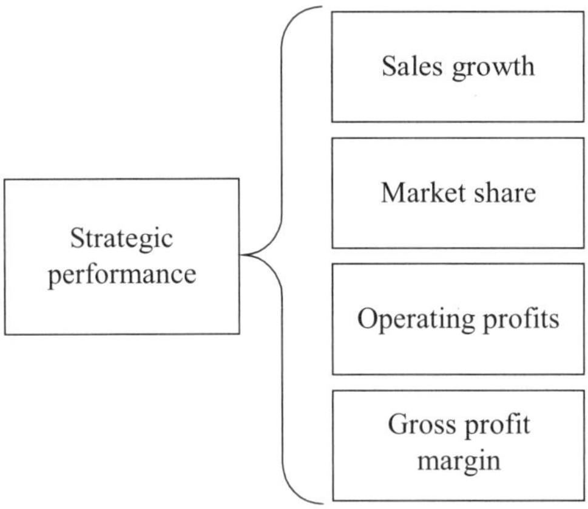

Figure 5.2 Conceptualization and dimensionalization of the performance variable

found, providing enough confidence to include the four indicators in a 'strategic performance survey'. This questionnaire was sent to the general managers of the business units from which organizational architecture data was available. The general managers were ones deemed to have considerable insight into the magnitude of their business unit's financial performance indicators, including the market share indicator, a key indicator of their unit's competitiveness. The managers were asked to indicate their own business unit's performance for two consecutive years and to compare the market share of their business unit with their immediate competitors on a five-point Likert-scale ranging from 1 (much worse/lower) to 5 (much better/higher). In the financial performance survey, a separate letter to these managers was enclosed. It emphasized that the survey served academic purposes only and that complete anonymity of the survey results was guaranteed. In this fashion, the subjective method of data gathering resulted in quantitative results on the four components of the dependent variable, strategic performance. The four performance indicators were added and averaged to arrive at the strategic performance variable.

ASSESSMENT OF THE ORGANIZATIONAL CAPITAL – ECONOMIC PERFORMANCE RELATIONSHIP

Since the mechanisms of value creation are outside the scope of this chapter, these are considered a black box. When the organizational capital of a corporation includes appropriate 'hard' as well as 'soft' capabilities and

Table 5.1 Multiple regression analysis (industry contingency)

Independent variables	N	r	R^2	R^2-change	F-value	p-value
Consumer goods	41	0.41	0.17	0.17	8.06	0.01**
Logistics	41	0.49	0.24	0.07	3.32	0.08^{+}
Percentage of total variance: 41						

Notes:
$^{+}$ Significant at the 0.10 level (2-tailed)
** Significant at the 0.01 level (2-tailed)

aligns and energizes the efforts of organization members, a synergistic result can be expected in which the outputs are greater than the sum of the inputs (Tomer, 1998).

Research Design

As mentioned earlier, data for the independent variable – conceptualized as organizational architecture – has been gathered with the help of MeyerMonitor, a computer-administered survey (Remenyi *et al.*, 1998). The instrument is extensive, comprising over 180 items that quantitatively characterize organizational architecture. Data on the dependent variable have been collected with the help of a self-administered survey (Bryman, 1989).

The research design can modestly be described as 'correlational in a cross-sectional setting' (compare: Dess *et al.*, 1993). The cross-sectional approach is expected to provide insight into the performance implications of organizational architecture (compare: Denison, 1984). The quantitative part of the research has been carried out in three steps. First, a contingency analysis was conducted, followed by correlation and multiple regression analyses.

Contingency Analysis

In order to control for other significant influencing variables (contingencies) on the dependent performance variable, a contingency analysis was conducted. This involved a multiple regression analysis with the help of dummy variables for industries. In the original research sample of 41 business units, two of the industries (logistics and consumer goods) were found to provide a statistically significant explanation of the variance of financial (or strategic) performance (see Table 5.1).

Since these two industries were highly associated with financial performance, data for them have been removed from the research sample. See Table 5.2 for the characteristics of the final research sample.

Table 5.2 Research sample after contingency analysis

Industry	Invited – responded BU's to Strategic performance survey (*response rate*):	Invited – responded** individuals of the MeyerMonitor linked to the responded BU's (*response rate*):
ICT	13*–13 *(100%)*	1685–939 *(56%)*
Logistics and mail	11–3 *(27%)*	46–27 *(59%)*
Finance	6–6 *(100%)*	260–147 *(57%)*
Financial services	33–8 *(24%)*	320–202 *(63%)*
Total	63–30 (48%)	2311–1315 (57%)

Notes:
BU: Business Unit ICT: Information and Communication Technology
* Maximum allowed by corporate headquarters (44% of total).
** After deleting invalid respondents (those who skipped items or did not finish the MeyerMonitor).

After this contingency analysis, 30 business units remained for which industry did not correlate significantly with financial performance, an indication that the contingency variable is controlled for adequately (Govindarajan and Gupta, 1985). Although this has resulted in a reduced sample size of 30 business units, for the remainder of the statistical analyses, it may be stated that if significant performance advantages exist, they are associated with the described organizational resources and not other variables such as company size, maturity, and so on (compare: Powell and Dent-Micallef, 1997; see Eikelenboom, 2005).

Correlation Analysis

Correlation analysis results are provided in Table 5.3. The last column provides the correlation coefficients of the five organizational architecture variables and total organizational architecture with strategic performance.

Overall, organizational architecture has a moderate positive and significant correlation with strategic performance ($p < 0.10$). Of the underlying factors of organizational architecture, only Quality and culture is significant ($p < 0.05$) and positively related to strategic performance.

Multiple Regression Analysis

The results of the multiple regression analysis of the organizational architecture factors on strategic performance are provided in Table 5.4.[2]

Table 5.3 Means, standard deviations and correlations

Variables	Mean	s.d.	*r*
Strategic performance	13.69	34.41	
Organizational architecture, total	3.85	1.10	0.30+
Quality and culture	3.57	1.25	0.45*
Personal development and empowerment	4.24	1.15	0.24
Quality of management	5.36	1.24	0.27
Benefits and rewards	2.67	1.39	0.00
Image	3.30	1.48	0.23

Notes:
+ Correlation is significant at the 0.10 level (2-tailed)
* Correlation is significant at the 0.05 level (2-tailed)
Dependent variable: strategic performance

The results indicate that the underlying dimensions Quality and culture and Benefits and rewards together explain 30 percent of the variance of financial performance. The factor Quality and culture is the most significant and most strong predictor with 20 percent explained variance. The found relationships are depicted in Figure 5.3 (on the right side are the correlation coefficient and explained variance of the two significant underlying dimensions of organizational architecture). Based on the empirical results of this study, it can be concluded that perceived organizational architecture correlates positively ($r = 0.30$) with strategic performance. In general, this percentage is considered moderately high for a latent construct. The underlying dimensions, Quality and culture and Benefits and rewards together correlate positively with strategic performance (r=0.54), and together explain 30 percent of strategic performance. However, we are cautious to interpret the results of the underlying dimensions of organizational architecture since a fairly high amount of multicollinearity has been found. The correlation matrix in Table 5.5 shows the medium to high inter-correlations between the underlying factors and the overall construct of organizational architecture.

The relatively high amount of multicollinearity reduces one's ability to discern the separate influences of the (underlying) independent variables on performance (Hair *et al.*, 1998).

Conclusions

Data from a sample of large, Dutch headquartered, multinationals has demonstrated significant, positive relationships between organizational capital and the economic performance of business units. Although the

Table 5.4 Multiple regression analysis

Independent Variables:	r	R^2	R^2-change	B	t-value	F-value	p-value
Quality and culture	0.45	0.20	0.20	18.26	3.36	6.95	0.01**
Benefits and rewards	0.54	0.30	0.10	−9.40	−1.92	3.69	0.07^{+}
Percentage of total variance: 30							

Notes:
$^{+}$ Significant at the 0.10 level (2-tailed)
** Significant at the 0.01 level (2-tailed)
Strategic Performance is the dependent variable.

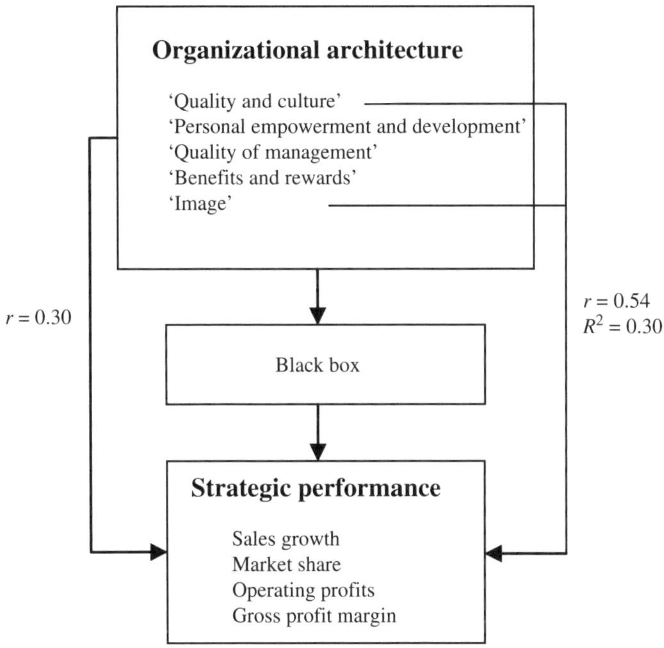

Figure 5.3 Found relationships

relationship is highly complex, the results indicate that improvement of multinationals' organizational capital may create a leverage for increased performance that otherwise would have been left on the table (Eikelenboom, 2005).

Does this tell us that positively perceived organizational architecture releases energies that increase the engagement and excitement of workers in the organization? Yes! Although the mechanisms related to increased performance were not examined in this study,[3] it can be concluded from the

Table 5.5 Multicollinearity (inter-correlations)

Variable	1	2	3	4	5
Organizational architecture					
Quality and culture	0.92**				
Personal development and empowerment	0.92**	0.76**			
Quality of management	0.76**	0.73**	0.63**		
Benefits and rewards	0.65**	0.46**	0.60**	0.26	
Image	0.83**	0.78**	0.69**	0.59**	0.35*

Notes:
* Correlation is significant at the 0.05 level (2-tailed)
** Correlation is significant at the 0.01 level (2-tailed)

results that higher scores on organizational architecture represent an organizational context that enables, nurtures, fosters and levers organizational behavior, which ultimately leads to higher strategic performance. Having corrected for the industry contingency and having dealt with complexities such as time lag issues by incorporating short and long-term performance indicators, the moderate, but statistically significant relationships indicate that an affirmative answer can be given to the question above.

Due to the degree of multicollinearity, it is difficult to reach firm conclusions about the impact on performance of each of the organizational architecture variables. It has been recognized that dimensionalization often can severely interfere with the representation of holistic phenomena such as organizational climate (and in our case: organizational architecture), 'because there is always much more to a context than can be encompassed by any list of dimensions or attributes' (Poole, 1985). The empirical results lead us to conclude that the influence of organizational capital is to a large extent holistic in nature. The nature of this influence is that although it is 'difficult to define and even more difficult to develop, it is nevertheless something easy to sense and experience: one manager described it as the "smell of the place" manifested in a thousand small details of how a company functions' (Bartlett and Ghoshal, 1995). In this study, the influence of organizational architecture as the conceptualization of organizational capital was found to be fairly pervasive, although hard to pinpoint exactly.

Limitations and Future Research Avenues

It is acknowledged that due to the relatively small sample size, causality, strictly speaking, could not be established. But significant correlation was demonstrated. Furthermore, additional longitudinal studies are recommended in order to incorporate time issues. Finally, alignment of organizational architecture with (formal) strategy may reveal important additional insights. This study may be considered a foundation on which further advances in the understanding of the relationships between intangibles such as organizational capital and economic outcomes may be built.

Managerial Implications

Ultimately, strategic performance is a management responsibility. It follows that general managers, in order to be successful, must take on the important role of shapers of organizational context or organizational architecture (Ghoshal and Bartlett, 1994). The term organizational architecture as used here implies that a sole focus on the hard organizational elements such as formal structure and systems is not sufficient for success; there needs to be an emphasis on both the soft organizational elements such as spirit, culture and leadership as well as the hard ones. Since organizational capital is perhaps the most inimitable of a company's resources, it is a key task of management to give shape to this resource (Ghoshal and Bartlett, 1994).

Hopefully, this study will help raise the awareness of managers concerning the importance of the inextricable combination of intangible, 'hard' and 'soft' organizational capital, as captured in the concept of organizational architecture, for bottom line, strategic performance. As hardware needs software and vice versa, an emphasis on only hard, formal, structures may lead to rigidness, inflexibility, insensitivity to individuals, emptiness and uninspired workers. Emphasis on only the soft aspects leads to fluidness, lack of goal orientedness, no synergy effects and inefficiencies. The one cannot work without the other. An inspiring culture cannot replace structure and systems, and a smoothly balanced organizational structure cannot replace a lack of spirit and leadership. This study implies that corporate (level) management in multinationals should not forsake either its management or its leadership roles. Clearly, it is not 'just a luxury' for corporate executives to work on organizational architecture in order to achieve the desired balance of the hard and soft and the desired balance of management and leadership.

FINAL CONCLUSIONS

The increasing pressures on corporate life are acknowledged: increasing competition, massive social and technological change, the evolution of global markets, and perhaps most importantly, an increasing change velocity. To cope with this along with growing insecurities, an increasing emphasis is being placed on the intangible aspects of organization such as motivation, spirit, enthusiasm, ideas and emotions and leadership (Tomer, 1998). Traditional hard factors such as tangible and financial assets are considered to be less important in the knowledge economy, and explanations of economic growth now focus more on intangible capital. The empirical evidence in this chapter indeed indicates support for this perspective in that it finds a very significant impact of one type of intangible capital, organizational capital, on economic performance.

NOTES

* Bart Eikelenboom, Business Universiteit Nyenrode, The Netherlands.

1. These two notions are used interchangeably (Robison *et al.*, 2002, Ray *et al.*, 2004).
2. The regression equation is SP = −26.45 + 18.26 Q&C − 9.40 B&R where SP is strategic performance, Q&C is quality and culture, and B&R is benefits and rewards.
3. This study uses a resource-based logic from strategic management which suggests that uniqueness springs from (organizational) resources (Barney, 2001). How the influencing process of organizational context to organizational behavior functions is not examined, as it is in the area of organizational psychology and outside the scope of this chapter.

REFERENCES

Andriessen, D. (2003), 'The value of weightless wealth: designing a method for the valuation of intangible resources,' Ph.D thesis, Universiteit Nyenrode.

Barney, Jay B. (2001), 'Is the resource-based "view" a useful perspective for strategic management research? Yes' *Academy of Management Review*, **26**(1), 41–56.

Barney, J.B. and W. Hesterly (1999), 'Organizational economics: understanding the relationship between organizations and economic analysis,' in R. Clegg and C. Hardy (eds), *Studying Organization. Theory and Method*, London: Sage.

Bartlett C.A. and S. Ghoshal (1995), 'Rebuilding behavioral context: turn process reengineering into people rejuvenation,' *Sloan Management Review*, **37**(1), 11–23.

Becker, G.S. (1964), *Human Capital: A Theoretical and Empirical Analysis, with Special Reference to Education*, New York: Columbia University Press.

Bryman, A. (1989), *Research Methods and Organization Studies: Contemporary Social Research*, Volume 20, London: Unwin Hyman.

Denison, D.R. (1984), 'Bringing corporate culture to the bottom line,' *Organizational Dynamics*, **13**(2), 5–22.

Dess, G.G. and R.B. Robinson Jr. (1984), 'Measuring organizational performance in the absence of objective measures,' *Strategic Management Journal*, **5**(3), 265–73.

Dess, G.G., S. Newport and A.M.A. Rasheed (1993), 'Configuration research in strategic management: key issues and suggestions', *Journal of Management*, **19**(4), 775–95.

Eenennaam, F. van. (2001), *Market-Based Strategies in a Converging Market: A Study on Marketing Standardisation of Consumer Goods in Western Europe*, Breukelen: Athenean Holding BV.

Eikelenboom, B.L. (2005), 'Organizational capital and bottom line performance: the relationship between organizational architecture and strategic performance of business units in Dutch headquartered multinationals', Ph.D dissertation, Business Universiteit Nyenrode, Breukelen (The Netherlands): Eburon.

Ghoshal, S. and C.A. Bartlett (1994), 'Linking organizational context and managerial action: the dimensions of quality of management,' *Strategic Management Journal*, **15** (Summer Special Issue), 91–112.

Govindarajan, V. and A.K. Gupta (1985), 'Linking control systems to business unit strategy: impact on performance,' *Accounting, Organizations and Society*, **10**(1), 51–66.

Hair Jr, J.F., R.E. Anderson, R.L. Tatham and W.C. Black (1998), *Multivariate Data Analysis*, London: Prentice-Hall International.

Hoopes, D.G., T.L. Madsen and G. Walker (2003), 'Guest editors' introduction to the special issue: why is there a resource-based view?: toward a theory of competitive heterogeneity,' *Strategic Management Journal*, **24**(10), 889–902.

Janson, F.W. (1991), *History of Art*, New York: Abrams.

Kaplan, R.S. and D.P. Norton (2004a), 'Measuring the strategic readiness of intangible assets,' *Harvard Business Review*, **82**(5), 52–63.

Kaplan, R.S. and D.P. Norton (2004b), 'How strategy maps frame an organization's objectives,' *Financial Executive*, **20**(2), 40–45.

Londen, H. Van (1998), *De waarde en waarden van concerns [The Value and Values of Concerns]*, Assen: Van Gorcum.

Makadok, R. (2001), 'Toward a synthesis of the resource-based and dynamic-capability views of rent creation,' *Strategic Management Review*, **22**(5), 387–402.

Muijen, J.J. van (1994), *Organisatiecultuur en organisatieklimaat, de ontwikkeling van een meetinstrument op basis van het 'competing values' model. [Organization Culture and Organizational Climate, the Development of a Measuring-Instrument on Basis of the Competing Values Model]*. Ridderkerk: Ridderprint BV.

Murray, J.Y., M. Kotabe and A.R.Wildt (1995), 'Strategic and financial perfomance implications of global sourcing strategy: a contingency analysis,' *Journal of International Business Studies*, **26**(1), 181–202.

Nadler, D.A. and M.L. Tushman (1997), *Competing by Design: The Power of Organizational Architecture.* Oxford: Oxford University Press.

Nadler, D.A., M. Gerstein, R. Shaw and associates (1992), *Organizational Architecture. Designs for Changing Organizations*, San Francisco, CA: Jossey-Bass.

Poole, M.S. 1985, 'Communication and organization climates,' In: L. Putnam and R.D. Thompkins (eds) *Organizational Communication: Traditional Themes and New Directions*. Beverly Hills: Sage.

Powell, Thomas C. and Anne Dent-Micallef (1997), 'Information technology as competitive advantage: the role of human, business, and technology resources,' *Strategic Management Journal*, **18**(5), 375–405.

Ray, G., J. B. Barney and W.A. Muhanna (2004), 'Capabilities, business processes, and competitive advantage: choosing the dependent variable in empirical tests of the resource-based view,' *Strategic Management Journal*, **25**(1), 23–37.

Remenyi, D., B. Williams, A. Money and E. Swartz (1998), *Doing Research in Business and Management*, London: Sage.

Robison, L.J., A.A. Schmid and M.E. Siles (2002), 'Is social capital really capital,' *Review of Social Economy*, **60**(1), 1–21.
Tomer, J.F. (1987), *Organizational Capital: The Path to Higher Productivity and Well-Being*, New York: Praeger.
Tomer, J.F. (1998), 'Beyond the machine model of the firm, toward a holistic human model,' *Journal of Socio-Economics*, **27**(3), 323–41.
Venkatraman, N. and V. Ramanujam (1986), 'Measurement of business performance in strategy research: a comparison of approaches,' *Academy of Management Review*, **11**(4), 801–14.

6. Personal capital and emotional intelligence: an increasingly important intangible source of economic growth

> Analyses done by dozens of different experts in close to five hundred corporations, government agencies, and nonprofit organizations worldwide have arrived independently at remarkably similar conclusions . . . Their conclusions all point to the paramount place of emotional intelligence in excellence on the job – in virtually any job.
>
> **Goleman 1998: 5**

The purpose of this chapter is to provide an explanation for a part of economic growth that has heretofore been unexplained. In seeking to explain economic growth, economists have naturally turned first to the most tangible factors, physical capital, natural resources and labor. Increasingly, however, they have turned to intangible or less tangible considerations like standard human capital. Because a significant part of economic growth still remains unexplained, it is necessary and important to explore the role of the most intangible factors, those of a social and psychological nature. That is why this chapter is concerned with personal capital formation and its contribution to explaining the previously unexplained growth in national output. This chapter focuses largely on one type of personal capital formation, that due to improvement in emotional intelligence.

ECONOMIC GROWTH AND INTANGIBLE CAPITAL FORMATION

Let's start with the standard neoclassical approach to economic growth in which the economy is viewed as a production function. Using a version of this theory, Edward Denison (for example, 1962 and 1974) and other economists have used 'growth accounting' methods to estimate the sources of economic growth. In particular, they have used data on the growth of certain inputs and outputs in order to indicate how much of the output growth is accounted for by the growth of these different inputs. The unaccounted for growth, the residual, is a measure of the magnitude of technological change as well as the effect of the unmeasured influences and mismeasurement (see Maddison, 1995: 40–46). Abramovitz (1993: 218) has referred to the residual as our 'measure of ignorance.' Despite some drawbacks, it is useful at least to begin with the standard approach because my intention is to reduce our ignorance (and the size of the residual) further by explaining about a number of inputs that have at best been little considered by economists.

In seeking to explain or account for a larger proportion of economic growth, economists have more and more included intangible inputs in their analyses, most importantly, human capital deriving from education and training. The noneconomic and/or intangible aspects have received less attention in part because they frequently do not lend themselves to measurement. Insofar as there is evidence available, there is reason to believe that noneconomic intangible sources of growth are more important now than they were formerly (Abramovitz, 1993).

Recall from Chapter 2 the essential nature of what economists call capital. Capital is that which is produced by humans, is long lasting, represents productive capacity, involves a cost, and might be invested in on the basis of a self-conscious calculation relating to the future. As many of us now realize, older definitions that emphasized capital as tangible assets are far too narrow. The importance of my broad, general definition above is that it allows us to conceive of other things that can serve as productive capacity. Certainly the enhanced human capacities owing to education and training are important, but there are other important intangible factors to consider.

The importance of the standard concept of human capital, in contrast to social and organizational capital, is fully accepted by the economic mainstream. Although this acceptance and interest in human capital has occurred in the last 40 years or so, the idea of human capital is far older. 'Economists who considered human beings or their skills as capital include such well-known names in the history of economic thought as Petty, Smith, Say, Senior, List, von Thunen, Roscher, Bagehot, Ernst Engel, Sidgwick, Walras, and Fisher' (Kiker, 1966: 481). Adam Smith (1937: 101, 265–6), for instance, explicitly recognized that human skills and useful abilities are just like expensive machinery in they can be acquired at a cost with the expectation of earning at least an ordinary rate of profit. These skills and abilities, however, are very different from tangible capital in that they are embodied in a person. Unlike tangible capital, human capital cannot be removed or alienated from an individual in order to be sold. Thus, recalling Chapter 2, human capital refers to mental, social and physical attributes that are produced, are embodied in humans, are not alienable, and contribute to a person's productive capacity, enabling the possessor to earn higher income as a consequence.

Another type of intangible capital is social (and organizational) capital; both are the product of activities that create social relationships.[1] Despite their lack of recognition as capital by economists, social and organizational capital should definitely be considered types of capital. This is because these social relationships provide lasting productive capacity that is used by economic entities to achieve their purposes. Both social and organizational capital are forms of human capital because in each the productive capacity is embodied in humans. However, the productive capacity is embodied, generally speaking, not in individuals per se but in the relationships or connections between people. There is a growing literature in economics and other social science disciplines (especially sociology) that attempts to explain and document the contribution of various types of social capital to economic growth (see Chapter 3 for a review of some of the important contributions to this literature). Recall from Chapter 2 that social capital refers to enduring features of the social landscape that provide productive capacity by enabling important recurrent social activities.

PERSONAL CAPITAL AS A SOURCE OF ECONOMIC GROWTH

Is it possible to account for all or most of the variation in human economic performance using as explanatory variables: (a) individual endowments of the standard types of human capital; and (b) the social and organizational capital endowments related to these individuals? There is good reason to think the answer is no. This is because there are other types of human capacity that must be considered, in particular what I have previously called personal capital. To begin our exploration of this new concept, let's first inquire into the nature and magnitude of individual differences in productivity.

Individual Differences in Productivity

Hunter *et al.* (1990) find very sizable variations among employees in their measured workplace output, and the amount of this variability is positively related to the complexity level of the job. They find, for example, that for routine clerical or blue collar work the top 1 percent of workers produced a dollar value of output worth 52 percent more than the average worker. For jobs of medium complexity, the top 1 percent added 85 percent more value than the average performer, and for the most complex jobs such as insurance salespeople, account managers, lawyers and physicians, the top 1 percent added 127 percent more value (see also Goleman, 1998: 34–5 and 336). This variability suggests that firms, and colleges as well, have much to gain from selecting applicants likely to be high performers.

Traditionally, in their efforts to select high performers, businesses and colleges have relied greatly on school grades and intelligence tests. Unfortunately, as David McClelland (1973) indicates, both of these have a very low correlation with job and life success. In McClelland's view, high job performance is frequently related more strongly to many other competencies than those pointed to by the traditional academic measures. Thus, he believes that businesses and colleges should try to select applicants on the basis of those competencies that have demonstrated a close relationship to the desired performance behavior, and they should educate and train people to improve these competencies as opposed to improving general academic aptitude. Included among the nonscholastic competencies that McClelland thinks are highly related to success are: (a) moderate goal setting; (b) patience; (c) ability to communicate emotions; (d) initiative; (e) ability to respond well in unclear situations; and (f) moral development (pp. 9–12). Economists acknowledge that the influence of such 'personality' factors 'in productivity is detectable and is rewarded by employers. But most economists, unlike psychologists, have taken the position that personality is either unobservable or unmeasurable' (Goldsmith *et al.*, 1997: 815). Let's now examine the concept of personal capital which refers to these very intangible competencies that economists and others have tended to ignore.

The Concept of Personal Capital

Personal capital is a kind of human capital because it relates to capacity embodied in individuals. However, personal capital differs from standard human capital in that the human capacity involved is not the type developed by academic education or by the usual types of job related training. The personal capital capacities are fundamentally different from cognitive intelligence or intellectual knowledge. Personal capital relates to an individual's basic personal qualities and reflects the quality of an individual's psychological, physical and spiritual functioning (Tomer, 1996: 626–7; Tomer, 2001: 251). Further, it mirrors one's internal biochemical balance, one's physical health and conditioning, one's psychological strengths and weaknesses, and one's purpose in life. A person's stock of personal capital is partly a product of one's genetic inheritance, partly a result of the life-shaping events that one has encountered, and partly an outcome of one's efforts to mature and to grow in nonintellectual ways.

Thus, it is in part produced intentionally. Personal capital qualities are related to a person's capacity to work or consume in that they underlie the more specific capacities (standard human capital and consumption capital) that a person invests in in order to be qualified for work tasks or to be able to enjoy consumer goods. Moreover, certain personal capital qualities are a prerequisite for developing successful organizational relationships (social and organizational capital) (Tomer, 1999a: 46–8). The existence of these personal capital capacities in its members makes it possible for economic entities to achieve more than would be possible without them.

It is necessary to take note of other authors who have used the term personal capital, or similar terms, and whether they define it similarly. Recently, Gary Becker (1996: Chapter 1) has used the term personal capital in a quite different way. Personal capital in his usage is a capacity deriving from a person's past consumption and personal experience; it is a capacity that is a determinant of one's ability to get satisfaction from consumer goods. His personal capital concept is what I, and Becker in earlier works, have referred to as consumption capital. Another author, Daniel Goleman (1998: 209), has used the term personal capital to refer to a person's 'networks of personal contacts.' This is different from my usage and is essentially the same as the concept of social capital used by sociologists. Goldsmith *et al.* (1997: 815) use the term psychological capital to refer to 'those features of personality psychologists believe contribute to an individual's productivity. These may include a person's perception of self, attitudes toward work, ethical orientation, and general outlook on life.' Further, 'a person's psychological capital is likely to govern their motivation and general attitude toward work' (p. 816). Thus, as used by Goldsmith *et al.*, the psychological capital concept is similar to personal capital but somewhat narrower because it only relates to human psychological capacities.

In their book, *Personal Productivity*, John W. and John B. Kendrick (1988) do not use the term personal capital, but they do explain about many ways in which people can invest in themselves, raise their productivity, and thereby accomplish more of their personal goals. In their chapter on 'Investment in self: health and safety,' they explain how individuals can invest in their mental and spiritual health (Chapter 6). For example, the Kendricks explain: (a) how one's psychological difficulties might be overcome with or without the use of psychotherapy (p. 84); (b) how one can strengthen positive thinking and build a positive self image (p. 85); (c) how a person can recharge one's spiritual batteries; and (d) how one can take charge of one's life (p. 86). These are all activities involving investments in what I call personal capital.

Emotional Intelligence and Emotional Competence

A very important component of personal capital that has received much recent attention is the human capacity called emotional intelligence. Daniel Goleman (1995, 1998; Goleman *et al.*, 2002) in the three books, *Emotional Intelligence*, *Working with Emotional Intelligence* and *Primal Leadership*, is particularly notable for defining, applying, and popularizing this concept. My use of emotional intelligence (EI) draws heavily upon his second book which focuses on the important contribution that organization members' EI makes in the workplace.

According to Goleman (1998: 317),

> 'Emotional Intelligence' refers to the capacity for recognizing our own feelings and those of others, for motivating ourselves, and for managing emotions well in ourselves and in our relationships. It describes abilities distinct from, but complementary to, academic intelligence, the purely cognitive capacities measured by IQ.

Emotional intelligence has five elements: self-awareness, motivation, self-regulation, empathy, and adeptness in relationships (p. 24). These determine one's potential for mastering the 25 emotional competencies, the more specific human capacities essential for success in the workplace. For each of the five elements of EI, there are a number of corresponding emotional competencies (pp. 24–8). For example, there are three emotional competencies associated with self-awareness: (a) emotional awareness; (b) accurate self-assessment; and (c) self-confidence. See Box 6.1 for the complete list of EIs and their associated emotional competencies.

In contrast to IQ (or pure cognitive capacity) which remains relatively fixed throughout one's life, 'emotional intelligence develops with age and experience from childhood to adulthood' and, through effort, can be improved at any age (John Mayer as quoted in Goleman 1998: 239–40). For most people, EI grows steadily with advancing maturity, particularly as people learn: (a) to become more aware of their emotions, especially distressing ones; (b) to become more empathetic with others; and (c) to handle difficult social situations and relationships. The emotional competencies based on EI involve 'ingrained habits of thought, feeling and behavior' which can be learned and unlearned with effort and time (p. 243). In the process of acquiring these habitual patterns, neural connections associated with these patterns are strengthened and become the dominant path for nerve impulses.

BOX 6.1 THE EMOTIONAL COMPETENCE FRAMEWORK

Personal Competence

Self-Awareness

- Emotional awareness
- Accurate self-assessment
- Self-confidence

Self-Regulation

- Self-control
- Trustworthiness
- Conscientiousness
- Adaptability
- Innovation

Motivation

- Achievement drive
- Commitment
- Initiative
- Optimism

Social Competence

Empathy

- Understanding others
- Developing others
- Service orientation
- Leveraging diversity
- Political awareness

Social Skills

- Influence
- Communication
- Conflict management
- Leadership
- Change catalyst
- Building bonds
- Collaboration and cooperation
- Team capabilities

Source: Daniel Goleman (1998), *Working with Emotional Intelligence*, pp. 26–7.

It is important to note that different kinds of emotional competence are required by different industries, organizations, and jobs (Goleman, 1998: 28–9). Thus, individuals who improve their EI and emotional competence in ways that match the demands of their work situation can be expected to raise their job performance. Spending time and effort on such improvements is the essence of what successful investment in personal capital involves.

A number of other authors define EI somewhat differently from Goleman. For instance, Mayer and Salovey's (1997: 5) definition is more like a kind of intelligence in that it emphasizes thinking, perceiving, understanding, appraising, discriminating and identifying emotion. Goleman's concept of EI, on the other hand, relates to the way people function emotionally if their functioning is at its potential or at least is not problematic. Hendrie Weisinger's (1998) definition is relatively close to Goleman's. In his view, EI is the intelligent use of emotions.

Compared to Goleman's, Robert Cooper and Ayman Sawaf's (1997: 273) definition gives greater emphasis to the higher aspects of human behavior, particularly aspects associated with business leadership. Their concept includes factors such as intuition, integrity, personal purpose and creativity not emphasized by Goleman. Steve and John Simmons' (1997) approach to EI is very different from Goleman's. In their view, EI relates to 26 relatively invariant character traits. In subsequent discussion, this chapter relies largely on Goleman's concepts of EI and emotional competence.

Emotional Intelligence and Economic Performance

How does high emotional functioning translate into the competencies that make for successful job performance? And how does lack of these competencies make for failure? In *Working with Emotional Intelligence*, Goleman (1998) explains in great detail how the presence or absence of the 25 emotional competencies is a crucial determinant of specific kinds of work performance. To illustrate, let's consider a number of the emotional competencies listed in Box 6.1 in order to get a better idea how they contribute.

First consider trustworthiness which means acting ethically, building trust through reliability and authenticity, and admitting mistakes (Goleman 1998: 89). Its importance is indicated in the following:

> 'Of the general managers for sales who've worked for me and washed out, the single thing they lacked most was trustworthiness,' a senior vice president at a division of Automatic Data Processors told me. 'In sales, it's trade-offs – I'll give you this if you give me a concession on that. It's an ambiguous situation, where you have to take someone's word for it. A field like finance – that's more science than art, it's more clear-cut. But in sales it's grays, so being trustworthy is all the more important.' (pp. 90–91)

The second competency considered is achievement drive. People with this competency are results-oriented, set challenging goals, and pursue information related to how to improve their performance (Goleman, 1998: 113).

> Consider a study of fifty-nine entrepreneurs, most of them research scientists, each of whom had taken advantage of an innovative technology to found a high-tech firm. Five years after establishing their firms, those who were highest in achievement traits (like seeking out feedback on their performance and setting goals) were the most likely to have flourished – they had an average increase in sales of $1 million a year, increased the number of employees by fifty or more, or sold their company for a substantial profit. (p. 116)

Another competency is conflict management. People with this competence are able to negotiate and resolve disagreements, handle difficult people and tense situations, de-escalate conflict, and orchestrate win-win solutions (Goleman, 1998: 178).

> In a survey of retail buyers in department store chains, each of whom handled merchandise worth $15 million to $30 million, the style of negotiating was an accurate barometer of the health of the manufacturer-retailer relationship. Predictably, when negotiations were typically aggressive, revolving around threats and demands, it boded poorly for the future of the relationship; buyers ended up embittered and dissatisfied and often dropped the product line. But for those relationships in which aggressiveness was ruled out in favor of problem solving or compromise, the longevity of the relationship increased. (p. 181)

Finally, building bonds is a competence involving nurturing instrumental relationships. This includes cultivating extensive informal networks, building rapport, and maintaining friendships among work associates (Goleman, 1998: 206).

> Jeffrey Katzenberg, one of the three founders of the Hollywood creative company Dreamworks SKG, is a networker without equal. The motive for his manic flurries of calls is, mainly, just to stay in touch – not explicitly to 'do business.' But his telephone routine primes these relationships, keeping them fresh, so that when the business need comes along, he can call on them seamlessly: make a proposal, pin down a deal. In the entertainment industry, relationships are the key to doing business, because the projects – a film, a TV series, an interactive CD-ROM – are all short-term, goal-focused, and time-limited. They require knitting together an instant organization, a pseudofamily of director, producers, actors, and production people, all of whom dissolve back at the end into a loose network of potential players. Katzenberg keeps a weblike thread of connection out to everyone so that he can reel them in as needed. (pp. 206–7)

Each and every occupation has a unique profile of emotional competencies that, along with cognitive intelligence, education, training, mentoring and supervising, would be necessary for excellent performance. Because of the relative importance of emotional competencies in successful job performance, it makes sense for companies to assess jobs to determine their emotional competence requirements and to recruit employees with these competencies or to help existing organization members develop the needed competencies (Goleman, 1998: 251, 259–62). Increasingly, this is being done in systematic ways. 'Assessing the competencies that make someone outstanding at a particular job has become something of a mini-industry, with practitioners using a range of well-validated methods to tease out the ingredients of star performance' (p. 260). Consider strategic planners. It has always been thought that the key ingredient for their success is 'analytical and conceptual thinking,' that is, cognitive ability.

> It turns out there's more to success as a planner than brainpower. Emotional skills are essential as well. Studies reveal that the *outstanding* strategic planners are not necessarily superior in their analytic skills. Instead the skills that raise them above the crowd are those of emotional competence: astute political awareness, the ability to make arguments with emotional impact, and high levels of interpersonal influence. (p. 259)

Presumably businesses with the aid of this kind of assessment can be more successful in their recruiting and developing efforts, and thus, can be more successful in adding to their firm's stock of personal capital.

There is good reason to believe that EI matters not just for individual job performance but the performance of the organization as a whole. Outstanding companies are high in many organizational competencies that are similar to Goleman's list of emotional competencies (recall Box 6.1). These organizational competencies as a group are essentially the 'organization's collective level of EI' (Goleman, 1998: 297–301). It is the latter that 'determines the degree to which that organization's intellectual capital is realized – and so its overall performance' (p. 299; see also Druskat and Wolff, 2001).

EI is just one component of personal capital, albeit a very important one. There are a variety of other work related human capacities included under the rubric of personal capital. These others are personal capital capacities not related to emotional functioning or emotional management. It remains a subject for further research to define carefully the nature of these other capacities, to indicate how they differ from EI, and to indicate how they contribute to job or organizational performance.

It is important to mention that it is only recently that some firms have begun to pay significant systematic attention to personal capital capacities like EI, and thus, to make the kind of efforts necessary to raise their competitive performance through investments in personal capital. Firms, for example, are using psychological testing to identify the EI of prospective employees and employing search firms that explicitly screen job candidates for desired types of EI. Earlier, there was little or no effort to incorporate these considerations in the firm's joining-up process or the human resource development process. It is also important to note that more and more people on their own are making efforts to recognize their strengths and weaknesses and, as a consequence, are making personal capital investments in themselves through formal and informal experiences that develop their desired personal qualities. In some cases, people are correcting EI deficiencies (for example, overcoming addictions, attachments, psychological hangups and so on). In other cases, they are seeking various kinds of personal growth or maturity. Some of the self-help activities involved are targeted carefully to improve job capabilities; some are not. The specific activities involved range widely from going to seminars and workshops, to reading books and listening to tapes, to engaging in psychotherapy. In any case, what in the past was either not done or was done in a hit or miss way is increasingly being done in a big way and in a systematic way. Thus, one could argue that in the past it made little sense for economists to consider personal capital as a source of economic growth. However, now that firms and people are devoting significant resources to personal capital formation and that personal competence has become recognized as critical to successful business performance, this argument no longer makes sense. Economists today cannot afford to ignore personal capital formation in their investigations into the sources of economic growth.

MEASURING THE CONTRIBUTION OF PERSONAL CAPITAL TO ECONOMIC GROWTH

Advocates of neoclassical and endogenous growth theories, while differing in their theoretical perspectives, have sought to measure the most important contributors to economic growth using similar cross-country empirical analyses. The basic approach has involved regressing countries' rates of growth of real GDP per capita over long periods of time on a variety of key explanatory variables. While none of the variables used by Barro (1997), or other economists for that matter (see, for example, Mankiw *et al.* (1992)), directly or explicitly reflect personal capital or emotional intelligence, Barro's analysis is notable for using a life expectancy variable reflecting health status and the general quality of human capital and three regional variables for two low growth areas (sub-Saharan Africa and Latin America) and one high growth area (East Asia). Barro (1997) and Barro and Lee (1994) find that although school attainment contributes to growth, it is a less important contributor than life expectancy (p. 43). Life expectancy's strong positive relation to growth is apparently because it reflects not only good physical health but desirable behavior owing to good work and personal habits and other competencies (p. 18). Thus it would not be surprising if life expectancy was picking up some personal capital elements. Barro's regional variables might also pick up some personal capital aspects. This would be the case if there were, say, emotional intelligence patterns common to regions. Could the low growth performance of sub-Saharan Africa and Latin America and the high performance of East Asia reflect the emotional intelligence of the people in these regions? One of the geographical variables used by Sachs and Warner (1997) is tropical climate. While places with tropical climate may be 'associated with poorer soils and higher infectious disease endemicity' (p. 186), they might also be associated with lower emotional intelligence.

In their empirical study of economic growth, Sachs and Warner (1997) report that these 'cross-country growth studies are plagued by left-out-variable errors of great importance' (p. 186). This is indicated, for example, by Barro's (1997: 13) regression equations with R squared values not exceeding 0.60, suggesting that there is a need for additional and better independent variables to obtain greater percentage explanation of the dependent variable, the growth rate. One area, cited by Sachs and Warner, which is especially in need of better measures and understanding is human capital accumulation in poorer countries (p. 188).

In his analysis of human capital and growth, Paul Romer (1990) has broken down workers' human capital endowment into three types of skills that are relevant for production. These are: first physical skills like eye-hand coordination and strength; second, educational skills acquired in primary and secondary school; and third, scientific talent acquired in post-secondary education (p. 253). Surely there are more than three relevant major types of human capital skills. It would certainly make sense to add to the skill list the competencies included under the emotional intelligence rubric. It is useful to consider all of these human capital skills to be a kind of 'wetware.' Wetware, as distinguished from hardware and software, consists of 'the things that are stored in the "wet" computer of the human brain' (Romer, 1994: 143).

In connection with measuring the intangible contributors to economic growth using cross-country data, Keefer and Knack's (1997) study is important to note. They find that two social capital variables, trust and civic cooperation, have a strong positive and significant association with the rate of growth of per capita income for a sample of 29 countries. Among the other independent variables in their regression equations are initial GDP, two human capital (education-related) variables, and an investment variable. If the growth contribution of social capital can be measured in this way, presumably the contribution of personal capital can be as well.

Robert Hall and Charles Jones' (1999) thesis is that 'differences in capital accumulation, productivity, and therefore output per worker are driven by differences in institutions and government policies, which we call social infrastructure' (p. 1). A social infrastructure conducive to economic growth is one that encourages desirable efforts and discourages undesirable efforts by enabling individuals to 'capture the social returns to their actions as private returns' (p. 2). Hall and Jones' cross-section 'results indicate that differences in social infrastructure account for much of the difference in long-run economic performance throughout the world, as measured by output per worker' (p. 14).

One obvious difficulty involved with measuring the personal capital contribution to economic growth is identifying the best measures of investment in personal capital and obtaining data on these. It would naturally be desirable to have one or two overall personal capital measures. However, this is problematic because, for example, emotional intelligence alone has five main elements with 25 specific associated emotional competencies. If these elements and competencies were highly independent of each other, this would be a significant difficulty. One possible source of personal capital data is the assessments of people's attitudes, interests, motivations, preferences, orientations and competencies deriving from the type of 'tests' used to determine people's suitability for different types of careers. 'Psychological' tests provide another possible source of data to the extent that they measure aspects of a person's self-discipline, honesty, empathy, key social skills and so on. In the absence of satisfactory test data for many countries, one would have to rely on nontest proxies. Ideally, adequate proxy data could be found among the nation's social indicators. Resolving this data difficulty is beyond the scope of the present research.

EVIDENCE FROM STUDIES EXPLAINING EARNINGS

While a definitive empirical analysis indicating the size of the personal capital contribution to economic growth is probably not possible at this time, results from a number of past empirical studies can give us an idea of the importance of this contribution. In general, these studies have found that certain noncognitive personal traits are strongly associated with differences in earnings among workers. See Chapter 3 for a review of these important studies.

Bowles *et al.* (2001) have provided a critical evaluation and summary of studies explaining earnings; they give special attention to the noncognitive determinants of earnings. In general, they find that what successful parents pass onto their children goes beyond superior schooling, inherited wealth, and genetic inheritance of cognitive ability. They suggest that the unexplained variance of earnings in conventional earnings equations can be explained by 'unobserved skill,' particularly noncognitive skills/traits which are difficult to measure (p. 1140). Moreover, based on their review, they find that 'seemingly irrelevant personal characteristics . . . even whether one keeps a clean house, are often robust predictors of earnings' (p. 1138). Among the skills/traits which have been considered by researchers are attitude, motivation, fatalism, self-directedness, impatience, integrity, conscientiousness, perseverance, and leadership. The authors find reason to believe that a set of traits they call 'incentive enhancing preferences' are especially important determinants of earnings (p. 1144). Among this set of traits are low time discount rate, predisposition to truth telling, identification with the objectives of the owners and managers, high marginal utility of income, and low disutility of effort (p. 1145). Such traits are thought to be valuable to employers because they attenuate the costs of enforcing employment contracts in situations where workers have effort discretion. In general, the studies reviewed provide much evidence that a variety of noncognitive skills/traits are significant determinants of worker earnings.

If the studies cited here and in Chapter 3 are right that noncognitive skills/traits are an important, and neglected, determinants of earnings, it is not unreasonable to infer that investment in these noncognitive human capital factors ought to be important in explaining economic growth. The noncognitive skills/traits considered in existing studies do not encompass all the elements of emotional intelligence, but they do include some of the more important EI elements. Thus, these empirical studies are interesting and provide general support for the thesis that investment in personal capital, especially that related to EI, is an important determinant of economic growth.

THE RELATIONSHIP BETWEEN PERSONAL CAPITAL AND SOCIAL CAPITAL

In some situations, personal capital and social capital are complements; in other situations, they are substitutes. When successful social capital formation requires that the individuals involved possess certain types of personal capital, personal capital can be considered a complement to social capital.

With respect to organizational capital which is a type of social capital, pre-organizational capital is the term used in my earlier writing to refer to the type of personal capital qualities antecedent to successful organizational capital formation (Tomer 1999a: 46–8).

> An individual's endowment of . . . pre-organizational capital qualities determines a person's generalized capability for being successfully joined to an organization. Individuals with a high endowment of these qualities are expected to develop a more effective psychological contract with the organization, develop more cooperative, trusting, and efficacious relationships with other organization members, and make deeper commitments that integrate their own purposes with those of the organization than do others with comparatively low endowments. (p. 47)[2]

Among the pre-organizational capital qualities whose presence is critically important if organizational capital is to be built and maintained are certain of Goleman's emotional competencies. Included among these are the last five social skills: (a) leadership; (b) change catalyst; (c) building bonds; (d) collaboration and cooperation; and (e) team capabilities (Goleman 1998: 27). Two of the empathy competencies, understanding others and developing others, are particularly important. And a variety of other qualities and virtues including: (a) self-control; (b) trustworthiness; (c) conscientiousness; (d) commitment; and (e) optimism are important (p. 26) (see also Tomer, 1999a: 46–7). These are the types of personal capital qualities that when present, especially in key people such as organization leaders, determines the organization's capability for forming and maintaining successful organizational relationships, thus indicating the complementary nature of personal capital and social capital.

There are two senses in which personal capital and social capital can be substitutes. First, suppose the organizational capital formation has gone very well and the organizational relationships developed provide plenty of structure, focus, and comfort to organization participants. Such relationships are likely to have the effect of calming people's negative emotions that might otherwise be a contaminant to organizational efforts. It is in this sense that strong social capital substitutes for personal capital deficiencies of organization members. Second, suppose the organization's workers have strong personal capital qualities and have a low likelihood of manifesting any negative, contaminating emotion. With these workers, there is less need for the kind of social capital that calms and structures their interactions because these workers are more likely to cooperate and coordinate their efforts spontaneously. Thus, their strong personal capital is able to substitute to an extent for investment in social capital.

IMPLICATIONS

As indicated earlier, there are important reasons to believe that personal capital formation has in recent years become a significant part of total capital formation in economically advanced countries. This theme is echoed by Goleman (1998: 9–10):

> The globalization of the workforce puts a particular premium on emotional intelligence in wealthier countries. Higher wages in these countries, if they are to be maintained, will depend on a new kind of productivity . . . As business changes, so do the traits needed to excel. Data tracking the talents of star performers over several decades reveal that two abilities that mattered relatively little for success in the 1970s have become crucially important in the 1990s: team building and adapting to change. And entirely new capabilities have begun to appear as traits of star performers, notably change catalyst and leveraging diversity. New challenges demand new talents.

Despite the increasing importance of personal and social capital for business performance, several trends suggest that countries like the US are in some respects not meeting this challenge. Even though test scores indicate that children's average IQ scores have made a significant gradual rise over the last 80 years, there is evidence that from the mid-1970s to the late 1980s children's emotional intelligence was steadily worsening, a decline shared by all socio-economic groups in many countries (Goleman, 1998: 11–12). According to Robert Putnam (1995a,b), there is also significant evidence that America's stock of social capital was declining over the last generation. Could it be that the increasing intentional investment in personal capital and social capital has been for the purpose of counteracting the growing 'natural' deficiencies in these human capacities?

Does it make sense for government to play a role with respect to personal and social capital formation? According to Simon Kuznets (1971: 346–7), the government needs to play a crucial supplementary role to foster economic growth as an entrepreneur or organizer of the 'socially required infrastructure' and as a facilitator of adjustment in economic and social institutions. With respect to social capital, Putnam (1995a: 77) is explicit: 'High on America's agenda should be the question of how to reverse these adverse trends in social connectedness, thus restoring civic engagement and civic trust.' Thus, Putnam (1993: 42) favors government efforts to revitalize the US stock of social capital. Presumably, a good case could also be made for a government role to encourage the development of certain key types of emotional competence.

Personal capital and social capital are not just important for understanding the economic performance of advanced economies. These concepts are also important for understanding whether less developed countries are likely to 'take off' on the path of sustained economic growth. Some LDCs may 'naturally' have the kind of culture that fosters the development of, for example, the types of EI critical to initiating the economic growth process. Other LDCs may naturally have important deficiencies in this regard. According to Fidelis Ezeala-Harrison (1995), 'human factor depravity' deriving from past colonial economic exploitation and current lack of leadership is an extremely important reason why so many LDCs remain underdeveloped. For satisfactory economic and social development, the basic human factor attributes such as 'honesty, respect for the rule of law, individual innate self-discipline, accountability, and commitment to patriotic and selfless efforts' must be present (p. 3). '*Human factor depravity* . . . occurs as society fails to instil such ideals as honesty, respect for the rule of law, individual innate self-discipline, and social accountability into the basic training and development of its human resources' (p. 4). It seems that human factor depravity can be understood as a deficiency of a variety of personal capital, and perhaps social capital, capacities. Thus, a key part of overcoming LDCs' economic underdevelopment is making the appropriate investments in personal and social capital.

CONCLUSIONS

This chapter has made the case that personal capital formation is a source of economic growth which is increasingly important. The soft nature of intangible inputs, like personal capital, the difficulty of measuring them, and their interrelationship with psychological and social processes which are normally outside the scope of economic inquiry are no doubt important reasons why economists have in the past ignored their contribution. Now, however, as explicit investment in it is increasing, and its contribution to economic performance has become more and more evident, economists can no longer afford to neglect the economic role of personal capital. This is especially true now that Daniel Goleman's writings have enabled us to see very clearly that our management of our emotions, our ability to motivate ourselves, and our social skills are in most cases a more important determinant of our work performance than our IQ, intellectual preparation or task training.

Very important research remains, especially empirical research. Among the important questions are the following. Is it possible to measure accurately the stocks of personal capital? What portion of the rate of economic growth can be explained by including these stocks in the analysis?

What are the important trends in personal capital formation? How are these trends likely to change in the future? Based on the answers to these questions recommendations for government policy can be made. Important government initiatives to encourage personal capital formation may be required in order for a nation to achieve its economic growth goals, to maintain its business competitiveness, or to become economically developed.

NOTES

1. Social capital has been defined more specifically in a variety of ways by different researchers; see Tomer (1999b).
2. One should note that people's personal (pre-organizational) capital endowment is distinctly different from the actual relationship (the bonds or connections between people) developed, that is the organizational capital formed.

REFERENCES

Abramovitz, Moses (1993), 'The search for the sources of growth: areas of ignorance, old and new,' *Journal of Economic History*, **53**(2), 217–43.

Barro, Robert J. (1997), *Determinants of Economic Growth: A Cross-Country Empirical Study*, Cambridge, MA: MIT Press.

Barro, Robert J. and Lee, Jong-Wha (1994), 'Sources of economic growth,' *Carnegie-Rochester Conference Series on Public Policy*, **40**, 1–46.

Becker, Gary S. (1996), *Accounting for Tastes*, Cambridge, MA: Harvard University Press.

Bowles, Samuel, Herbert Gintis and Melissa Osborne (2001), 'The determinants of earnings: a behavioral approach,' *Journal of Economic Literature*, **39**(4), 1137–76.

Cooper, Robert K. and Ayman Sawaf (1997), *Executive EQ: Emotional Intelligence in Leadership and Organizations*, New York: Grosset/Putnam.

Denison, Edward, F. (1962), 'The sources of economic growth in the United States and the alternatives before us,' Supplementary Paper No. 13, Committee on Economic Development, New York.

Denison, Edward F. (1974), *Accounting for United States Economic Growth, 1929–1969*, Washington, DC: Brookings Institution.

Druskat, Vanessa Urch and Steven B. Wolff (2001), 'Building emotional intelligence of groups,' *Harvard Business Review*, **79**(3), 81–90.

Ezeala-Harrison, Fidelis (1995), 'Human factor issues in the history of economic underdevelopment,' *Review of Human Factor Studies*, **1**(1), 1–25.

Goldsmith, Arthur H., Jonathan R. Veum and William Darity, Jr (1997), 'The impact of psychological and human capital on wages,' *Economic Inquiry*, **35**, 815–29.

Goleman, Daniel (1995), *Emotional Intelligence*, New York: Bantam Books.

Goleman, Daniel (1998), *Working with Emotional Intelligence*, New York: Bantam Books.

Goleman, Daniel, Richard Boyatzis and Annie McKee (2002), *Primal Leadership: Learning to Lead with Emotional Intelligence*, Boston, MA: Harvard Business School Press.

Hall, Robert and Charles Jones (1999), 'Why do some countries produce so much more output per worker than others?,' *Quarterly Journal of Economics*, **114**(1), 83–116.

Hunter, John E., Frank L. Schmidt and Michael K. Judiesch (1990), 'Individual differences in output variability as a function of job complexity,' *Journal of Applied Psychology*, **75**(1), 28–42.

Keefer, Philip and Stephen Knack (1993), 'Why don't poor countries catch up? A cross-national test of an institutional explanation,' IRIS Center Working Paper No. 60, University of Maryland, College Park.

Kendrick, John W. and John B. Kendrick (1988), *Personal Productivity: How to Increase Your Satisfaction in Living*, Armonk, NY: M.E. Sharpe.

Kiker, B.F. (1966), 'The historical roots of the concept of human capital,' *Journal of Political Economy*, **74**, 481–99.

Kuznets, Simon (1971), *Economic Growth of Nations: Total Output and Production Structure*, Cambridge, MA: Harvard University Press.

Maddison, Angus (1995), *Monitoring the World Economy 1820–1992*, Paris: Organization for Economic Cooperation and Development.

Mankiw, N. Gregory, David Romer and David N. Weil (1992), 'A contribution to the empirics of economic growth,' *Quarterly Journal of Economics*, **107**(2), 407–37.

Mayer, J.D. and P. Salovey (1997), 'What is emotional intelligence?,' in P. Salovey and D. Sluyter (eds), *Emotional Development and Emotional Intelligence: Implications for Educators*, New York: Basic Books, pp. 3–31.

McClelland, David C. (1973), 'Testing for Competence Rather Than for "Intelligence",' *American Psychologist*, **46**, 1–14.

Putnam, Robert D. (1993), 'The prosperous community: social capital and public life,' *The American Prospect*, **21**(13), 35–42.

Putnam, Robert D. (1995a), 'Bowling alone: America's declining social capital,' *Journal of Democracy*, **6**(1), 65–78.

Putnam, Robert D. (1995b), 'The strange disappearance of civic America,' *Policy*, **12**(1), 3–13.

Romer, Paul M. (1990), 'Human capital and economic growth: theory and evidence,' *Carnegie-Rochester Conference Series on Public Policy*, **32**, 251–86.

Romer, Paul M. (1994), 'Economic growth and investment in children,' *Daedalus*, **123**(4), 141–50.

Sachs, Jeffrey D. (1997), 'Fundamental sources of long-run growth,' *American Economic Review*, **87**(2), 184–8.

Sachs, Jeffrey and Andrew Warner (1997), 'Sources of slow growth in African economies', *Journal of African Economies*, **6**(3) (October), 335–76.

Simmons, Steve and John C. Simmons (1997), *Measuring Emotional Intelligence*, Arlington, TX: Summit.

Smith, Adam (1937 [1776]), *An Inquiry into the Nature and Causes of the Wealth of Nations*, New York: Modern Library.

Tomer, John F. (1996), 'Good habits and bad habits: a new age socio-economic model of preference formation,' *Journal of Socio-Economics*, **25**(6), 619–38.

Tomer, John F. (1999a), *The Human Firm: A Socio-Economic Analysis of its Behavior and Potential in a New Economic Age*, New York: Routledge.

Tomer, John F. (1999b), 'Social and organizational capital,' in Phillip Anthony

O'Hara (ed.) *Encyclopedia of Political Economy*. Vol. 2, London: Routledge, pp. 1049–51.
Tomer, John F. (2001), 'Addictions are not rational: a socio-economic model of addictive behavior,' *Journal of Socio-Economics*, **30**(3), 243–61.
Weisinger, Hendrie (1998), *Emotional Intelligence at Work: The Untapped Edge for Success*, San Francisco, CA: Jossey-Bass.

7. Intangible factors in the Eastern European transition: a socio-economic analysis

INTRODUCTION

Given the state of economic ideology and the predominance of neoclassical economic theory, given the loss of confidence in the communist system among many of the citizens of the formerly communist countries in the late 1980s, and given these people's impatient desire to move quickly to scrap the old system, it is hard to imagine that the Eastern European economic transition could have occurred much differently (Adam, 1999: 3; Gora, 1991: 146). Western economists' advocacy of a rapid radical transition was what many, especially the post-communist political elite, wanted to hear. There was not much opportunity for alternative voices to be heard. Although these historical forces were no doubt irresistible at that time, this should not prevent us from trying, even at this late date, to learn how the transition process could have gone better and how our understanding of the economics of transition could be improved.

The transition in Eastern Europe has provided a severe test for economists and economic ideas, and despite some successes, it looks like, overall, the test has failed. Too few of the transition economies have achieved sustained economic growth a decade later. Mainstream theory's most notable failure is its inability to appreciate the intangible or softer side of how economic systems and organizations operate. In the context of large scale change, it is particularly important to appreciate not just the structured, explicit and definite aspects of relationships but also the holistic, intangible, social, psychological, and even spiritual aspects of these relationships. This is why it is important to utilize a socio-economic conception of socialism and capitalism when thinking about the transformation of these systems. Thus, this chapter attempts to develop a socio-economic theory of transition success that first can explain the differing degrees of transition success that Eastern European countries have had and second can provide guidance on alternatives to neo-liberal transition strategy and policy.

The first task of this chapter is to develop models of socialism and capitalism that incorporate both the hard and soft elements of these socio-economic systems. Following that, the mainstream economic approach to understanding countries' transition success and to developing transition strategy is explained and critiqued. Next the transition outcomes, both successes and failures, are considered. Finally, a socio-economic theory of transition success is developed, explained, and its implications for strategy and policy are explored.

MODELS OF SOCIALIST AND CAPITALIST SYSTEMS

The Hard and Soft Elements of a Socio-Economic System

A socio-economic system such as the socialist system or the capitalist system, is defined by its typical structure. This structure has both hard and soft attributes. As explained elsewhere (Tomer, 1999a: 3), the hard attributes are relatively tangible, physical, measurable, capable of being expressed in mathematical relationships or legal language, visible and explicit. The opposite, soft attributes, are intangible, less definite, holistic aspects of the world. Financial relationships, ownership and organizational structure (hierarchy) are relatively hard; whereas enthusiasm, fairness, kindness, harmony, compassion are relatively soft. One of the hard features generally associated with capitalism is that owners of capital assets are entitled to claim the returns (profits) that are left after paying the specific claims of all the other input owners. On the soft side is the spirit of capitalism which is associated with risk taking, innovation adventure, and discovery. A hard feature typical of socialism is central planning whereby definite plans are made for allocating national resources in line with political priorities. The high value that socialists place on equality as an ideal is a soft feature of socialism.

The hard aspects of a socio-economic system's structure are not only very definite but tend to control or channel the behavior of people within the system. These controls may have a legal, organizational, financial or even political nature. Even though the soft elements of the structure are less definite and less visible, they may nevertheless be long lasting and capable of having a significant influence on human behavior. The soft aspects are generally thought to be linked or attached to the hard structure, but they are often more separate and independent of the hard structure than is commonly supposed. Soft features are often mental attributes such as attitudes, outlooks or perspectives, expectations, values, ethical orientation, inspiration, enthusiasm, and commitment. Socio-economic systems work best if their hard and soft elements are aligned or at least compatible, and they work least well when there is tension or conflict between them. This view is similar to what Pejovich (1997: 246) calls 'the interaction thesis.' According to this thesis, if society's 'formal rules are in harmony with its informal rules . . . [it] reduces the transaction costs of maintaining and protecting the rules of the social game and frees resources for the production of wealth' (p. 246). Vice versa if they are not in harmony.

Kornai's Models of Existing Socialism and Capitalism

In order to be clear about when the transition from socialism to capitalism is over, Janos Kornai (2000: 28–9) has developed models of these systems' essential attributes. While the two systems' various historical manifestations have had a great variety of characteristics, each system has a common core of characteristics, what Kornai calls 'system-specific attributes.' Kornai's models are 'parsimonious, minimalist characterizations,' and thus, leave out much of the flesh of the two systems (p. 29); they just focus on the essentials. These models are not models of ideal systems; they are models of 'existing' socialism and capitalism in the sense that they are based on these systems historically established actual attributes. See Figure 7.1 for Kornai's models of the socialist and capitalist systems.

> The first three blocks of the diagram sum up the fundamental features of each system: what characterizes political power, the distribution of property rights, and the constellation of coordination mechanisms. Once these are in place, they largely determine the fourth block, the type of behavior typical of the economic actors, and the fifth block, the typical economic phenomena. (p. 29)

Similar to most economic models, Kornai's models include only more or less hard attributes.

DEVELOPING SOCIO-ECONOMIC MODELS OF SOCIALISM AND CAPITALISM

Introducing the Soft Features: Revising the Kornai Models

What is missing from Kornai's models are the soft attributes of the people and social relationships in the two systems. Each soft attribute generally corresponds to one of Kornai's hard, system-specific attributes (see especially the first three blocks in Figure 7.1). Consider first the soft features of

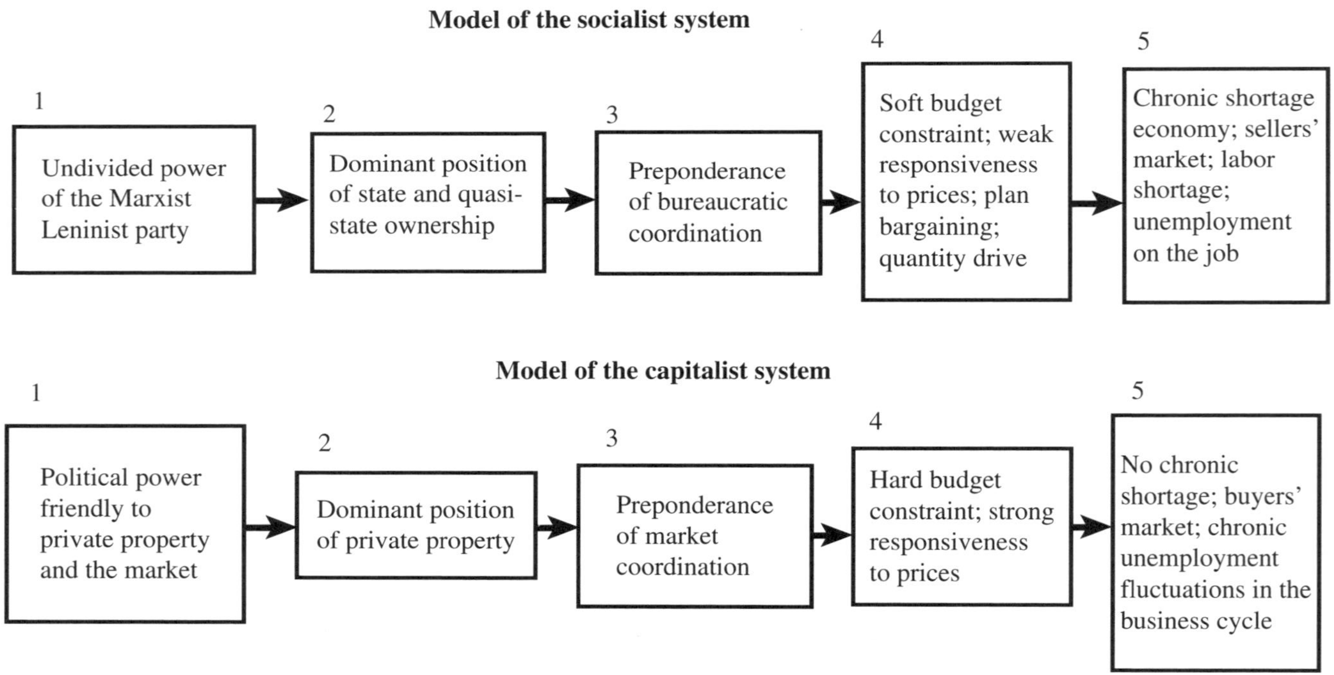

Source: Kornai (2000: 29)

Figure 7.1 Models of the socialist and capitalist systems

the socialist system. Associated with the first block related to the power of the (communist) party are the following soft attributes: (a) attitude of disciplined obedience to the authority of the party; (b) behavior in line with socialist ideology and norms; (c) little orientation to following the rule of law; and (d) acceptance of coercive actions by, for example, the secret police. Associated with the second block related to the dominant position of state ownership are the following: (a) orientation to collective and societal goals, with correspondingly little orientation to individual goals and individualism; (b) a low value on consumer goods; and (c) dependence of people on the socialist system for their well-being. The third block, preponderance of bureaucratic coordination, has the following soft features associated with it: (a) a planning mentality involving an orientation to achieving bureaucratic goals and targets set at higher levels of the hierarchy; (b) an orientation to using social networks to accomplish goals and to get needs satisfied; and (c) an image of the good manager as someone who maintains positive relationships with authority and has concern for the security of workers. Another important socialist soft attribute is the high value placed on equality and economic security.

Consider the soft features of capitalism. Associated with block one, political power friendly to private property and the market, are the following soft attributes: first acceptance of the ideology and norms of capitalism; second orientation to individual rights and private property rights; and third orientation to following the rule of law. The soft features below are associated with the dominant position of private property: (a) orientation to taking responsibility and being self-reliant; (b) orientation to seeking wealth accumulation and economic security; (c) orientation to making investments (this involves acquiring skill and knowledge, being patient, having a long-term perspective, and willingness to take risks); and (d) orientation to enjoyment of consumer goods. Finally, the preponderance of market coordination is associated with: (a) orientation to individual gain (profit or satisfaction); (b) tendency for opportunistic behavior to be tempered by adherence to ethical precepts and moral values (and if not, at least by government regulation); (c) free flow of information (especially if democracy is present) and market participants' attentiveness to relevant economic information; and (d) tendency to view other market participants as competitors. In capitalism, people generally place a high value on individual progress and the notion that individuals will be rewarded commensurate with their contributions.

Personal Capital in the Systems

There is another level to the soft features of the two systems. Beneath the attitudes, orientations, and values cited above are personal capacities (or personal capital) which do not have as obvious a relationship to the respective systems. Nevertheless, because people tend to develop those personal capacities that are compatible with their socio-economic system and with their economic sector and professional category, we would expect the personal capital investments of people in socialist societies to differ markedly from those of people in capitalist societies. Note that personal capital is a type of human capital unrelated to cognitive intelligence or intellectual knowledge. Personal capital reflects the quality of an individual's psychological, physical, and spiritual functioning (Tomer, 2003: 457). A very important component of personal capital is emotional intelligence (see Daniel Goleman, 1995, 1998).

> Emotional intelligence has five elements: self-awareness, motivation, self-regulation, empathy, and adeptness in relationships. These determine one's potential for mastering the twenty-five emotional competencies, the more specific human capacities essential for success in the workplace. For each of the five elements of emotional intelligence, there are a number of corresponding emotional competencies. (Tomer, 2003: 16)

No doubt, all of the emotional competencies have some importance and usefulness in any system. However, there is reason to believe that some competencies are more important for a particular system. For example, in my judgment the following cluster of competencies will be more important in a capitalist system: self control, trustworthiness, adaptability, innovation, initiative, optimism, service orientation, change catalyst and self confidence. In contrast, the following group of competencies is in my judgment more important in a socialist system: conscientiousness, commitment, political awareness, conflict management, collaboration and cooperation, and achievement drive. Obviously, other characteristics of a socio-economic system, besides its basic classification, will affect what emotional competencies are most compatible with it. For example, an advanced, post-industrial, dynamic capitalism would presumably differ from a newly industrialized capitalism in these respects. Further, as societies pass through new stages of development or as they make dramatic systemic transitions, people in these societies will feel the need to develop new competencies, and thus, will need to make new kinds of investment in personal capital. Typically then, one might expect emotional competencies to lag behind important economic evolutionary or revolutionary changes, always trying to catch up to what business needs. It is possible, of course, that society somehow anticipates the needs for new competencies and signals people to make the appropriate personal investments in a timely way.

Social Capital in the Systems

Besides personal capital, the capitalist system and socialist system have quite different social capital requirements. Note that social capital is the product of activities that create social relationships (Tomer, 1999b). Social capital is a type of human capital in which the capacity is embodied not in individuals per se but in the relationships or connections between people. Because the social relationships in the two systems differ greatly, it is to be expected that the types of social capital (and organizational capital, a type of social capital) involved will be very different. Social capital reflects both the hard and soft aspects of relationships. Formal social relationships, for example, the formal organizational structure of an enterprise, are generally hard while informal or less formal aspects of social and organizational relationships are typically soft. There is a big difference between the implicit social contracts and communication patterns that are relatively soft features of capitalism compared to those of socialism. For example, the socialist system emphasizes vertical communications and discourages horizontal communications, whereas there is less emphasis on vertical communications in capitalism. One interesting aspect of organizational relationships within the enterprise is that decision making in socialist enterprises is much more politically motivated, and there is a greater obligation to provide for the social security of organization members than is the case for the capitalist firm. Note that the main elements of the socio-economic models of socialism and capitalism are now in place.

Implications for System Change

According to Peter Murrell (1992: 41), the organizational routines in the centrally planned economies were selected in accordance with the needs of the bureaucratic system of administrative allocation and control and are largely suited to that situation. Also, because personnel allocation has occurred within that system, it 'will have an allocation of human capital and of management styles that matches the dictates of a nonmarket environment' (p. 41). For similar reasons, the stock of behavioral patterns and expectations are unlikely to be suited for a new market environment. It follows that a change from a centrally planned economy to a market economy would require a lengthy and difficult period of investment in personal and social capital before performance in the new system could reach anywhere near its potential. As Murrell indicates, because of the personal and social capital 'still adapted to the bureaucratic environment of central planning, a swift changeover to the market could be very destructive of the capacity of the existing enterprises to produce output' (p. 42). From the standpoint of the interaction thesis, part of the decline in productive capacity will occur because of a rise in transaction costs, 'the costs of making an exchange . . . and the costs of maintaining and protecting the institutional structure' due to the conflict between formal and informal rules (Pejovich, 1997: 244–6).

TOWARD A THEORY EXPLAINING TRANSITION SUCCESS

To understand better the importance of the intangible factors in the transition process, it is helpful to develop a theory explaining the medium term (say, five to ten years) transition success of Central and Eastern European countries. In this theory, the dependent variable is the degree of transition success of one of these nations, and the explanatory variables include the different policy actions undertaken by and conditions existing in this country. Transition success here does not necessarily mean achieving a full-fledged transformation of the nation's socio-economic system, and thus, say, becoming socio-economically comparable to the leading Western European nations. Transition success in the present usage means two things: first making reasonable progress in the process of transforming the nation's socio-economic system from socialism to capitalism; and second keeping the social and economic costs associated with this transition low. Transformation progress would be indicated by: (a) the extent of the transformation of the hard and soft features of socialism to those of capitalism; and (b) the favorable macroeconomic performance of the new system. The economic costs of transition include such things as: (a) a falling national output; (b) a rising unemployment rate; (c) rising inflation; (d) decreasing real wages; (e) falling real consumption of goods and services; and (f) higher incidence of poverty. Among the noneconomic costs of transition are: (a) lower life expectancy; (b) higher infant mortality; (c) lower marriage rate; (d) higher emigration to immigration rate; (e) increase in health problems; (f) lower fertility rate; and (g) higher age-specific mortality rates. The longer the time period over which these economic and noneconomic costs are incurred and the more severe are these costs, the higher is that nation's cost of transition. A nation which has made little progress on the transformation process and which has incurred high social and economic transition costs has obviously had a low degree of transition success.

MAINSTREAM ECONOMICS AND TRANSITION SUCCESS

Is there a mainstream economic theory explaining transition success? Strictly speaking, the answer is no; there is no explicit neoclassical theory of transition success (Murrell, 1991a; Horne, 1995: 379). Despite the absence of neoclassical theory, many Western mainstream economists have definite opinions on economic transition matters and have been eager to give advice regarding these (Murrell, 1991b: 9). Most noteworthy are the economists favoring a rapid transition (a neo-liberal strategy) who have been in the majority in the Western academic community (Murrell, 1992; 52). For a variety of political and economic reasons, the crucial role of formulating the transition strategy was largely entrusted to a small group of these economists (Adam, 1999: 1–3). An important leader of this group has been Jeffrey Sachs of Harvard University (pp. 4–5) who has advised in Poland, Russia, Slovenia, Estonia, Mongolia and elsewhere. Implicit in these economists' advice are at least elements of a mainstream transition theory.

At an early stage of the economic transition, there was a great deal of agreement on the standard (neo-liberal) approach. It involved proceeding 'as fast as possible on macroeconomic stabilization, the liberalization of domestic trade and prices, current account convertibility, privatization, and the creation of a social safety net, while simultaneously creating the legal framework for a market economy' (Murrell, 1995: 164; see also Fischer and Gelb, 1991; Lipton and Sachs, 1990a,b). With respect to privatization, this approach involved privatizing small and medium size enterprises fast, by sale or using special financial arrangements. In the case of the core of large industrial and commercial firms, the process was inevitably slower and involved converting state owned enterprises into corporate form with boards of directors and stocks, and then, selling or distributing the stock by a number of methods to a variety of groups including citizens, employees, foreigners, mutual funds and the state (Fischer, 1992). Two other elements of the standard approach are: (a) creating in enterprises a hard budget constraint; and (b) creating a market based financial system.

The essence of the neo-liberal transition strategy has been to replace the important hard features, notably the political, organizational, and legal structures, of socialism with those of capitalism and to replace them quickly. In doing so, it is not necessary to take much account of the old system's soft features; informal structures and idiosyncratic historical and cultural features are of little importance (Murrell, 1995; Stiglitz, 2000: 58). Further, according to Ericson (1991: 11), a centrally planned economy is a coherent whole system that is dramatically different qualitatively from a market economy; it is different in its inherent logic and in the interaction of its components.

> The defining characteristics of the Soviet-style system are interconnected and mutually supporting; altering one or a few is merely disruptive of the stable functioning of the system and of its effectiveness. Hence, a meaningful reform must eliminate all nine [major] characteristics . . ., more or less simultaneously. (p. 24)

Regardless of the socialist society's history and institutions, neo-liberals aim at the same imagined transition endpoint, their model of ideal capitalism (Murrell, 1993: 122–4). In the neo-liberal view, transitional change is akin to an exercise in comparative statics; it involves moving from one equilibrium position to another. Like their neoclassical brethren, neo-liberals assume swift, unproblematic, uncostly adjustment, and thus, soft features accommodate to hard ones frictionlessly (Etzioni, 1991: 4). Once the hard features of the new system have replaced those of the old system, the correct incentives embodied in the new system will automatically produce the desired behavior as individuals rationally respond to the new incentives (Murrell, 1993: 117–19). No learning, adjusting, or reorienting is necessary. Thus, neo-liberals maintain that it is important to destroy all vestiges of the old system and quickly to replace it with the new one. It is not a process involving modifying existing institutions and structures. While these ideas on transition strategy do not amount to a full-fledged transition theory, they do reveal clearly the neo-liberal conceptions of the nature of economic systems and their change processes.

TRANSITION OUTCOMES

Neo-liberal transition advice by Western economists was highly influential on the policies pursued in many of the Soviet-bloc countries of Eastern Europe. One reason for this is that the rapid collapse of the socialist system caught domestic politicians and economists unprepared, and there was a need for quick action (p. 5). Second is that 'the new, post-communist political elites had typically only a vague idea of what economic reforms to introduce and in what sequence to introduce them' (Stanislaw Gomulka as quoted in Adam, 1999: 5). Thus, these transition leaders had a great need for economic advice. Third, according to Stiglitz (2000: 58), the neo-liberal

> school won the debate in the Treasury Department and in the IMF. Or, to be more accurate, the Treasury Department and the IMF made sure there was no open debate and then proceeded blindly along the second route. Those who opposed this course were either not consulted or not consulted for long.

Thus, in countries like Poland and Czechoslovakia and quite a few others, the design of the strategy of transformation was 'entrusted to a small group of [neo-liberal] academics' (Adam, 1999: 5), who have been called 'economic technocrats.' The implementation of this strategy by Eastern European political leaders was nothing short of a revolutionary effort at complete reconstruction of these nations' socio-economic systems in a top-down manner (Murrell, 1993: 115).

Before proceeding to the outcomes of the implemented policies, it is important to note that a series of political-economic collapses, the first one occurring in September 1989 in Poland, preceded the launching of the economic transition efforts. According to Vaclav Havel (1991: 19), a leading author and politician in Czechoslovakia who had been President of the Czech Republic, 'the old system has collapsed, the new one is not yet built.' Similarly, Yegor Gaidar (interviewed by Desai (2000: 14–15)), a leading politician, economic writer, and a principal architect of Russia's reforms in 1992, said of the situation that existed in 1990–1, 'The existing institutions stopped functioning and new institutions could not be created overnight. We had a severe economic crisis in the Soviet Union because the past regime, the past system, stopped operating, and new arrangements did not work.'

During the early 1990s, the Central and Eastern European nations experienced both the shock of the collapse of the old system and the shock(s) associated with the imposition of neo-liberal radical reform. Much of the evidence indicates that the shocks were anything but therapy. Even Andrew Berg and Jeffrey Sachs (1992: 142) recognized the negative psychological experience of Poland in the period immediately following 1989. He mentions

> the undoubted rise in anxiety and uncertainty in the Polish population as the result of the collapse of the old economic system. There are widespread fears of involuntary unemployment and job layoffs, a largely novel phenomenon, and even a sense of doom or despair among parts of the population. There may also be a loss of the hope that was held by some during the worst times of the 1980s, that getting rid of the Communists would quickly and painlessly give Poland a Western-European economy.

Vaclav Havel, then President of Czechoslovakia, (1991: 19) said

> Our society is still in a state of shock. It could have been predicted, but no one predicted that the shock would be so profound . . . In this atmosphere of general impatience, anxiety, disappointment, and doubt, elements of spitefulness, suspicion, mistrust, and mutual recrimination are creeping into public life.

An important indicator of the severity of the shock is its impact on these nations' health and demography. Russia and East Germany both experienced unprecedented peacetime changes in their vital trends.

> In Russia from 1991 to 1993, for example, the birth rate dropped by 12 percent, the death rate increased by 26 percent, the marriage rate declined by 20 percent, the infant mortality rate increased by 4 percent, and the mortality rate of middle-aged adults rose by 13 percent. The changes have been most dramatic for males, especially those in middle age. Coronary disease, cancer and social ills such as suicide, alcoholism and murder are the prime culprits. In Russia from 1989 to 1994, male life expectancy dropped from 64.4 to 57.3 years. (Murrell, 1996: 39–40)

East Germany experienced an outmigration of over one million people between 1989 and 1992 bringing its population to 16 million (Eberstadt, 1994: 137). Live births declined by 56 percent from 1989 to 1992 (p. 142); marriages in 1992 were only 37 percent of the 1989 amount (p. 144); and in 1990–1 age-standardized mortality rates were 28 percent higher for males and 29 percent higher for females in East Germany compared to West Germany (pp. 147–8). Three major types of ailments were responsible for most of the increase: cardiovascular disease, injuries (including suicide), and cirrhosis of the liver. As Eberstadt states, this 'portrays a society convulsed by its stresses' (p. 145).

A related, widely noted outcome occurring to various degrees in the different transition economies is the rise of crime, corruption, rent-seeking, and other opportunistic behavior which has been encouraged by the breakdown of external constraints and inhibitions against this behavior. Rampant opportunistic behavior has been most observed in Russia and other countries of the former Soviet Union. Much of this behavior involves a variety of methods of rent-seeking, that is, 'extracting monetary benefits [directly or indirectly] from the government' (Aslund 1999a: 52). Among these methods are 'arbitrage: to buy cheaply anything at fixed state prices and to sell at a high free-market price,' especially raw materials such as oil, natural gas, and metals (p. 53). A second method involved import subsidies in which people (generally high government or party officials) have taken advantage of the difference between the international market exchange rate and the government rate. A third method involved taking advantage of government loans at highly subsidized interest rates (p. 53). Incredibly, according to Aslund (p. 53), rents associated with arbitrage activities amounted to 30 percent of Russian GDP in 1992; rents associated with import subsidies were 15 percent of 1992 GDP; and credit subsidies 30 percent of 1992 GDP. Also, many have taken advantage of the unfortunate existence of 'incentives for asset stripping [of enterprises] rather than wealth creation' (Stiglitz, 1999: 33, 50). For more analysis of these and 'various forms of predatory anticompetitive behavior,' see Rosefielde and Stein (1999) and Kaufmann and Siegelbaum (1996).

The basic story regarding macroeconomic conditions is well known. The bad news is that output declined by historically unprecedented amounts. According to Brenton *et al.* (1997: 114), in the former Soviet Union, the deepest decline in real GDP between 1989 and 1994 averaged 40.9 percent; in Central Europe, this decline averaged 26.5 percent. The good news is that 'By the end of 1994, GDP per capita was increasing in more than half of the countries' (Murrell, 1996: 37). Poland started growing in 1992, followed by the Czech Republic, Slovenia, and Romania in 1993 and Hungary and the Republic of Slovakia in 1994 (Brown, 1999: 93). Poland's growth in the mid- to late 1990s was particularly impressive. However, by 1997, the Ukraine was still experiencing declining output, and some countries have still not established a sustained pattern of growth. For the great majority of the transition economies, inflation rates peaked between 1991 and 1994, and these rates dropped to low double-digit or single-digit rates by the late 1990s (Fischer *et al.* 1996: 52; Brown, 1999: 94). For Armenia and the Ukraine, the maximum annual inflation rate exceeded 10 000 percent, and only a few transition nations escaped hyperinflation in the early 1990s.

> With only one exception, the countries under question have done more poorly since the transition to the market economy than before . . . For eighteen of the twenty-five countries for which we have data, poverty on the average has increased from 4 percent to 45 percent of the population, using the $4-a-day standard, revealing the devastating changes in standards of living. (Stiglitz, 1999: 26–7)

In all the transition economies, the private sector has increased dramatically relative to the government sector, partly due to privatization of state owned enterprises and partly due to the growth of new private firms. Unquestionably, the new firms have been of greater significance (Murrell, 1996: 39). This is true even in Poland where the decent performance of state enterprises has been a pleasant surprise. Whereas privatization of small to medium sized firms has generally occurred fairly quickly and has been more or less successful, the outcomes of the privatization of large state enterprises have varied greatly. On the one hand, Marshall Goldman (2000: 28) has called Russia's privatization experience a 'dreadful mistake.' (p. 28). In his view, Russia privatized much too fast through the issue of vouchers (p. 33). The result was that: (a) ownership was too diffuse; (b) the process of privatization was corrupt; (c) there were incentives for management to strip assets; (d) the program was not tailored to the special circumstances of Russia; (e) government was insufficiently supportive; and (f) a competitive infrastructure was lacking (pp. 32–8). On the other hand, Poland's experience with privatizing large enterprises was favorable despite the fact (or in retrospect because of the fact) that their privatization was delayed until 1995 due to the political difficulty of reaching an agreement on a plan

(p. 35). 'The delay gave them time to learn from the mistakes of others who had moved too impetuously' (p. 35).

As the above evidence indicates, the transition outcomes are quite varied. Certainly, there are some successes. Nevertheless, the outcomes are strongly suggestive of the failure of the neo-liberal radical reform strategy. The most important outcomes, the profound social and psychological shock experienced by the people in transition, the very negative health and demographic outcomes, the great rise in corruption and opportunistic rent-seeking, the severe economic downturns typically accompanied by hyperinflation, and the large increase in poverty, are not exactly ringing endorsements of the shock therapy programs. These factors indicate that for most of the transition economies, the degree of transition success was very low as indicated by the extremely high economic costs of transition and the as yet very low transition benefits. Overall, this suggests the need for a better transition strategy, one that is based on a more adequate understanding of the socio-economic processes involved in transition.

A SOCIO-ECONOMIC THEORY OF TRANSITION SUCCESS

A Metaphor

A man named Traecon was unhappy; his unhappiness was focused on his body that was no longer functioning very well at least compared to the bodies of the men he knew who lived in a city named Weseur some distance from his. He reasoned that he would function much better and be happy if he could replace his body parts with those of Weseurian men. He sought the advice of distinguished doctors about the body part transplant process. A majority thought he would be better off transplanting all the parts at once (a 'big bang') because the body parts of Weseurian men needed to function together as a whole. A minority counseled in favor of a gradual, step-by-step, approach to the transplants. Traecon who had little understanding of these matters naturally went with the majority and had one big operation. After recovering from the operation, he definitely looked like a Weseurian man. However, there were problems. Not all the parts fit together very well or worked together very well. Also, his attitudes, values and motivation were unchanged and did not jibe with those of Weseurians. These unpleasant results were a shock to him. Overall, he was functioning worse than before, and he was still unhappy, maybe more so. He wonders whether he should have taken the gradual approach. On good days, he thinks that maybe things will work out in the long run.

The Theoretical Framework for Explaining Transition Success

The medium-term transition success of a country is explained by two main kinds of explanatory variables: first the conditions existing in the country at the beginning of the transition; and second the transition policy measures implemented subsequently. It is useful to distinguish among a number of different types of initial country conditions. First are the set of conditions relating to the nation's social, cultural, psychological and spiritual circumstances as well as its history. Second are the economic and geographic conditions, particularly its macroeconomic circumstances, its location (for example, closeness to Western Europe) and its resources. Third is the status of the socialist system. Has the system involved full-fledged central planning? Have reforms to the system been introduced? How long has the system been functioning and how well? Fourth are the political conditions. Has the communist party system collapsed? Is there widespread support for and consensus on the move to capitalism? Is there a strong group of leaders committed to the transition process? Are these leaders committed to a democratic process? Depending on the answers to these and similar questions about initial conditions, a nation's prospects for a successful transition could be rated.

Consider the initial conditions in Poland. By September 1989, Poland's 'revulsion against the failures of communism' led it to be the first country to attempt a transition to a market economy under a noncommunist government (Lipton and Sachs, 1990a: 76–7). Among the Polish people, there was a high degree of consensus that they wanted a return to Europe, to markets, and to an economy like Western Europe (ibid. pp. 75–6). Janos Kornai observed that 'Poland is fortunate to have a strong government enjoying popular support . . ., [a nation] united behind the Solidarity government' (ibid. p. 138). Besides Solidarity, the Catholic Church is also considered a strong unifying element (ibid. p. 143). In light of its dismal economic performance in the 1980s, Poland, which had had a communist economic system for over 40 years, embarked on a series of significant reforms, most significant of which were those during the last years of the decade (Murrell, 1993: 126). These 1980s reforms included gradually reducing the role of central planning along with greater decentralization and the beginnings of liberalization. Poland already had privately owned farms. In addition, the rights of property ownership were being enhanced; privatization became legal; and by 1989, many prices had been freed from regulation (pp. 126–7). Despite these reforms, or perhaps partly because of them, by September 1989, the 'economy [was] in deep crisis: Inflation was raging, shortages of virtually all goods were rampant, and the black market was all pervasive' (Wellisz, 1991: 211). Nevertheless, Poland's economy benefited from its underlying strengths in human capital, natural resources, physical capital and its closeness to Western Europe (Lipton and Sachs, 1990a: 131–2). All things considered, Lipton and Sachs believed that Poland had very good long-term prospects for a successful transition and for reducing the gap between its economic performance and that of Western Europe. In contrast, based on the initial conditions of the countries of the former Soviet Union, there was much less reason to be sanguine about these nations' transition prospects.

Besides initial conditions, the group of transition policy measures chosen and implemented (strategy) is the other main determinant of transition success. At this point in the chapter, the main types of transition measures and strategy characteristics are simply listed. Explanations relating to them can be found in several of the following sections. The first group of transition measures are the ones most prominently mentioned by neo-liberals. Recall that they include: macroeconomic stabilization, liberalization of domestic trade and prices, current account convertibility, privatization, creation of a social safety net and creation of the legal framework for a market economy. Other policy measures include policies to encourage tangible investment and policies to encourage intangible investment (developing the capacity of the needed soft factors). Strategy characteristics which affect decision making on and implementation of the policy measures include: (a) the degree of democracy in the transition process; (b) the degree of creativity in blending the new system's features with the nation's legacy from the past and with the useful features of the socialist system; and (c) the speed and sequencing of policy changes.

Findings on Transition Success

One important measure of a country's transition success or failure is, of course, its rate of growth of real GDP per capita. A number of economists have undertaken empirical investigations to account for the substantially different growth rates among the Eastern European countries. Sachs (1996), for example, finds that an 'overall index of reform progress' with nine different dimensions is positively associated with growth during 1989–95 in a study of 25 countries. Fischer *et al.* (1996), in a study of 20 nations over the 1992–4 period, similarly find that countries making progress in reforms and stabilizing inflation grow faster and end their recessions sooner. Selowsky and Martin (1997) in a study of 25 transitional economies in the 1990–5 period find that reform policies may have an initial negative effect but a cumulative positive effect. They also find that countries involved in regional military conflicts have paid a high price in terms of lower GDP growth. The study of de Melo *et al.* (1997) found that in addition to reform policies, country initial conditions provide a significant

a fixed, theoretically determined endpoint (p. 122). This means, for example, that

> The Russian model has to be different because Russia has another history, other problems, and distinct traditions . . . If someone were to introduce the American constitution and American laws from A to Z in another society, he would fail miserably. The American model functions in America because of its history. (Gaidar quotation from Desai, 2000: 27)

Difficulty of reconstructing existing organizations

One might expect that reconstructing existing state owned enterprises would be less costly than organizing entirely new enterprises, but there are important reasons why this may not be the case. According to Murrell (1992: 44),

> An existing organizational structure entails the adaptation of behavior and language of communication to existing conditions, the alignment of organizations with an existing structure of physical plant, and many commitments to existing members that are costly to negate. Because of the difficulties of changing such organizational features, the reconstruction of existing organizations involves costs that are not present in the construction of new organizations.

When these costs of transforming organizational capital are high, privatization will be inferior to the gradual rise of new private enterprise with its entirely new organizational capital.

Soft elements fostering transition

Contrary to the impression that one might have gotten from the above, some soft or relatively intangible factors can foster the transition. One such soft factor is the 'period of extraordinary politics' which may occur at the very beginning of the transition period. This is a period of grace 'when out of idealism the population accepts a great deal of change' (Aslund, 1999a: 63); it is a period 'devoid of effective pressure groups able to oppose the adverse impact that economic reforms would have on many established sectors and enterprises' (Gelb, 1999: 42–3). Gelb also believes that optimistic expectations, say, of rejoining Western Europe, can act as a stabilizing force during the difficult years (p. 43). When these types of soft factors are present, they can make the transition easier.

To the extent that civil society, the public's capacity to organize itself to defend its interests, is strong, this can foster the transition. In Kornai's (1992: 4) view, civil society in Eastern Europe is in the process of awakening. According to Aslund (1999a: 58), with the exception of Poland, the strength of civil society in the transition economies has been mostly weak. In Poland, strong trade unions, workers' councils, the Catholic Church, and private peasants exerted their collective powers to rein in the opportunistic rent-seeking activities of some of the elites. Another important intangible factor is the role of the media, particularly its quality and independence. According to Aslund (p. 58), Central Europe, the Baltic countries, and Russia (initially) benefited from the media's pressures on rent-seekers. Kornai (p. 4), commenting on the role of the press in Hungary, said 'Anyone trying to abuse the state's power or to mismanage the state's money runs a risk of being exposed in the press.'

The Intermediate Variables: Shock and Capitalist Productive Capacity

In an earlier section outlining the basic theoretical framework, a country's transition success was said to be determined by two main kinds of explanatory variables: first initial country conditions, and second the transition policy measures utilized. Here two intermediate variables, shock and capitalist productive capacity, are introduced. These two variables are intermediate between the explanatory variables and transition success. In other words, the initial conditions together with the transition policy measures determine the country's shock level and its capitalist productive capacity which, in turn, determine its transition success. If the initial conditions and policy measures cause the degree of shock to rise above a certain threshold level, this will cause the transition process to be retarded. To the extent that policy and initial conditions directly contribute to raising the productive capacity of the emerging market system (or enhance the likelihood of this), this should raise economic performance and lead to transition success.

Shock

Shock refers to a particularly sudden increase in transition costs. The transition will inevitably produce such a shock when the transition effort involves a drastic change from one socio-economic system to another all at once. In this case, the shock will be profound because it will involve a collapse of the institutions of the old system without time for the new ones to be built. Consequently, people will experience severe emotional losses associated with the lack of reliable norms and expectations. In this situation, the hard and soft features of the socio-economic system will be severely out of alignment. Further, there is reason to expect that the effects of the shock will be proportionately greater if the reform measures producing it had been imposed in an undemocratic manner. With respect to economic effects, 'large shocks – whether intentional or not – invariably have large and negative effects on output and investment . . . usually because they generate high levels of uncertainty' (Kozul-Wright and Rayment, 1997: 645). According to Murrell (1992: 41), significant shocks bring adversity which undermines the prevailing patterns of cooperation. Moreover, there appears to be a nonlinear relation between the magnitude of the shock and the amount of the decline in system performance (p. 42). There is evidence that after some point an increase in shock produces a more than proportional decline in performance due to increasing social dysfunction.

Neo-liberal advocates of rapid radical reform do not deny that countries following their recommendations will experience shock. Instead, they argue largely on pragmatic, not theoretical, grounds that because the several types of reforms are interdependent, it is necessary to introduce all of them at the same time (Horne, 1995: 382). Neo-liberals also argue that fast reform will lessen the chances of political opposition to the reforms mobilizing. The latter reasoning highlights the undemocratic nature of their reform strategy. In any case, neo-liberals expect that this strategy will lead to a severe, but short, decline in the system's economic performance followed by a rapid recovery, overall a more favorable result, in their view, than a gradual, less shocking, transitional strategy (see, for example, Hoen, 1995: 60–2). Apparently, neo-liberals implicitly assume no lasting impairment of the system's productive capacity during the shock period and no impairment of people's ability to function while in a state of shock. In general, as indicated by these assumptions, neo-liberal rapid reformers have failed to appreciate how detrimental the effects of shock can be on the transitional socio-economies and their people.

In the wake of rapid radical reform, people will experience shock as their social bonds and connections associated with the old system are torn and broken. This is especially true when these relationships (social and organizational capital) are destroyed in a way over which people have little or no control. Not surprisingly, people will experience this as a collectively painful and traumatic event which is uprooting, disorienting, and often severely disturbing. Even though many of the people may have consciously wanted the transition, they still inevitably will experience the pain of giving up their sense of identity, habits, expectations and beliefs. Thus, it is to be expected that many will experience depression, anxiety, confusion, fearfulness and other painful emotions. This pain may be similar to the pain associated with marital divorce; the difference is that it is experienced in common by large numbers of people. The amount of distress experienced by people will, one expects, be related to (a) the degree that people have invested themselves in the relationships of the old system and (b) the cultural distance between the old and new socio-economies.

People's painful experience of shock is expected to have a negative effect on transition success for several reasons. First, to the extent that the population is suffering from anxiety, confusion, depression, and general emotional upset, their ability to make decisions and manage situations will be impaired. Such people will not be in the mental states most conducive to managing change processes and making the crucial decisions that will affect the course of their nations for a very long time. Second, people in a state of shock will not be able to focus clearly on their ultimate goals and may begin to doubt their original goals. Thus, they will have difficulty advancing confidently and competently toward their goals. Further, these doubts and confusions will be reflected in the political sphere making it difficult for political leaders to be coherent and focused in their deliberations. Third, many people experiencing shock will naturally exert political pressure to reduce the factors perceived as causing the shock, thereby slowing the pace of transitional reforms. On the one hand, this might be desirable if the pace had been too fast. On the other hand, it might succeed in getting the reform process off track, thus negatively affecting transition success. Fourth, the destruction of social and organizational capital, not to mention drastic declines in value in socialism-specific capital, other types of intangible capital and tangible capital, will directly reduce productive capacity markedly, thereby lowering transition success. Fifth, the shock loosens important constraints on behavior, encouraging opportunistic behavior, especially destructive forms of rent-seeking, thus undermining the possibilities for transition success. Needless to say, this view of what shock involves and how it affects transition success is dramatically different from the neo-liberal view. It should be noted that shock appears to have been present in all the transitional socio-economies to varying degrees. East Germany and Russia are notable for the high degree of shock experienced by their populations.

Capitalist productive capacity

The whole purpose of the transition is to transform a socialist society into a capitalist one. Thus, it is a straightforward proposition that when transition policy measures or initial country conditions contribute to raising the productive capacity of the new socio-economic system or encourage this, it will lead to greater transition success.

IMPLICATIONS FOR TRANSITION STRATEGY

The purpose of this section is to draw together some of the important general implications of the foregoing for transition strategy. It is beyond the scope of this chapter to spell out in detail a full-fledged transition strategy. Naturally any such strategy would need to be tailored to the specific circumstances of the country involved.

One thing is quite clear. Neoclassical economics is ill-suited to contribute to the formation of transition strategy. This is because it lacks the ability

> to deal with issues such as how much one can rush the change of a culture, what it takes to evolve a new set of social institutions, how long a political regime can withstand pain, and to what extent a given people has or lacks the predispositions democracy presumes and capitalism requires. (Etzioni, 1992: 41)

Further, the neoclassical comparative static method of analysis is deficient from the standpoint of transition economics because it analyzes equilibrium states, not the processes of change from one state to another. In other words, it does not feature dynamic analysis. Evolutionary economics comes to mind as an alternative to neoclassical economics because of its emphasis on continuously changing phenomena. However, evolutionary economics tends to focus on long run endogenous change and does not offer much in the way of concrete advice regarding transitional strategy (Horne, 1995: 382).

The neo-liberal strategy (based on neoclassical economics) of rapid radical (all at once) reform has been shown to cause the population of a transitional economy to experience significant levels of shock, and therefore, for reasons discussed above, leads not to transition success but to failure. Also, neo-liberals have taken little or no account of the soft features of socio-economic systems. They, therefore, have not appreciated the reasons for socio-economic friction and the reasons why a nation's culture and history make a difference for transition strategy.

The transition strategy question has often been framed as a choice between rapid radical reform and gradualism. Since, as indicated above, shock therapy is decidedly not therapeutic, this rules out radical reform. But that is not the end of the matter; it is important to consider the principles that can help us decide what kind of gradualist approach would be most desirable. First, it is clear that transition policy should be gradualist in the sense of going slower than the speed associated with the shock threshold. Second, the transition speed should be adjusted to the socio-economy's readiness or capacity for change. Change should not be forced, and the change program should allow time for learning, time for people and enterprises to acquire the relevant types of intangible capital (standard human, social, organizational and personal) and for these to become aligned with the system's hard features.

There is considerable agreement among the advocates of gradualism on the desirability of a two track approach. The first track involves the rapid, spontaneous creation of new private enterprise. This phase ought to be fostered while at the same time holding off on changing the old state sector, that is, holding off on privatization (Murrell, 1993: 125; 1992: 44–5). Once a sizable, robust, competitive, new private sector has emerged along with infrastructural supports and sufficient soft features to complement the new hard structures, then the second track involving large scale privatizations can proceed. Presumably, at this point, the new firms will be pulling employees from the old enterprises (Etzioni, 1992: 9–10). The second track is much more likely to succeed after competitive structures and sufficient intangible capital formation have been established. It should be noted that until new social and organizational capital specific to the emerging market economy has been put in place, it is important for the transition country to utilize existing structures of the old regime 'on a selective and temporary basis to exert control over the state enterprises in the period before privatization and creation of market institutions can take place' (Murrell, 1992: 50). Thus, it is important for these countries not to be too quick in taking actions that might destroy existing organizational capital.

As mentioned earlier, there is good reason to believe that the most successful transitions will involve a patient, step by step, democratic process. The desired gradualism should be one that is chosen with the understanding and consent of all the important societal participants; it should not be a gradualism that is merely the result of political turmoil and reactions to severe shock. The most successful economic development experiences in East Asia, namely those of Japan, Singapore, South Korea, and Taiwan, involved evolutionary processes in which the resulting form of capitalism was a creative blend of old collectivist traditions with modern capitalist institutions. 'The Czech Republic, thanks primarily to Vaclav Klaus, is [unfortunately] the only East European country taking this approach' (Pejovich, 1997: 249).

The evidence on the success of gradualism is subject to different interpretations. In Anders Aslund's (1999b) view, radical reform, not gradualism, is associated with transition success (as measured by change in output). But Aslund's interpretation is suspect; there is after all considerable evidence in favor of gradualism. The countries of Uzbekistan and Slovenia, for example, both of which had been criticized for the slowness of their reforms, are now performing well (Stiglitz, 1999: 29). According to Murrell (1993: 126–31), although Poland started out in January 1990 with a 'big bang,' Poland's success can be attributed to the fact that 'society took back the reforms from the shock therapists' as 'gradually many of the elements of the initial program were withdrawn or weakened' (pp. 126, 129). Further, Poland delayed the privatization of most of its larger enterprises until about 1995 (Goldman, 2000: 35). As indicated earlier, this delay was fortunate as it gave the Poles an opportunity to learn from the experience of other countries who were quicker to privatize. Whereas Aslund counts Poland as a success for radical reform, it should, as Murrell and others point out, be counted as a success for gradualism. Of course, the biggest success for gradualism is China. Unfortunately, space does not permit us to analyze this case.

OVERVIEW OF THE SOCIO-ECONOMIC THEORY OF TRANSITION SUCCESS

The essentials of the socio-economic theory of transition success developed here are depicted in Figure 7.2. The country's initial conditions and the transition policy measures carried out in line with the overall transition strategy determine the country's intermediate variables, the level of shock and the magnitude of the capitalist productive capacity, which in turn determine the country's likelihood of transition success. Again, consider Poland. Earlier some of Poland's initial conditions were reviewed, and Poland's prospects for transition success were found to be relatively favorable. With respect to transition policy measures, Poland is somewhat mixed. On one hand, the initial radical reform measures along with the collapse of communism undoubtedly produced detrimental levels of shock. On the other hand, as indicated above, it did not take Poland very long to back off of these radical policies and choose a more gradual transition path through a relatively democratic process. Our prediction based on the theory of transition success in this case seems consistent with the actual results. As would be predicted, the early high level of shock led to significant declines in the system's performance as indicated by output and other measures, but predictably the performance improved as shock declined, gradualist policy actions were taken, and needed investment in both tangible and intangible capital occurred. Thus, Poland is an important example of transition success, one that our theory would predict. It would be interesting to apply this theory to all the transition economies, comparing predictions with outcomes.

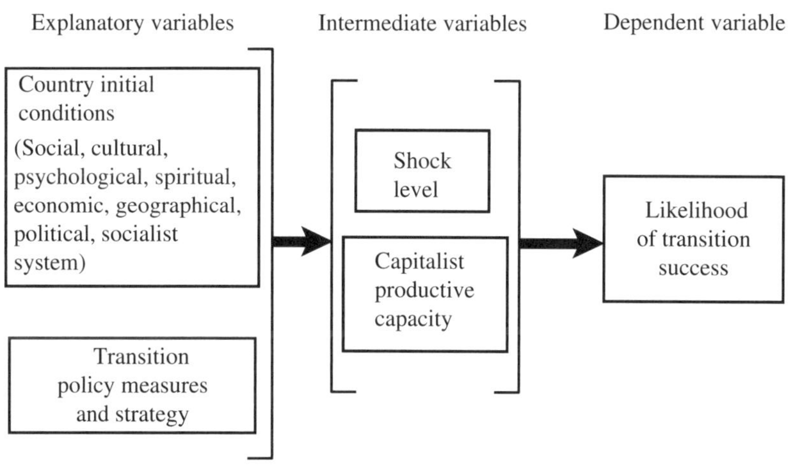

Figure 7.2 Socio-economic theory of transition success

CONCLUSION

The transition from socialism to capitalism is generally conceived of as a substitution of the organizational structures and the legal, financial and political relationships of capitalism for those of socialism, that is, a substitution of capitalism's hard features for socialism's. But this conception of socio-economic systems leaves out the important soft aspect. If our conception of these systems is flawed in this respect, our transition strategies are also likely to be flawed, thereby leading to disastrous transition experiences. Soft factors such as attitudes, behavioral orientations, values and beliefs must mesh with the hard elements of socio-economic systems. Otherwise, the performance of these systems will be nowhere near their potential. Accordingly, when all the hard features are changed quickly without attention to the soft features, as in the neo-liberal radical reform strategy, the result is inevitably a deep shock which greatly retards the transition process. To avoid this, the architects of transition must make sure that the process is democratic and gradual, and that sufficient attention is paid to the need for intangible capital formation in order to replace the old soft features with new ones.

An important contribution of this chapter is the development of a socio-economic theory of transition success that is designed to explain and predict countries' medium term transition success. In this theory, a nation's success is explained by the country's initial conditions and the transition policy measures they have implemented. As indicated above, there is reason to believe that this theory will correctly predict the transition successes and failures of the different Eastern European countries. Careful empirical research, which is beyond the scope of this chapter, would be necessary to confirm this. Finally, there is also reason to believe that our theory of transition success may provide a good basis for constructing a theory explaining less developed countries' economic development successes and failures.

REFERENCES

Adam, Jan (1999), *Social Costs of Transformation to a Market Economy in Post-Socialist Countries*, New York: St Martin's.

Aslund, Anders (1999a), 'The end of rent-seeking: the end of postcommunist transformation,' in Annette N. Brown, *When Is Transition Over?* Kalamazoo, MI: W.E. Upjohn Institute, pp. 51–68.

Aslund, Anders (1999b), 'Post-Communist economic transformation,' in Aurel Braun and Zoltan Barany (eds) *Dilemmas of Transition: The Hungarian Experience*, New York: Rowman and Littlefield, pp. 69–88.

Benacek, Vladimir (1995), 'Small businesses and private entrepreneurship during transition: the case of the Czech Republic,' *Eastern European Economics*, **33**(3–4), 38–75.

Berg, Andrew and Jeffrey Sachs (1992), 'Structural adjustment and international trade in Eastern Europe: the case of Poland,' *Economic Policy*, **14**, 118–73.

Berg, Andrew, Eduardo Borensztein, Ratna Sahay and Jeromin Zettlemeyer (1999), 'The evolution of output in transition economies: explaining the differences,' IMF Working Paper 99/73.

Brenton, Paul, Daniel Gros and Guy Vandille (1997), 'Output decline and recovery in the transition economies: causes and social consequences,' *Economics of Transition*, **5**(1), 113–30.

Brown, Annette N. (1999), *When Is Transition Over?* Kalamazoo, MI: W.E. Upjohn Institute.

de Melo, Martha, Cevdet Denizer, Alan Gelb and Stoyan Tenev (1997), 'Circumstances and choice: the role of initial conditions and policies in transition economies,' World Bank Policy Research Working Paper No. 1866.

Desai, Padma (2000), 'A Russian optimist: interview with Yegor Gaidar,' *Challenge*, **43**(3), 5–27.

Eberstadt, Nicholas (1994), 'Demographic shocks after Communism: East Germany, 1989–93,' *Population and Development Review*, **20**(1), 137–52.

Ericson, Richard E. (1991), 'The classical Soviet-type economy: the nature of the system and implications for reform,' *Journal of Economic Perspectives*, **5**(4), 11–27.

Etzioni, Amitai (1991), 'Eastern Europe: the wealth of lessons,' *Challenge*, **34**(4), 4–10.

Etzioni, Amitai (1992), 'How is Russia bearing up?' *Challenge*, **35**(3), 40–3.

Fischer, Stanley (1992), 'Privatization in East European transformation,' in Christoper Clague and Gordon C. Rausser (eds) *The Emergence of Market Economies in Eastern Europe*, Cambridge, MA: Blackwell, pp. 227–43.

Fischer, Stanley and Alan Gelb (1991), 'The process of socialist economic transformation,' *Journal of Economic Perspectives*, **5**(4), 91–105.

Fischer, Stanley, Ratna Sahay and Carlos A. Vegh (1996), 'Stabilization and growth in transition economies: the early experience,' *Journal of Economic Perspective*, **10**(2), 45–66.

Gelb, Alan (1999), 'The end of transition,' in Annette N. Brown (ed.) *When is Transition Over?* Kalamazoo, MI: W.E. Upjohn Institute, pp. 39–49.

Goldman, Marshall (2000), 'Reprivatizing Russia,' *Challenge*, **43**(3), 28–43.

Goleman, Daniel (1995), *Emotional Intelligence*, New York: Bantam Books.

Goleman, Daniel (1998), *Working with Emotional Intelligence*, New York: Bantam Books.

Gora, Marek (1991), 'Shock therapy for the Polish labour market,' *International Labour Review*, **130**(2), 145–63.

Havel, Vaclav (1991), 'The New Year in Prague,' *The New York Review of Books*, 7 March, 19–20.

Heybey, Berta and Peter Murrell (1999), 'The relationship between economic growth and the speed of liberalization during transition,' *Journal of Policy Reform*, **3**(2), 121–37.

Hoen, Herman W. (1995), 'Theoretically underpinning the transition in Eastern Europe: an Austrian view,' *Economic Systems*, **19**(1), 59–77.

Horne, Jocelyn (1995), 'The economics of transition and the transition of economics,' *Economic Record*, **71**(215), 379–92.
Kaufmann, Daniel and Paul Siegelbaum (1996), 'Privatization and corruption in transition economies,' *Journal of International Affairs*, **50**(2), 419–58.
Kornai, Janos (1992), 'The postsocialist transition and the state: reflections in the light of Hungarian fiscal problems,' *American Economic Review*, **82**(2), 1–21.
Kornai, Janos (2000), 'What the change of system from socialism to capitalism does and does not mean,' *Journal of Economic Perspectives*, **14**(1), 27–42.
Kozul-Wright, Richard and Paul Rayment (1997), 'The institutional hiatus in economies in transition and its policy consequences,' *Cambridge Journal of Economics*, **21**(5), 641–61.
Lavigne, Marie (1999), 'What is still missing?,' in Annette M. Brown (ed.) *When Is Transition Over?* Kalamazoo, MI: W.E. Upjohn Institute, pp. 13–29.
Lipton, David and Jeffrey Sachs (1990a), 'Creating a market economy in Eastern Europe: the case of Poland,' *Brookings Papers on Economic Activity*, **1**, 75–147.
Lipton, David and Jeffrey Sachs (1990b), 'Privatization in Eastern Europe: the case of Poland,' *Brookings Papers on Economic Activity*, **2**, 293–333.
Litwack, John M. (1991), 'Legality and market reform in Soviet-type economies,' *Journal of Economic Perspectives*, **5**(4), 77–89.
Murrell, Peter (1991a), 'Can neoclassical economics underpin the reform of centrally planned economies,' *Journal of Economic Perspectives*, **5**(4), 59–76.
Murrell, Peter (1991b), 'Symposium on economic transition in the Soviet Union and Eastern Europe,' *Journal of Economic Perspectives*, **5**(4), 3–9.
Murrell, Peter (1992), 'Evolution in economics and in the economic reform of the centrally planned economies,' in Christopher Clague and Gordon C. Rausser (eds) *The Emergence of Market Economies in Eastern Europe*, Cambridge, MA: Blackwell, pp. 35–53.
Murrell, Peter (1993), 'What is shock therapy? What did it do in Poland and Russia?,' *Post-Soviet Affairs*, **9**(2), 111–40.
Murrell, Peter (1995), 'The transition according to Cambridge, Mass.,' *Journal of Economic Literature*, **33**(1), 164–78.
Murrell, Peter (1996), 'How far has the transition progressed?,' *Journal of Economic Perspectives*, **10**(2), 25–44.
Neace, M.B. (1999), 'Entrepreneurs in emerging economies: creating trust, social capital and civil society,' *Annals of the American Academy of Political and Social Science*, **565**, 148–61.
Pejovich, Svetozar (1997), 'Law, tradition, and the transition in Eastern Europe,' *The Independent Review*, **2**(2), 243–54.
Rosefielde, Steven and Howard Stein (1999), 'An introduction to the symposium,' *Eastern Economic Journal*, **25**(4), 379–87.
Sachs, Jeffrey D. (1996), 'The transition at mid decade', *American Economic Review*, **86**(2) (May), 128–33.
Selowsky, Marcelo and Ricardo Martin (1997), 'Policy performance and output growth in transition economies', *American Economic Review*, **87**(2), 349–53.
Stiglitz, Joseph (1999), 'Who will guard the guardians?' *Challenge*, **42**(6), 26–67.
Stiglitz, Joseph (2000), 'The insider: what I learned at the world economic crisis,' *New Republic*, 17 and 24 April, 56–60.
Tomer, John F. (1999a), *The Human Firm: A Socio-Economic Analysis of its Behavior and Potential in a New Economic Age*, New York: Routledge.
Tomer, John F. (1999b), 'Social and organizational capital,' in Phillip Anthony

O'Hara (ed.) *Encyclopedia of Political Economy*. Vol. 2, London: Routledge, pp. 1049–51.

Tomer, John F. (2003), 'Personal capital, and emotional intelligence: increasingly important intangible sources of economic growth,' *Eastern Economic Journal*, **29**(3), 453–70.

Wellisz, Stanislaw (1991), 'Poland Under "Solidarity" Rule,' *Journal of Economic Perspectives*, **5**(4), 211–17.

PART III

Intangible capital, human well-being and rationality

The four chapters of Part III are concerned with the contribution of intangible capital to human well-being and rationality. Chapter 8 develops a concept of human well-being that synthesizes the ideas of many others and integrates both economic and noneconomic aspects of life. The concepts of social capital and personal capital are important to understanding how human development is related to well-being. Chapter 9 explains why addictions, contrary to mainstream economists who follow Gary Becker's lead, are not rational and are unwise, excessive, overindulgent, compulsive, something to be regretted and destructive. This chapter develops a socio-economic model of addictive behavior in which several types of intangible capital play a key role. Chapter 10 develops a socio-economic model of preference formation that explains how one's actual preferences may change due to various influences such as those from true preferences and metapreferences. Intangible capital, in the form of personal capital and consumption capital, is an important element in this model. Chapter 11 develops a normative conception of rationality, true rationality, that arguably is a more appropriate conception than the mainstream version associated with economic man. True rationality includes both instrumental rationality and rationality of ends, and intangible capital, especially personal capital and consumption capital, is essential to understanding it.

8. Human well-being: a new approach that considers the overall quality of people's lives

> Sen . . . believes that it is the responsibility of government to promote the overall good of society, and that it is the job of the economist to produce an operational definition of that good and to identify the policies that will best promote it.
>
> **Robert Sugden, 1993, p. 1948**

INTRODUCTION

There is no shortage of ideas about the nature of human well-being. The ideas on what well-being is range from the material, for example, consumption of goods and services, to the spiritual, for example, enlightenment or union with God. The problem is that the notion of well-being incorporated into mainstream economics is severely limited; it does not adequately reflect even many of the good ideas concerning the economic aspect of well-being. And, important philosophic and religious ideas of what constitutes the essence of a good quality life are not considered at all. Therefore, this chapter proposes to develop a concept of human well-being usable by economists and others, a concept that integrates the economic and noneconomic aspects of life in order to satisfy the important objections to the mainstream economic approach. The well-being concept developed here is a synthesis utilizing the ideas of many others along with the relatively new concept of social capital and the newer concept of personal capital. This concept of well-being will be considered successful if it makes sense in light of: (a) research findings on well-being; (b) wise thinking regarding well-being; and (c) our intuitive sense of what well-being means for us. Is a person's well-being the highest when he or she is wealthy?, virtuous?, self-actualized? or enlightened? What factors should be added to or deleted from this list?

To begin, it is important, first, to review the mainstream economic approach and objections to it, consider economic alternatives to the mainstream approach, and then proceed to the great variety of noneconomic ideas on well-being. Based on this foundation, the construction of a revised concept of well-being begins. Then the implications of the new concept are explored.

WELFARISM: THE MAINSTREAM ECONOMIC APPROACH TO WELL-BEING

The mainstream economic approach to well-being, which is a version of utilitarianism, has been labeled welfarism by Amartya Sen and Bernard Williams (1982: 3). According to welfarism, people's well-being comes from the satisfaction or utility they get from consuming what they prefer. Over the years, the objections to welfarism have increased. The following briefly indicates some of the main types of objections. First, according to Daniel Hausman and Michael McPherson (1996: 73), 'Real individuals are not exclusively self-interested. They are sometimes altruistic and all too often malevolent.' Second, there are problems if preferences change (p. 75). Would the individual be better off by satisfying the original preferences? Third, people's preferences may be based on beliefs that are false or unreasonable (p. 76). Will Mary be better off drinking the glass of poison she believes to be medicine? Fourth, some people may have preferences that are obnoxious in the sense of being obviously unfair, racist, sadistic or otherwise antisocial (pp. 77–8). Wouldn't it be a bad thing to satisfy those preferences? Thus, Hausman and McPherson (1996: 73) state that 'there are such obvious objections to a preference-satisfaction view of well-being that one wonders how economists could possibly endorse it.'

Strictly, to determine the well-being of a society, a welfarist economist should sum up the utility of all individuals. Because utility is not easy to measure, economists have generally adopted the 'crude' commodity approach, that is, they have measured the total societal output (GNP, GDP and so on). The advantage of this latter approach is that economists have become better and better at measuring this output. There are, however, a number of very important disadvantages as Sen has emphasized. One is that commodities are not intrinsically good; they are not the desired end; they are only the means to the end (well-being) (David Crocker, 1992: 590–91). The second is the 'interpersonal variability argument.' 'Due to variations among individuals, the same commodity either may help some and harm others or may promote the well-being of some a lot and of others only a little' (p. 591). The upshot is that a certain quantity of GDP, although it may be viewed as a means to an end, does not translate directly into a certain amount of well-being.

REVISING WELFARISM

Because of the aforementioned disadvantages (as well as others) of using a crude commodity approach to measuring well-being, a number of authors have suggested revisions involving the use of a suitably modified output measure. One such approach is the basic needs approach (BNA) worked out by economists and policymakers such as Paul Streeten, Frances Stewart and Mahbub ul Haq in the field of economic development (Crocker, 1992: 602–3). To raise well-being according to the BNA, developing countries should focus on meeting certain basic or human needs (pp. 603–5) and allocate fewer resources to satisfying many subjective preferences or wants.

A second approach involves developing an output measure revised to reflect welfare. The US Income and Product Accounts have been criticized as giving a misleading impression of the growth of national well-being. In response to these criticisms, William Nordhaus and James Tobin (1972) have made the first serious attempt to produce a comprehensive measure of output that is more closely associated with welfare than the traditional production-oriented measures. They have attempted 'to adjust, modify, and supplement the Income and Product Accounts for the kinds of welfare-producing activities, both positive and negative, that are either not included as part of real product or are included as final rather than intermediate product' (p. xv).

Subsequently, other economists have made similar efforts to correct GNP or GDP in order to obtain a measure more indicative of well-being. Worth noting in this regard is the Physical Quality of Life Index 'which develops an index summarizing infant mortality, life expectancy at age one, and basic literacy on a zero to 100 scale' (Romesh Diwan, 2000: 321). Also important is the United Nations Development Programme's Human Development Index (HDI) (UNDP, 1998). HDI reflects three basic dimensions of human development; it utilizes measures of life expectancy, educational attainment (adult literacy and educational enrollment of children) and adjusted income.

The most notable and ambitious well-being indicator based on output is the Genuine Progress Indicator (GPI) developed by an organization called Redefining Progress. GPI is computed by making no less than 24 adjustments to (mostly additions and subtractions) personal consumption. These adjustments reflect: (a) crime and family breakdown; (b) household and volunteer work; (c) income distribution; (d) resource depletion; (e) pollution; (f) long-term environmental damage; (g) changes in leisure time; (h) defensive expenditures; (i) lifespan of consumer durables and public infrastructure; and (j) dependence on foreign assets (see literature available from Redefining Progress). For example, there is an addition to reflect the value of volunteer work, and there are subtractions to reflect the costs of family breakdown, automobile accidents, air pollution and ozone depletion. GPI is important because its trend is dramatically different than that of GDP.

> The GDP would tell us that life has gotten progressively better since the early 1950s – that young adults today are entering a better economic world than their parents did. GDP per American has more than doubled over that time. The GPI shows a very different picture: an upward curve from the early fifties until about 1970, but a gradual decline of roughly 45 percent since then. This strongly suggests that the costs of increased economic activity – at least the kind we are locked into now – have begun to outweigh the benefits, resulting in growth that is actually uneconomic. (Cobb *et al.*, 1995: 72)

SOCIO-ECONOMIC THEORIES REGARDING THE DETERMINANTS OF WELL-BEING

Relative Status

According to one class of theories, a person's well-being is determined to a large extent by the individual's social position or status relative to those to which one compares oneself or relative to one's own previous status. According to Richard Easterlin (1974: 118), 'In judging their happiness, people tend to compare their actual situation with a reference standard or norm, derived from their prior and ongoing social experience.' One variant of this type of theory is 'that the utility a person obtains from his consumption expenditure is a function, not of the absolute level of his expenditure, but of the ratio of his current [consumption] expenditure to that of other people' (p. 112). The relevant amount for other people could refer to an average for the nation as a whole or possibly to an average for a peer or reference group, depending on how the consumption norm or reference standard is determined. Over time it is not uncommon for consumption norms to change, especially movement upward reflecting adaptation to a nation's increase in per capita income.

Relationships

According to Romesh Diwan (2000), human well-being is a function of two kinds of wealth, material wealth and relational wealth. Relational wealth (RW) reflects the harmoniousness of a society's relationships, in particular the ability to be 'in harmony with oneself, one's social relations, and one's [natural] environment.' RW reflects the quality of relationships in families, communities, and neighborhoods. Further, RW reflects the degree to which relationships are loving, caring and ethical. Diwan, citing evidence of lower well-being (that is, lower GPI) in recent decades, suggests that the problem is a result of declining RW. This clearly implies a need to build RW in order to counter family breakdown, the destruction of communities, the deterioration of the natural environment, and the excesses of consumer behavior.

SUBJECTIVE WELL-BEING

Another approach to studying well-being is simply to ask people to evaluate the quality of their lives. The responses provide the data on what is known as subjective well-being (see Diener and Suh, 1999). 'These evaluations include both cognitive judgments of life satisfaction and affective [positive and negative] evaluations of moods and emotions' (Diener and Lucas, 1999: 213; see also Argyle 1996). Although subjective well-being (SWB) can reflect transitory influences, researchers have found much evidence that SWB is moderately stable over time and across many situations suggesting that SWB is a viable concept with long-term validity (Diener and Lucas, 1999: 214; Easterlin, 1974: 96–8).

In analyzing international differences in SWB, one of the most significant findings is the diminishing marginal utility associated with economic growth after some point. According to Ronald Inglehart (1996: 518), when a country goes from poverty and scarcity to become a productive industrial country, there is a dramatic increase in SWB. 'But we find a threshold (at roughly the economic level of Ireland in 1990) where economic growth no longer seems to increase SWB significantly.' According to Inglehart, nations that once put the highest priority on narrow economic achievement, now that they have become economically secure, come to place a higher priority on noneconomic, quality of life considerations such as self-expression. Inglehart calls this societal transition the shift from Materialism to Postmaterialism (or Postmodernism).

As a result of his many years studying well-being, especially the factors explaining SWB in the US, Angus Campbell (1981) has arrived at a number of important conclusions which are relevant to our concerns here. According to Campbell, well-being is not simple; 'it relates to life as a whole and to the specific domains of life' (p. 223). A person's well-being depends on being able to satisfy three basic kinds of needs: having (material and impersonal resources), relating (love, companionship and solidarity), and being (self-actualization and obverse of alienation) (pp. 6–7, 224–30) (see also Erik Allardt, 1993). Campbell finds that objective circumstances such as economic progress do not reliably satisfy all these needs, and thus, the relationship between these objective conditions and well-being is weak (Campbell, 1981: 224, 230). 'If all these objective indicators are taken together as predictors of feelings of well-being, they succeed in accounting for less than a fifth of the variation' (p. 230).

FUNCTIONINGS

Because of the many objections to welfarism (recall the ones cited earlier), Amartya Sen (1987: 13) has rejected this approach to understanding well-being. Sen also rejects the crude commodity approach which utilizes a person's possession of goods (opulence) as a measure of well-being (pp. 15–16). Thus, Sen (along with help from others such as Martha Nussbaum) (see, for example, Nussbaum and Sen, 1993) has attempted to develop an important alternative approach to welfarism, not just a revised version of welfarism or a new/revised measure of well-being. According to Sen (1987: 16), it is important to focus on the 'life we lead and what we can or cannot do, can or cannot be' rather than 'the resources and means one has to lead a life.' In Sen's (1985; 28) view, well-being is the achievement of valuable functionings defined as 'what the person is succeeding in "doing" or "being".' Functionings range from the fairly specific, such as being well-dressed, being well-nourished, ability to obtain pleasure from food or music, to the broad and/or vague, such as having self-respect, acting freely, keeping track of what's going on, appreciating beauty, being psychologically well-adjusted, and being wise and contented. As these examples suggest, well-being *a la* Sen is a complex, intrinsically ambiguous concept (Robert Sugden, 1993: 1953).

Sen's approach is motivated by the desire to find a true answer to a question that engaged Aristotle's thinking: 'What makes a good life?' (Sugden, 1993: 1952). The answer, according to Sen, is that a good life includes many intrinsically important functionings, ones which are general enough to apply across all cultures. These functionings include everything from basic material ones such as being in good health and being adequately fed to others such as ability to act freely. To evaluate a person's or a people's well-being is to make a 'reasoned assessment' of their life situation(s). To illustrate an advantage of this approach, consider Sen's (1985: 73–80) comparison of five developing countries using data on GNP per capita and four other characteristics (for 1982) that reflect level of functioning. Sri Lanka stands out among these nations because although its GNP per capita was far lower than Mexico and Brazil and close to that of China and India, it had the highest life expectancy, the lowest infant mortality, the lowest child death rate and the highest adult literacy rate. Judging by the traditional criteria (GNP per capita), Sri Lanka was at or near the bottom of the list, but judging by its rating on the four functionings, a very different picture of well-being in Sri Lanka emerges. In general, using Sen's functionings approach provides much richer and more nuanced information regarding a people's level of well-being than does a measure of output or resources per capita. The difficulty with Sen's approach is the question of how to rank or value the different functionings in order to arrive at an overall measure of well-being (Sugden, 1993: 1952–3).

HAPPINESS, GENES AND SET-POINTS

Most of us tend to think of our well-being as resulting from a combination of external events and our behavior. Could it be, however, that our happiness is largely determined by our genetic inheritance? Researchers who answer in the affirmative have hypothesized that everyone has a happiness set-point, a baseline happiness level. Even though positive and negative events (for example, winning the lottery, becoming paralyzed) may move people temporarily away from their baseline level, their happiness eventually returns to this set-point (Diener and Lucas, 1999: 221; Dalai Lama and Cutler, 1998: 20–2; Lykken, 1999: 19–22). Researchers have postulated that these set-points are related to an individual's temperament or personality and are biologically determined (Diener and Lucas, 1999: 221). One kind of interesting evidence on this comes from studies of twins. The most significant piece of evidence is for well-being scores for identical twins (who have identical genes) raised apart. David Lykken (1999: 55–7) and his collaborator, Auke Tellegen, found the current happiness levels of these identical twins to have a correlation of 0.53. This indicates that more than 50 percent of the variation across people in current happiness is associated with genetic differences. These results, however, are underestimates of the true genetic similarity of identical twins because current happiness levels include a significant transitory component. After adjusting the estimates to remove the transitory factor, Lykken (p. 58) finds that 'nearly 100 percent of the variation across people in the happiness set-point seems to be due to individual differences in genetic makeup!' It should be noted that despite this, Lykken has come to believe that people who learn good habits can achieve happiness levels above their set-points and people with bad habits will tend to have levels below their set-points (p. 60).

HUMANISTIC PHILOSOPHY AND PSYCHOLOGY

On the subject of well-being, Aristotle is the preeminent philosopher. According to Aristotle, human well-being emerges from what we do and what we become, not from what we have (Jerome Segal, 1991: 304) (a view consistent with Sen's approach). Further, 'the good life is one in which a person most fully, and at the highest level of excellence, fulfills his deepest nature . . . [It is] a life in which there is a flourishing of one's truest self' (Segal, 1991: 289). This kind of life cannot be in any sense a means to other ends; it is an end in itself. Moreover, happiness is not the same as pleasure, amusement, nor utility from consumption activity, although there is nothing wrong with these things per se. Thus, according to Aristotle, 'the happy man is one whose activity accords with perfect virtue and who is adequately furnished with goods' (Campbell, 1981: 56).

No doubt, many would agree that Abraham Maslow is the preeminent humanistic psychologist. Maslow is in accord with Aristotle on the nature of the good life. It is a life in which man is able to fulfill his lowest and highest human needs, especially his need for self-actualization.

> What a man *can* be, he *must* be. This need we may call self-actualization . . . It refers to man's desire for self-fulfillment, namely to the tendency for him to become actualized in what he is potentially. This tendency might be phrased as the desire to become more and more what one is, to become everything that one is capable of becoming. (Maslow, *A Theory of Human Motivation*, 1943, as quoted in Hoffman, 1999: 143)

In general, economists have ignored the issues such as self-actualization and character development raised by Aristotle, Maslow and many others in connection with human well-being (Kiron, 1997: 173). One exception to this is found in the writings of a number of important humanistic economists. For example, the nineteenth century Swiss economist and historian, Sismondi, wrote that the ultimate end of an economic system is an 'enobling of human nature' and the 'perfection of Man' (Lutz, 1999: 130). A second example is John A. Hobson, an Englishman and a humanistic social economist whose life spanned the nineteenth and twentieth centuries. He anticipated Maslow's hierarchy of needs and advocated institutional reforms that would help people realize the higher dimensions of their human nature, especially self-actualization (pp. 93–9, 130–1).

PRUDENTIAL VALUES

James Griffin (1986), a philosopher, has developed an approach to well-being which is an alternative to welfarism and also an attempt to go beyond Sen's functionings and capabilities approach. Like Aristotle, Griffin considers a person's well-being to come from living a good life as a whole, a flourishing life (p. 63). What Griffin objects to is assessing a person's overall level of well-being by adding up 'lots of small, short-term utilities' (p. 34). His objection applies both to welfarism (and other variants of utilitarianism) and Sen's approach which involves attaching a value to the many functionings and adding them up (p. 36). In Griffin's view, satisfaction of desires per se does not necessarily contribute to well-being; only satisfaction of 'informed desires' does. Satisfaction of irrational, immoral, trivial, abnormal, cheap, disgusting, and vicious desires does not make one better off (p. 39). Note that Tomer (1996: 623) has developed a concept similar to informed desires, that is, true preferences, a 'person's unique set of preferences that represent what is really and truly the best for that person.' In this view, only satisfaction of true preferences leads to well-being.

According to Griffin (1986: 58, 63), the ideal life, the perfect way for a human to function, contains the right balance of virtues; it is a life lived in agreement with prudential values. Griffin's (p. 67) list of prudential values includes: (a) accomplishment; (b) the components of human existence (choosing one's own course – autonomy, basic capabilities enabling one to act, liberty); (c) understanding; (d) enjoyment; and (e) deep personal relations (see also Mozaffar Qizilbash's (1996: 156) similar but longer list). These are values that would be valuable in any life regardless of culture. Moreover, these values or ends of life are intended to be 'an important standard for judging most (ordinary) lives' (Griffin, 1986: 70). 'They let us say roughly . . . how good the life is and how it could be better. They do, because they rest on general features of human nature' (p. 70). Qizilbash (1996: 146) believes that Griffin's approach is an improvement over Sen's particularly because Sen 'fails to give a list of valuable functionings' that is, an adequate account of what the good life is. To sum up, progress toward greater well-being, or human development, occurs, in Griffin's view, when people's lives increasingly reflect the prudential values (p. 157).

RELIGION AND WELL-BEING

Religions and spiritual traditions inevitably incorporate ideas concerning what the good life is, how one should live one's life, and the rewards (and penalties) one can expect in this life or possible future lives. Almost all religions specify some ultimate or ideal state that their members aim for such as enlightenment or oneness with God. In a sense, this state provides the member with the ultimate of well-being; but since typically only a very small proportion of the religion's members achieve the ideal, the most important thrust of a religion is its guidance on how to live one's life, and thus, how to achieve a measure of increased well-being on the path to, but far short of, the religious ideal.

In the case of Hinduism, there are four basic aims in life that contribute to well-being (Koller 1985: 42–6). The ultimate aim of Hindus is self-liberation or self-realization (moksha). The other three are: (a) enjoyment of the fullness of life or pleasure (*kama*); (b) means of life, success, prosperity or wealth (*artha*); and (c) virtuous living, righteousness, guide to action, or moral and ethical duty (*dharma*).

> In order to achieve the spiritual goal of *moksha*, it is necessary to first satisfy the physical and psychological needs of the individual by attaining the necessary means of life (*artha*) and the enjoyment (*kama*) they make possible. In turn, in order to regulate the activities of *artha* and *kama*, virtue – or *dharma* – is necessary (pp. 42–3).

According to Hinduism (Smith, 1991: 21–2), everyone has hidden within them a true self with infinite awareness and infinite bliss. Why is this unlimited self not readily apparent? It is because this self is like a lamp 'covered with dust and dirt to the point of obscuring its light completely. The problem life poses for the human self is to cleanse the dross of its being to the point where its infinite center can shine forth in full display' (p. 22). Hindus can make significant progress along this path, and increase their well-being, by bringing artha, kama and dharma into the right relationship.

With respect to well-being, the essence of Buddhism is quite similar to Hinduism. This is not very surprising because the historical Buddha, the founder of Buddhism, was in a sense a reformer of Hinduism. According to Buddhism, there are four factors contributing to happiness (or well-being): (a) wealth; (b) worldly satisfaction; (c) spirituality; and (d) enlightenment (Dalai Lama and Cutler, 1998: 24). In regard to the third, spirituality, 'your state of mind is the key' (p. 24). In particular, it is important to have the 'right mental attitude' and 'maintain a calm, peaceful state of mind' (p. 25). Buddhists, similar to Hindus, seek to reach the ultimate state, enlightenment, through disciplined practices that remove the 'dust from the lamp', alleviate suffering, and allow the Buddha's nature to shine through.

It is less easy to characterize Christianity on the subject of well-being. For one thing, Christianity is very big in terms of number of adherents and very diverse. There are three main divisions: Roman Catholicism, the Eastern Orthodox Church and Protestantism; and there are more than 1000 Protestant groups and many Eastern Orthodox branches. Christianity is distinguished by a strong belief in one God and by its adherents' experience of God's love as expressed particularly by sending his only son, Jesus Christ, to earth. Christians are asked to reciprocate God's love by loving all others. According to Christianity, people have only one life to determine whether in the afterlife they will go to heaven or hell (see Smith, 1991: 330–46). With respect to how one should behave in order to experience well-being, Christianity as a whole emphasizes loving, compassionate actions and not committing sins. The ultimate of well-being in Christianity is to experience oneness with God along with the love of God and the love of others.

Due to the space limitations of this chapter, the other major religions (most notably Judaism and Islam) are not considered here. While considering these other religions would be interesting, this would contribute relatively little toward the development of the well-being approach that is the focus of this chapter.

HUMAN NATURE A LA KEN WILBER

To properly understand well-being, it is important to have a comprehensive, accurate conception of human nature. No one has taken a more embracing and comprehensive view of human nature than Ken Wilber (see for example, 1996a,b) who has systematically studied the path of human development. Wilber's full spectrum model is a map of the entire range of human potential. His view is that human development unfolds in predictable stages. These stages of consciousness include not only those recognized by Western psychologists but those recognized by Eastern religions, most notably Hinduism and Buddhism. In Wilber's (1996a) model, there are ten stages of development which in turn are classified into three main categories: subconscious (the prepersonal stages), self-consciousness (the personal stages) and superconsciousness (the transpersonal stages). Wilber's (1996a: 4–5) developmental stages are also usefully divided into two halves. The first, the Outward Arc, is the movement from subconsciousness to self-consciousness and is characterized by self-assertion, individuation, and conquering outer worlds. The second, the Inward Arc, is the movement from self-consciousness to superconsciousness and is characterized by self-realization, going within, transcending self, and achieving oneness.

According to Ken Wilber (1996a: Chapter 10), human development proceeds from stage to stage, proceeding to successively higher-order wholes and unities and integrations. Typically, individual development stops far short of reaching a person's full potential. On the one hand, there is an innate tendency for humans to seek to evolve until there is only one Unity, self-liberation, enlightenment, the ultimate of well-being. On the other hand, there is a typical level of human development consistent with a society's culture, institutions, ethics and norms, and these act like a pacer of development. 'This cultural center of gravity acts like a magnet on individual development. If you are below the average level, it tends to pull you up. If you try to go above it, it tends to pull you down' (Wilber, 1996b: 139). Although Wilber does not say so explicitly, it seems almost implied in his work that a person's well-being is related to the person's attained stage of human development as well as the development stage corresponding to his/her society's center of gravity.

PERSONAL CAPITAL AND SOCIAL CAPITAL

> The personal capital concept can be used to gain further insight into well-being's nature. *Personal capital* is a kind of human capital that differs from standard human capital in that the human capacity involved is not the type developed by academic education or by the usual types of job related training. The personal capital capacities are fundamentally different from cognitive intelligence or intellectual knowledge. Personal capital relates to an individual's basic personal qualities and reflects the quality of an individual's psychological, physical, and spiritual functioning. A very important component of personal capital that has received much recent attention is the human capacity called emotional intelligence which Daniel Goleman (1995, 1998) has written about. (Tomer, 2003).

The importance of personal capital is that as people grow, moving along the human development path, becoming more mature, more capable, and more conscious, a good part of this development can be characterized as personal capital formation. Presumably, there are some aspects of standard human capital formation involved, but the basic story is that people are becoming more capable due to psychological or emotional, physical and spiritual growth. These people are becoming more capable in all spheres of life, not just the work sphere and the personal sphere. Another way to look at this is that people who have experienced personal growth (accumulation of personal capital) have raised the quality of their existing functionings and have added new functionings to their repertoire. If the investment in personal capital raises emotional intelligence, it may be because of greater social skills, increased motivation, or increased awareness and ability to regulate one's emotions that people have more and better beings and doings. From Sen's standpoint, clearly, these people have increased their well-being. To the extent that this personal growth has moved people to a higher stage of human development, this represents a rise in well-being from Wilber's standpoint, and presumably, the standpoints of Hinduism and Buddhism.

Another form of intangible capital, social capital, is also important in gaining insight regarding well-being. Social capital is the product of activities that create social relationships, relationships providing lasting productive or personal capacity. Unlike the standard forms of human capital, the capacity is embodied, generally speaking, not in individuals per se but in the relationships or connections between people (Tomer, 1999). According to sociologist James Coleman (1988: S98), 'Like other forms of capital, social capital is productive, making possible the achievement of certain ends that in its absence would not be possible.'

Arguably, investment in many kinds of social capital increases well-being. When people are successful at transforming their relationships for the better, that is, when these relationships become more loving, compassionate, and joyful, this involves a well-being increasing investment in social capital. From Sen's standpoint, to the extent that certain functionings (for example, giving and receiving social support, being nurtured by one's family) require strong relationships, social capital contributes to well-being. It should be noted that social capital is quite similar to relational wealth which according to Romesh Diwan (2000) is an important contributor to well-being.

WELL-BEING AND FUNCTIONING: A NEW APPROACH

As Aristotle and others have stated, the essence of human well-being is a life well-lived. According to Henry Bruton (1997: 19), it is 'a life rich in meaning and personal growth, a life that reflects the fact of one's humanness and one's membership in a community, and, finally, a life built from some sort of conscious thought and reflection as to its content and purpose.' And as James Griffin (1986) has pointed out, one cannot tell if a life has been truly well-lived by adding up all the things a person has consumed or even adding up the value of all their functionings *a la* Sen. To summarize this larger aspect of a person's or a society's well-being satisfactorily, what is needed is a somewhat different concept of functioning, that is, overall human functioning. Overall human functioning has to do with the spirit in which one 'approaches life, meets its trials, decides on goals and action' (p. 63). This overall functioning refers also to the degree to which one has fulfilled one's deepest nature, found one's purpose in life, and lived according to it. It is correlated with Wilber's stages of human development. In general, the higher the stage of human development, the higher the overall human functioning.

To further appreciate the overall human functioning concept, consider a page containing a list of many types of human functionings. At the bottom of the page is listed all the kinds of functionings that would come to one's mind most readily. Included here are functionings related to nourishment, safety, security, health, longevity, literacy, recreation, entertainment, sexual relations, comfort, housing, transportation, social relationships, and so on, the functionings Sen writes about. Let's call these ordinary adult human functionings. At the top of the page is a somewhat smaller, different list of functionings. Included here are functionings related to such things as: appreciation of one's life purpose, wisdom, accomplishment, orientation to serve others, degree of harmony and peace, joy, commitment, mental clarity and balance, discipline, and life integrity. Let's call these higher human functionings. Overall human functioning is essentially a suitable cluster of these higher human functionings.

To characterize adequately a person's well-being, that is, whether in fact a person's life is going well, requires us to consider both the higher and lower aspects of functioning. Thus, the approach to well-being proposed here has two elements: overall human functioning and the ordinary adult human functionings. Let's call it the overall/ordinary functioning approach to well-being. According to this approach, high well-being people are those who have not only become capable in many aspects of life as evidenced by their many ordinary functionings, but they are people whose life makes sense as a whole, and thus, who experience the deep satisfaction and joy that comes from a coherent, meaningful life. In other words, well-being is partly about the essence or core of one's life and partly about all the specific elements of it. It is about both the higher and the lower aspects. Note that there is a significant correspondence between the higher functionings and the prudential values that Griffin writes about.

The idea of two levels of human functionings, higher and ordinary, is akin to the higher and lower needs on Maslow's hierarchy of human needs. Just as one would have to satisfy one's lower needs on a regular basis before one could focus much attention on satisfying one's higher needs, one is likely to be focused largely on attainment of many of the ordinary functionings before one can give much attention to the higher human functionings. People in poor or modest circumstances probably are concerned mostly with the ordinary functionings. Then as material circumstances improve along with greater economic security, there is at least the possibility that people will attend more to their higher human functionings.

Every society has a typical pattern of both the ordinary and higher human functionings realized by its citizens. We would expect this typical functioning level to act as a magnet (recall Wilber) that either pulls people up to or pulls them down to the typical or conventional level. To realize this conventional level of functioning (or any other level) requires certain kinds of investment in personal and social capital as well as in standard types of human capital (not to mention tangible capital). A society's institutions presumably have been developed in such a way as to help people gain the required level of intangible capital formation. The types of institutions involved range from educational ones to a variety of other institutions organized to enable the required level of family, community and employment functioning. If one understands this societal pattern of functionings as well as deviations from it, one can gain a good appreciation of that society's well-being. This understanding would also enable one to appreciate that society's well-being deficiencies and the degree of well-being inequality.

THE IDEAL

If a society were to adopt the overall/ordinary functioning approach to well-being as opposed to the welfarist approach, one would expect that instead of focusing its efforts on increasing economic efficiency and raising production, this society would attempt more directly to improve important aspects of how people's lives are going. Certainly, well-being might be improved by producing more goods and services and accumulating resources, but from the standpoint of the new approach these material improvements would be viewed simply as means to well-being, not as ends. According to the new approach, the ideal society would be one in which: (a) everyone is well nourished, well housed, healthy, secure, safe, literate/educated, comfortable, entertained, and so on; and (b) everyone is experiencing the deep satisfaction and joy coming from living a very meaningful life, one lived in accord with one's true purposes. Despite the fact that no society is close to the ideal, this ideal can be very useful in that it may point clearly to what societies need to do to raise well-being.

In the approach to well-being developed here, individuals are assumed to have ultimate purposes, and individual well-being is determined in part by whether people live in accord with their purposes. It is, however, conceivable that social collectivities, for example, organizations, communities, societies and so on, have ultimate purposes that are not simple aggregations of the purposes of their members. If so, people's well-being would be related to their membership in these collectivities and the extent to which these groups' efforts were in accord with the group's purposes. Were this true, some modification of our new approach to well-being would be needed to accommodate this reality.

IMPLICATIONS

It is important to note that the approach to well-being developed here is not consistent with the utility maximizing concept of rationality incorporated in mainstream economic theory. A rational person acting consistent with our approach would seek to make decisions that would enhance his/her long-term well-being. An important aspect of this is making decisions consistent with one's ultimate life purposes

This new approach to well-being has implications for what socio-economies, presumably in many cases through government action, should do to enhance well-being. One is that society should help its citizens to discover their true purposes and to cast off their addictions, fixations/obsessions and attachments. Second, it should help citizens to integrate their purposes with the common purpose and to proceed enthusiastically to achieve these. Third, it should help its citizens to develop the understanding, skill, and emotional and social competencies that will enable them to travel as far as possible on the path to high well-being. Fourth, it should be alert to obstacles along the path and seek to remove these. According to Robert Lane (1996: 282):

> If a high quality of life, intensely desired by all, is thus dependent upon the qualities of persons leading those lives, we should expect the public to demand governmental programs devised to promote [qualities such as] cognitive complexity, a sense of autonomy and effectiveness, self-knowledge, self-esteem and so forth. Why is this not the case?

The concept of well-being advocated here has both an objective and a subjective aspect. It has an objective aspect because there are external, observable conditions that affect one's functionings, and thus, one's well-being. The subjective aspect has to do with the mental, emotional, spiritual and so on factors, the internal and largely unobservable factors, that affect well-being. Well-being depends on both objective and subjective considerations; the objective factors are necessary but not sufficient for well-being, and the same goes for the subjective factors. It is interesting to note that the objective factors, by themselves, largely correspond to mainstream economists' conception of well-being, and the subjective factors, by themselves, roughly correspond to mystical religious views especially those of Eastern religions.

ACCOUNTING FOR WELL-BEING

There is obviously a need to measure well-being. People will want to know whether well-being is increasing or not and whether one nation's well-being is higher than another's. The concept of well-being defined here will obviously not be as easy to measure as gross domestic product or other output or consumption measures. But it is not impossible. What would be required is the development of a kind of socio-economic accounting for a nation. National socio-economic accounting would be to national income accounting what a corporate social audit is to a financial accounting audit. The social audit, which is voluntary in the US but nevertheless performed by some corporations, assesses the socio-economic performance of a corporation by comparing its behavior to certain norms or standards of business behavior. Similarly, a national socio-economic 'audit' would assess people's major types of functionings (higher and lower) in comparison to other nations and to societal standards. The data collected would be both objective and subjective as well as both qualitative and quantitative in nature. It should be noted that this is not the first proposal of this kind. According to Campbell (1981: 236), others have urged the creation of a 'system of social accounts intended to represent the social conditions of the nation.'

With respect to a national socio-economic audit, the most difficult type of data to obtain would be on the higher human functionings. The following is a list of types of data that would help assess a people's overall level of functioning:

- Degree of people's awareness of their lives' higher purpose.
- Degree to which people's lives manifest higher purpose, especially serving others.
- Degree to which people's lives have ethical, spiritual or religious discipline.
- Degree to which people have developed a strong sense of wisdom out of reflection, reading, and thinking.
- Degree to which people's accomplishments make sense as a whole.
- Degree to which people experience joy, bliss, deep satisfaction, and so on.
- Degree of harmony and balance evident in people's lives (or lack of disharmony and imbalance).
- Degree to which people have made and kept important commitments.
- Degree to which people hold dearly important and consistent moral values and attempt to live by these.
- Degree to which people's lives reflect imagination and creativity.
- Degree to which people feel good about themselves and confident in their ability to chart their own life course.
- Degree to which people feel free to be what is truly right for them.
- Degree to which people have established deep personal relationships that are mutually supportive of their life purposes.

- Degree to which people are supported and helped to search for wisdom and what is right for them.

Presumably, through survey means, reasonably good data on the above could be obtained. If so, this would enable us to make at least an adequate assessment of a society's overall human functioning.

CONCLUSIONS

As indicated before, the essence of well-being is living a good life. The biggest problem with the welfarist approach to well-being is that it leads us to counting incomes and commodities which are at best means to a good life. Revised versions of welfarism, even valuable ones such as the Genuine Progress Indicator approach, are a great improvement over crude commodity approaches but inevitably leave out important components of the good life. Sen's functionings and capabilities approach makes a very important advance over welfarism. In Sen's view, people's well-being comes from their intrinsically important doings and beings. It is not about how much food one consumes; it is about eating tasty food and being well-nourished. It is not about how many and what types of cars you have; it is about your ability to get where you want to go freely and in an efficient manner. Although very important, Sen's functionings approach for the most part does not capture the higher, broader aspect of life suggested by the questions: Has life gone well as a whole? Has life flourished?

Philosophers such as Aristotle, humanistic psychologists like Maslow, broad thinkers like Wilber, and religious traditions such as Hinduism and Buddhism have been very helpful in pointing out the true potential of human life, and they have given important advice on how to live life to its fullest. A complete concept of well-being, therefore, must in some fashion include these higher aspects of human life. The approach to well-being developed here is called the overall/ordinary approach to well-being. In addition to the ordinary adult human functionings, basically the functionings Sen mentions, the new approach includes a group of higher human functionings which, together, are called overall human functioning. To adequately assess a person's or a society's well-being, that is, to get a true picture of how well people's lives are going, it is necessary to consider both people's ordinary (or lower) functionings and their overall (or higher) functionings. Finally, to raise the level of a society's well-being requires a variety of kinds of capital formation, particularly investment in personal and social capital.

REFERENCES

Allardt, Erik (1993), 'Having, loving, being: an alternative to the Swedish model of welfare research,' in A. Sen and M. Nussbaum (eds), *The Quality of Life*, Oxford: Clarendon Press.

Argyle, Michael (1996), 'Subjective well-being,' in Avner Offer (ed.), *In Pursuit of the Quality of Life*, Oxford: Oxford University Press, pp. 18–45.

Bruton, Henry J. (1997), *On the Search for Well-Being*, Ann Arbor, MI: University of Michigan Press.

Campbell, Angus (1981), *The Sense of Well-Being in America: Recent Patterns and Trends*, New York: McGraw-Hill.

Cobb, Clifford, Ted Halstead and Jonathan Rowe (1995), 'If the GDP is up, why is America down?' *Atlantic Monthly*, **October**, 59–78.

Coleman, James S. (1988), 'Social capital in the creation of human capital,' *American Journal of Sociology*, **94**(Supplement), 95–120.

Crocker, David A. (1992), 'Functioning and capability: the foundation of Sen's and Nussbaum's development ethic,' *Political Theory*, **20**(4), 584–612.

Dalai Lama and Cutler, Howard C. (1998), *The Art of Happiness: A Handbook for Living*, New York: Riverhead Books.

Diener, Ed and Lucas, Richard E. (1999), 'Personality and subjective well-being,' in Daniel Kahneman, Ed Diener and Norbert Schwarz (eds), *Well-being: The Foundations of Hedonic Psychology*, New York: Russell Sage Foundation, pp. 213–29.

Diener, Ed and Suh, Eunkook Mark (1999), 'National differences in subjective well-being,' in Daniel Kahneman, Ed Diener and Norbert Schwarz (eds), *Well-being: The Foundations of Hedonic Psychology*, New York: Russell Sage Foundation, pp. 434–50.

Diwan, Romesh (2000), 'Relational wealth and the quality of life,' *Journal of Socio-Economics*, **29**(4), 305–40.

Easterlin, Richard A. (1974), 'Does economic growth improve the human lot? Some empirical evidence,' in Paul A. David and Melvin W. Reder (eds), *Nations and Households in Economic Growth: Essays in Honor of Moses Abramovitz*, New York: Academic Press, pp. 89–125.

Goleman, Daniel (1995), *Emotional Intelligence*, New York: Bantam Books.

Goleman, Daniel (1998), *Working with Emotional Intelligence*, New York: Bantam Books.

Griffin, James (1986), *Well-being: Its Meaning, Measurement, and Moral Importance*, Oxford: Clarendon Press.

Hausman, Daniel M. and Michael S. McPherson (1996), *Economic Analysis and Moral Philosophy*, Cambridge: Cambridge University Press.

Hoffman, Edward (1999), *The Right to be Human*, New York: McGraw-Hill.

Inglehart, Ronald (1996), 'The diminishing utility of economic growth: from maximizing security toward maximizing subjective well-being,' *Critical Review*, **10**(4), 509–31.

Kiron, David (1997), 'Economics and the good: individuals,' in F. Ackerman, D. Kiron, N. R. Goodwin, J. M. Harris and K. Gallagher (eds), *Human Well-Being and Economic Goals*, Washington, DC: Island Press.

Koller, John M. (1985), *Oriental Philosophies*, 2nd edn, New York: Scribner.

Lane, Robert E. (1996), 'Quality of life and quality of persons: a new role for government?,' in Avner Offer (ed.), *In Pursuit of the Quality of Life*, Oxford: Oxford University Press.

Lutz, Mark A. (1999), *Economics for the Common Good: Two Centuries of Social Economic Thought in the Humanistic Tradition*, London: Routledge.

Lykken, David (1999), *Happiness: What Studies on Twins Show Us about Nature, Nurture, and the Happiness Set-Point*, New York: Golden Books.

Maslow, A. H. (1943), 'A theory of human motivation,' *Psychological Review*, **50**, 370–96.

Nordhaus, William and James Tobin (1972), 'Is growth obsolete?,' in National Bureau of Economic Research *Economic Growth*, 50th Anniversary Colloquium V, New York: National Bureau of Economic Research.

Nussbaum, Martha (1993), 'Non-relative virtues: an Aristotelian approach,' in M. Nussbaum and A. Sen (eds), *The Quality of Life*, Oxford: Clarendon Press.

Nussbaum, Martha and Sen, Amartya (eds) (1993), *The Quality of Life*, Oxford: Clarendon Press.

Qizilbash, Mozaffar (1996), 'Capabilities, well-being and human development: a survey,' *Journal of Development Studies*, **33**(2), 143–62.

Segal, Jerome M. (1991), 'Alternative conceptions of the economic realm,' in Richard M. Coughlin (ed.), *Morality, Rationality, and Efficiency: New Perspectives on Socio-Economics*, Armonk, NY: M.E. Sharpe.

Sen, Amartya (1985), *Commodities and Capabilities*, Amsterdam: North-Holland.

Sen, Amartya (1987), *The Standard of Living*, Cambridge: Cambridge University Press.

Sen, Amartya and Bernard Williams (Eds) (1982), *Utilitarianism and Beyond*, Cambridge: Cambridge University Press.

Smith, Huston (1991), *The World's Religions: Our Great Wisdom Traditions*, San Francisco, CA: HarperCollins.

Sugden, Robert (1993), 'Welfare, resources, and capabilities: a review of *Inequality Reexamined* by Amartya Sen,' *Journal of Economic Literature*, **31**(4), 1947–62.

Tomer, John F. (1996), 'Good habits and bad habits: a New Age socio-economic model of preference formation,' *Journal of Socio-Economics*, **25**(6), 619–38.

Tomer, John F. (1999), 'Social and organizational capital,' in Phillip Anthony O'Hara (ed.), *Encyclopedia of Political Economy*, Vol. 2, London: Routledge, pp. 1949–51.

Tomer, John F. (2001), 'Economic man vs. heterodox men: the concept of human nature in the schools of economic thought,' *Journal of Socio-Economics*, **30**(4), 281–93.

Tomer, John F. (2003), 'Personal capital, and emotional intelligence: increasingly important intangible sources of economic growth,' *Eastern Economic Journal*, **29**(3), 453–70.

United Nations Development Programme (1998), *Human Development Report*, New York: Oxford University Press.

Wilber, Ken (1996a), *The Atman Project: A Transpersonal View of Human Development*. Wheaton, IL: Quest Books.

Wilber Ken (1996b), *A Brief History of Everything*, Boston, MA: Shambhala.

9. Addictions are not rational: a socio-economic model of addictive behavior

INTRODUCTION

Intuitively, most of us think of addictive behavior as unwise, excessive, overindulgent, compulsive, something to be regretted, ultimately destructive, and, of course, irrational. Mainstream economists, following Gary Becker's lead, know better. Addictive behavior, they say, is like all other economic behavior; it is economically rational. There are two main purposes of this chapter. One is to explain why addictive behavior is not rational. The other is to develop a socio-economic model of addictive behavior that is an alternative to economists' rational addiction theory. The explanation and the model draw on the insights of a variety of behavioral disciplines, especially psychologists, and combine these with economic concepts. It is hoped that these interdisciplinary theoretical perspectives will help us see addiction in a true light and help us connect to our natural intuition and wisdom concerning these matters.

The plan of this chapter is as follows. The first section reviews the concept of addiction in the theory of rational addiction. The second section explores the essential nature of addiction including why people become addicted and the brain physiology of addiction. The third section explains why addictive behavior is not a form of rational economic behavior. It also argues that economic man needs to be replaced by 'human man.' Our socio-economic model of addictive behavior is developed in the fourth section. Some of the implications of the model are explained in the fifth section, and the final section provides conclusions.

THE CONCEPT OF ADDICTION IN THE THEORY OF RATIONAL ADDICTION

The theory of rational addiction was developed by Gary Becker and his coauthors (see, for example, Becker and Stigler, 1977; Becker and Murphy,

1988; Becker *et al.*, 1991; Becker, 1996) to explain why addiction, rather than being a form of irrationality, is a form of rational economic behavior. Becker and Murphy (1988: 675) 'claim that addictions, even strong ones, are usually rational in the sense of involving forward-looking maximization with stable preferences.' In this view, addicts or would-be addicts attempt to maximize their utility over long time periods by making consistent choices with respect to addictive commodities, choices that consider the present value of the person's expected future benefits and costs from using the commodity. Addictions are simply strong habits with two essential characteristics: first reinforcement in which 'greater current consumption of a good raises its future consumption'; and second tolerance in which 'given levels of consumption are less satisfying when past consumption has been greater' (p. 682). Becker and coauthors recognize beneficial as well as harmful addictions depending on whether the human capital accumulated in the process of consuming the objects of addiction 'have negative or positive effects on utility and earnings' (p. 684). In sum, rational addiction theory views addictive behavior as merely a special case of consumption behavior.

While few would deny that rational addiction theory involves a creative application of mainstream economic theory, even some mainstream economists have criticized it for being hard to reconcile with certain important realities of addictions. In particular, this theory depicts addictions without any pathology. It implies that addicts happily, without regret, and with careful consideration of all alternatives choose addiction. In other words, people 'are never fooled or "hooked" into addiction' (Orphanides and Zervos, 1995: 740). Orphanides and Zervos propose several revisions to rational addiction theory to make it more realistic. In their version, individuals some of whom have high addictive tendencies are uncertain of the harm associated with consuming an addictive good and learn through experimentation. Some of these persons recognize their addictive tendency too late (after going beyond a critical level of consumption) and become addicted, an outcome they come to regret. While this version of the theory provides added realism, addiction is still not depicted as a departure from rational consumer behavior.

Gordon Winston's (1980) theory builds on rational addiction theory but is an improvement because his theory explicitly recognizes the compulsive aspect of addiction. As evidence that people 'get hooked' and desire to extricate themselves from addictions, Winston cites the existence of 'anti-markets' (p. 299). In these markets, people pay for services that enable them not to consume the objects of their addiction, whether it be liquor, cigarettes, gambling, overeating or drugs. In Winston's theory, an addicted person's preferences fluctuate between two states, one of which reflects the addictive compulsion and the other of which reflects long-run preferences (pp. 302–5). Winston's addicts experience the conflict of strongly desiring the addictive commodity while knowing that it may not be in their best long-run interests. Another valuable feature of Winston's theory is that it recognizes that 'the consumption of addictive commodities reduces the human capital – skills and sensitivities – employed' in other aspects of life (for example, physical fitness) (pp. 305–7). Although Winston incorporates the compulsive aspect of addiction, his theory is weak on psychological realism in depicting this aspect.

According to Andrew Yuengert (1997), rational addiction theory fails because it does not consider the ongoing internal struggle between passion and reason. In this view, passion intervenes at the expense of reason leading people to consume more of certain types of goods than they want. Unlike Orphanides and Zervos' (1995) version in which regret follows from people's imperfect information about their tendency toward addiction, regret in Yuengert's formulation is present even in the presence of complete information. The latter regret follows from people not being fully competent to resist consuming an excessive amount of 'passion goods.' In Yuengert's theory, a person's realized consumption is a weighted average of first the desired consumption in line with passion preferences and second the target consumption in line with reason preferences.

THE NATURE OF ADDICTION

Inadequacy of Rational Model

As the massive literature on addiction can attest, actual addictions do not conform to the model of rational consumer behavior in line with preferences, even if passion preferences and compulsive preferences are considered. To understand why, it is important to consider the nature of addiction. In what follows, I have attempted to distill the most important and general features of addiction from the writings of leading noneconomist authors in this field.

Defining Addiction

All five of the following features define addiction and distinguish addictive behavior from other behaviors. First, an addiction is a habit. This means it is a behavioral pattern done often, easily, automatically, and triggered by a particular situation. It is not instantaneously acquired; it is 'the result of a long stream of choices' (Herrnstein and Prelec, 1992: 336); and it is a pattern that is difficult to break. Second, it is harmful, that is, it is a bad habit. Consuming the addictive commodity is expected to result in significant negative side effects of a psychological, social or physical nature. For example, excessive, prolonged consumption of alcohol is expected to cause cirrhosis of the liver and damage to family and work relationships, among other things. Third, the user is dependent on the commodity. Rather than depending on themselves and their own faculties, addicts come to depend on the addictive substance or activity for certain rewards and come to view this involvement as essential to their functioning. For addicts, using this commodity becomes the center of their existence, and they are controlled by it (Peele, 1985: 104; Hirschman, 1992: 158). Fourth, addiction involves compulsive consumption and craving. Addicts do not simply desire, want or need a specific object or activity. Instead, they experience craving, an uncomfortable, intrusive, obsessional response compelling the addict to obtain the commodity (Ruden, 1997: 48). Fifth, deprivation of the commodity causes significant withdrawal symptoms. These symptoms involve 'upset to the person's overall social, psychological, and physical system' (Peele, 1985: 104).

The above means that there are no positive addictions, but that not all bad habits, attachments, and behavior involving addictive substances are addictions. Occasional binges and thrill use of addictive substances are not addictions. Presumably most coffee habits, habitual gum chewing, and similar behavior are not addictions as defined here. Imagine a continuum of human behavior; on one end is behavior involving no attachments or craving, on the other end is behavior involving extreme attachments and craving. Addictive behavior is only the behavior on the latter end of this continuum. Addictions, thus, are part of the ordinary human condition in which we are all attached to a variety of behavior patterns, styles, religious, political and other ideas, material possessions, and so on; they are simply a more severe and problematic form of these attachments.

Who Gets Addicted and Why

It is hard to make generalizations about addiction because there are many different addictive behavior patterns corresponding to the different specific types of addiction. Nevertheless, there are some broad commonalities to all types of addiction. Consider first what kind of people do not get addicted. In general, people who are able to obtain feelings of joy, competence, and meaningfulness while participating in life's activities are unlikely to be attracted to addictive activities (Peele, 1985: 157). Conversely, people who do become addicts generally are those with some kind of significant imbalance that impairs their ability to obtain real satisfactions and rewards from life's activities. Without the ability to obtain these positive feelings from functioning in the real world, individuals will naturally be tempted by the alternative artificial rewards offered by addictive experience (Peele, 1985: 155–7).

The kinds of imbalance leading to addiction can be psychological, physical, spiritual or some combination of these. While there are too many specific imbalances to enumerate here, we can gain some perspective on this subject by examining some important types of imbalance considered by authors on this subject. What follows is not intended to be a definitive classification of types of imbalance, it is only intended to be suggestive.

One important kind of imbalance relates to a person's self-identity. According to Elizabeth Hirschman (1992: 174–5), addicts lack an authentic self-identity, and lacking a sense of inner stability, they are prone to experience radical swings from extreme rigid self-control to extreme lack of control. 'The addict's early childhood self is already one that is emotionally inadequate and whose identity is false – an inauthentic self.' The addict's self never grew to wholeness because of dysfunction within the family of origin.

Another aspect of an addict's imbalance relates to a person's failure to develop the competence necessary to deal with life situations. According to Alfred Adler (Hoffman, 1994: 198), all children strive to overcome feelings of inferiority and maintain a satisfactory degree of self-esteem. Turmoil will be experienced 'when the particular strategy for obtaining self-esteem stops working, or even starts to become counterproductive.' In many people, these stressful situations will be accompanied by negative emotional and physical states such as anxiety, depression, inferiority, isolation, fear that one's inadequacies will be discovered, pain, and so on (Hirschman, 1992; Peele, 1985). Rather than face these emotions and struggle to find better ways to manage their emotions and difficult life situations, addicts seek refuge in addictive commodities. Thus, for example, we find that addicts 'become stuck, unaware, and unable to deal with their thoughts, feelings, and actions' (Apostolides, 1996: 35). According to Khantzian (1987: 234), cocaine dependent individuals 'are impaired in their capacity to recognize and regulate their emotions, suffer with significant problems of self-esteem, experience major difficulties in their relationships, and can be very erratic and deficient in matters of self-care.' Stimulant users report feelings of boredom and emptiness (p. 235). These are only a sample of the kinds of imbalance relating to people's failure to develop the required competence in response to life's demands.

Still another aspect of imbalance is spiritual in nature. Abraham Maslow characterized addiction as one of the 'metapathologies,' that is, as a 'spiritual illness that emerges when people's inborn need to find meaning in their lives is thwarted' (Schwartz, 1995: 90). Similarly, Victor Frankl (1984: 164–8) observed that it was feelings of emptiness and meaninglessness that led to addictions, particularly among young people who feel they have 'no future.' Referring to the research findings of Annemarie von Forstmeyer, Frankl noted that '90 percent of the alcoholics . . . suffered from an abysmal feeling of meaninglessness. Of the drug addicts studied by Stanley Kripner, 100 percent believed that "things seemed meaningless"' (pp. 167–8).

Because of the above imbalances and others not mentioned, addicts, not surprisingly, use addictive substances and activities in order to gain a feeling of balance otherwise missing from their lives. For example, addicts lacking a stable, authentic self-identity use addictive commodities to escape themselves, their minds, and their thoughts (Hirschman, 1992: 178). Addicts experiencing unpleasant feelings use addictive commodities in a variety of ways to self-medicate themselves, getting relief from negative states and heightening positive sensations. Cocaine can help users overcome lack of energy, complete tasks and relate better to others (Khantzian, 1987: 235). Stimulants provide users with a sense of mastery, control, invincibility and grandeur, as well as a defense against depression and/or feelings of unworthiness and weakness. In general, drug experiences offer 'enhanced sense of control, power, and self-esteem' and provide 'addicts control over areas of behavior or emotions that they otherwise feel unable to cope with' (Peele, 1985: 101).

The Physiology of Addiction

Another important commonality to addictions is the physical aspect of how the brain functions. Ronald Ruden (1997) has provided a careful explanation of what occurs in the addict's brain to cause unstoppable cravings for addictive commodities. In normal, nonaddictive operation, the nucleus accumbens (part of the limbic system) becomes sensitized and dopamine levels rise when a person perceives a distress pattern indicating the need to satisfy survival needs (food, sex, safety) or deal with pain. The dopamine focuses the person's attention on the need and motivates urgent action to satisfy the need. If the action is successful, serotonin levels rise, and the person's craving is replaced by a sense of balance called biobalance.

Addicts or people predisposed by genetic, environmental, or hormonal factors to addiction have a different 'brain terrain,' one characterized by a sensitized nucleus accumbens and low levels of serotonin (Ruden, 1997: Chapters 2 and 3). Chronic inescapable stress is the most important factor causing this kind of terrain. When such an addict perceives a pattern associated with an addictive good, a pattern conditioned by learning experience, this triggers increased dopamine and the focused compulsion or craving to 'get it.' In this case in contrast to the one above, once the good has been acquired there is no rise in serotonin and return to balance, no satiation. Thus, the person will continue to crave the alcohol, drug, etc. 'The "got it" never happens; . . . the "gotta have it" becomes unstoppable' (p. 65).

ADDICTIONS AND RATIONALITY

Rationality and Economic Man

In light of the above, what can be said about the rationality of addicted people? Recall that rational addiction theory maintains that an addicted individual is a rational economic man in the sense of making choices that maximize one's self-interest or expected utility. Such rational people could make mistakes, but they would correct them. They could highly discount expected future costs, but they would nevertheless consider them. In what follows, we indicate specifically the ways in which the essential nature of addictive behavior is not rational.

Thomas Schelling (1996) points out that there are many reasons why people have lapses from rationality, even if temporarily. These lapses make clear thinking and clear recall of relevant information unavailable to the decision maker. The reasons for these lapses are the following mental states: asleep, drowsy, depressed, euphoric, drunk, extremes of motivation (pain, fear, panic, rage, thirst), phobias, compulsions, captivations, nervous interaction (giggling, embarrassment), misbehaving minds, temptations, and addiction. The lapse from rationality central to our concerns is the craving experienced by addicts. According to Ruden (1997: 105), 'the craving response removes the ability to rationally decide our actions.' People in the throes of addictive craving (when dopamine levels have risen) do not have the ability to say no to the addictive good. Obviously, they do not have the mental ability to consider relevant information, consult their preferences, and make a decision based on these. Conceivably these people could be rational in moments when craving is not present.

Another source of irrationality is addicts' 'mental bookkeeping' concerning the benefits and costs of addiction. The benefits to using addictive commodities, even if inferior to life's genuinely pleasurable, satisfying involvements, are immediate, often providing significant relief from the addict's afflictions as well as providing positive feelings. The costs, on the other hand, usually come much later. Addicts, according to the clinical literature, practice a form of mental bookkeeping (a form of denial) in which the negative side effects are not charged against the addictive commodity (Herrnstein and Prelec, 1992: 347). For example, quarrels with one's spouse triggered by gambling are not tallied as a cost of gambling. This defective bookkeeping is an inherent feature of addictions, is clearly not rational, and is present even in the absence of craving.

According to George Akerlof (1991: 1–6), decision making by addicts is not fully rational because it fits the procrastination model. 'Most drug abusers, like most chronically overweight individuals, fully intend to cut down their intake, since they recognize that the long-run cost of their addiction exceeds its benefits. They intend to stop – tomorrow' (p. 5). Such procrastination occurs because individuals attach too much weight to the salient, early costs of changing their behavior.

It should be noted that the assumption of rational behavior is even questionable when addiction is not present. Daniel Kahneman's (1994) article considers the following reasons why decision making is often not rational. First is loss aversion where 'losses loom larger than corresponding gains' (p. 22). Second are framing effects where 'the same objective outcomes can be evaluated as gains or as losses, depending on the framing or reference state' (p. 22). Third is the endowment effect in which the value of a loss of a good (say, an addictive commodity) already possessed is rated higher than the value of a gain of the same good (pp. 22–5; see also the similar ideas of Hoch and Loewenstein, 1991). Kahneman also finds evidence that people have: (a) an inability to predict accurately their future utility from using goods; (b) an inability to predict changes in their tastes; and (c) an inability to accurately evaluate how much utility they have gained from an experience (pp. 25–32). There is reason to believe that these departures from rational behavior apply as much or more to addictive commodities as for conventional goods.

While the above are sufficient to indicate addicts' departure from rational behavior, there is an even more fundamental problem with rational addiction theory. This theory explicitly assumes stable preferences, and implicit is the assumption of a stable self, a self that knows what its unchanging preferences are, and thereby, is able to act consistently in accord with these preferences. Both these assumptions are false. First, the addict, by definition, is characterized by dependency, not by a strong stable, independent self. As indicated earlier, the addict typically has an inauthentic, unstable sense of self (Hirschman, 1992: 175). Far from behaving consistently and being in control of themselves, addicts generally depend on the addictive commodity to create and maintain a stable sense of self. Further, addicts typically 'do not like themselves' and feel 'unworthy and inadequate' (p. 178). Thus, they are not so much using the addictive commodity to feel better off, but using it to escape from themselves. Not infrequently, their indifference to the harmful consequences of addiction is accompanied by a desire for 'oblivion,' even possibly death (pp. 177–8).

Addictive behavior involves a surrender to a habit and implies a giving up on self and what is good for self. It is far from the idea of the rational man getting more of what he knows he wants and, thereby, becoming better off.

Recovered addicts are those who have 'woken up' to the realities of addiction, to the true dangers and costs of addiction. They are no longer denying the costs of addiction, relying on addictive goods to maintain a stable sense of self, or continually being controlled by craving. They realize the mistake involved in using addictive commodities in the way that they did, and they can see clearly the insanity of their former behavior. They, therefore, have good reason to regret their addictive involvement. In contrast, there is no reason for the rational addicts of mainstream economic theory, who have considered all expected benefits and costs carefully before deciding to use addictive commodities, to experience regret.

Rationality and Human Man

There is an even broader lesson to be drawn from the above analysis of the rationality of addiction. It is that the humans that get addicted or avoid addictions are much more than simply rational or irrational economic men. Ultimately, to comprehend what addiction involves for a human being, it is necessary to have a concept of what being human is that is dramatically different and broader than the economic man conception. Economic man, almost by definition, cannot be irrational. To understand fully departures from the rational, we need a concept of human man. Human man, unlike economic man, is capable of experiencing fully the rewards of life such as feeling great joy, competence and meaning. On the other hand, it is human to suffer from significant imbalances that impair our abilities in this respect. It is human man who experiments with and becomes hooked on addictive commodities and who denies the danger involved. It is human man who is capable of high mental, physical and spiritual well-being but often fails to achieve this potential. We need a concept of human man to understand addiction (not to mention other phenomena), and we need a concept of rationality more appropriate to use in connection with human man.

I propose a concept of rationality that is essentially the same as the quality Aristotle called virtue (Thomson, 1953). A virtuous person, according to Aristotle, is one who, because of having acquired good habits, regularly makes right choices, choices that leave one with no regrets and that contribute to one's happiness (Adler, 1978: 101). An important aspect of virtue is the quality of temperance which consists of 'habitually resisting the temptation to overindulge in pleasures of all sorts.' Moreover, temperance 'enables us to resist what appears to be good in the short run for the sake of what is really good for us in the long run' (p. 103). Virtue requires a mean between excess and deficiency in actions and passions. Quite clearly, addiction is not temperate; therefore, it is not virtuous, and, I would argue, neither is it rational. Rationality in this sense is associated with wisdom and reason, neither of which could be associated with addiction.

A SOCIO-ECONOMIC MODEL OF ADDICTIVE BEHAVIOR

Essence of the Model

The purpose of this section is to utilize the interdisciplinary insights above as well as others to develop a socio-economic model that explains whether an individual is likely to become addicted. The model is not designed to explain whether a person will simply try a potentially addicting substance or activity (henceforth addictive good) or even whether a person might occasionally abuse such a good. It is designed to explain who is likely to become fully involved in an addictive pattern of behavior as a result of an addiction forming process. The model can also be used to explain whether a person is likely give up an addiction.

According to the model, addictions occur to people who have 'significant imbalances' and who encounter situations where addictive goods are available, affordable, and attractive. The five external and internal influences that explain an individual's degree of imbalance and the factors that modify the strength of the imbalance are: (a) the individual's personal capital; (b) the individual's social capital; (c) the individual's consumption capital; (d) the societal and community influences on the individual; and (e) the stressfulness of the individual's current life situation. In essence, individuals with a degree of imbalance above a certain threshold are likely to have a biased perception of what the addictive good offers, tending to overvalue the expected benefits and undervalue the expected costs. Their resulting desire for the good is a key to whether they will become involved in an addiction. In what follows, the main elements of the model are considered in sequence.

Personal Capital

Personal capital, a kind of human capital, is the human capacity that derives from an individual's basic personal qualities (Tomer, 1996: 626–7).[1] Personal capital reflects the quality of an individual's psychological, physical, and spiritual functioning. This capacity is a mirror of one's internal biochemical balance, one's physical health and conditioning, one's psychological strengths and hangups, and one's purpose in life.

> One's endowment of personal capital reflects one's genetic inheritance and the events that have shaped one's life, but it also reflects one's self-improvement activities including psychotherapy/counseling, reading books, listening to or viewing audio and video tapes, attending seminars, seeking advice and wisdom from gurus or other religious/spiritual people, engaging in practices such as meditation and yoga, and undertaking a variety of other therapies and experiences. (p. 627)

These lasting qualities are related to a person's capacity to work or consume in the sense that they underlie or provide the basis for the more specific capacities that a person invests in in order to be qualified for work tasks or to be able to enjoy consumption goods. Examples of the latter include human capital due to on-the-job training and consumption capital related to athletic activity.

One important component of personal capital is what Daniel Goleman (1994) calls emotional intelligence. Emotional intelligence is quite different from cognitive intelligence which IQ tests are designated to measure. Emotional intelligence refers to a variety of emotional and social skills, habits and aptitudes. These include the ability to motivate oneself, to persist in the face of frustration, to control impulse, to delay gratification, to regulate one's moods, to keep distress from swamping the ability to think, to empathize, and to hope (p. 34). Our emotional intelligence, our ability to manage our emotions and social relationships, is a product of our genetic heritage, but it is also a product of the emotional lessons learned in childhood and adolescence and even adulthood (p. xiii). Persons with significant deficiencies in emotional intelligence are at greater risk for a variety of psychological ailments and for being involved in violent encounters. On the other hand, there is reason to believe that people with high emotional intelligence (even if their IQ is modest) are likely to be economically successful.

The physiological aspect of one's psychological functioning is another element in personal capital. According to Ronald Ruden (1997), as indicated earlier in connection to addiction, two critically important dimensions of a person's brain terrain are the degree of sensitization of the nucleus accumbens (of the limbic system) and the level of serotonin. The lower a person's nucleus accumbens sensitization and the higher the serotonin level, the greater is one's capacity to avoid addiction. With respect to a person's overall emotional functioning, Goleman (1994: 13–29) emphasizes the role of the amygdala (also part of the brain's limbic system) and the prefrontal lobes. The amygdala is the seat of emotion; its messages trigger emotional responses. These unrestrained emotional messages can be very strong and in an emergency very rapid. In contrast, the role of the prefrontal lobes is to comprehend the situation confronting a person and to coordinate, moderate and regulate the individual's emotional response in order that the response is appropriate to the situation. Complementary functioning of the amygdala and the prefrontal lobes is prerequisite for emotionally intelligent behavior. As people learn better ways to manage their emotions, new brain pathways and circuitry are created enabling the desired complementary functioning as well as inducing the desired biochemical balance. These become part of a person's expanded capacity for dealing with life, that is, their increased personal capital.

Imbalances and Personal Capital

At heart of the model is the idea that the people who become addicted have significant imbalances impairing their ability to obtain real satisfactions and rewards from life's activities. Because these imbalances are indicative of the poor level of an individual's psychological, physiological, and spiritual functioning, the individual's personal capital endowment will reflect this. It is when a person's degree of imbalance reaches a certain threshold and the individual finds an addictive good that seems to restore a sense of balance and control otherwise missing from his or her life that an addiction is likely to be formed.[2,3]

Daniel Goleman (1994) develops this theme with respect to those who have emotional imbalances. Those who become addicted use addictive goods as

> a way to soothe feelings of anxiety, anger, or depression . . . that have tormented them. Thus of several hundred seventh- and eighth-grade students tracked for two years, it was those who reported higher levels of emotional distress who subsequently went on to have the highest rates of substance abuse. This may explain why so many young people are able to experiment with drugs and drinking without becoming addicted, while others become dependent almost from the start: those most vulnerable to addiction seem to find in their drug or alcohol an instant way to soothe emotions that have distressed them for years. (p. 253)

According to Goleman (1994: 254–5), different emotional patterns lead to different addictive goods. There are two patterns associated with alcoholism. The first is chronically high levels of anxiety. The second is a high level of agitation, impulsivity, and boredom. People with these patterns turn to alcohol to calm their anxieties and sooth the agitation. Similarly, depression leads to cocaine, and chronic anger leads to heroin and other opioids.

Besides these emotional imbalances and the spiritual imbalance mentioned earlier, other types of imbalance have been implicated in addiction. Among these are: lack of proper nutrition, inadequate levels of brain chemicals such as serotonin, too high levels of brain chemicals such as histamine (a neurotransmitter regulating mood and energy), energy imbalance, and imbalances in the mind and body connection. Apostolides' (1996) *Psychology Today* article is suggestive of these imbalances and the therapies that can be used to correct them.

The personal story of Ken Daneyko, veteran hockey player for the New Jersey Devils, is illustrative (*NY Times*, 2 February 1998). Despite a successful hockey career, including helping his team win the Stanley Cup, Daneyko says, looking back, that 'he felt empty, all gaps and voids.' 'It's hard to explain. There was no balance in my life.' 'The only control in my life was hockey.' Thus, it is not surprising that he became an alcoholic.

Social Capital

An individual's endowment of social capital is the second main influence on whether a person is likely to become addicted. Social capital refers to the capacity that is embodied in an individual's social relationships or the bonds and connections between an individual and others. Social capital is embodied in families, institutions, civic communities, and the larger society. It is, strictly speaking, not embodied in individuals. Nevertheless, social capital enables a person to do more and attain his or her ends to a greater degree than without this resource. A person's social capital can be helpful in another way. In the presence of strong positive social relationships, people's imbalances are likely to be more muted and less problematic. Conversely, when social capital is weak and negative, people's imbalances are likely to be more pronounced and problematic.

This latter view is consistent with Francis Fukuyama's (1997) explanation of the causes of the dramatic rise in socially disruptive outcomes which began in the late 1960s in the US and other countries. According to Fukuyama, the increased labor force participation of women and the availability of improved birth control measures, namely the Pill, caused a dramatic decline of the nuclear family's social capital reflecting very important changes in the powerful social norms surrounding marriage. Most notable was the decline in the norm of male responsibility. That is, 'men felt liberated from norms requiring them to look after the women whom they had gotten pregnant' (p. 30). In Fukuyama's view, this decline in family social capital led to many negative and disruptive outcomes including rising rates of divorce, out of wedlock births, violent and property crime, child abuse, alcoholism and drug abuse. In the case of addiction, at least, the declining family social capital seems to have brought people's imbalances to the fore, thereby adding to their predisposition to become addicted.

Consumption Capital

A third influence on a person's likelihood to become addicted is the individual's consumption capital. It is one thing to have imbalances that predispose one toward an addictive good; it is another to have an actual addiction.

Forming an addiction involves an investment in consumption capital with respect to an addictive good. Accumulating consumption capital involves developing the capacity to use and appreciate a good, that is, developing an actual preference for a good not just a potential one (Tomer, 1996: 620–621).[4] The steps in this process include: (a) becoming oriented to the good; (b) gaining knowledge about the good; (c) learning how and where to acquire the good; (d) learning how to interact with and locate other consumers of the good; and (e) learning how the good's effects vary with particular mental states. It is through this process involving repeated choice that a person acquires a taste for the specific good and becomes habituated to it. Even if the addicted person stopped consuming the addictive good, the accumulated consumption capital would remain, albeit a bit depreciated. Such a former addict would retain the knowledge and appreciation regarding the good, and thus, have a susceptibility to it. This susceptibility, obviously, makes it easier and more likely for the addiction to begin again, other things being the same.

Society and Community

The general social and cultural influences from one's society and community are the fourth determinant of a person's likelihood of becoming addicted. These influences from leaders, peer groups, organizations, media, and so forth encourage people to have certain values, lifestyles and consumption patterns. They reflect the broader culture as well as local cultural influences. Do these influences encourage us to be temperate? Or do they encourage behavior that is characterized by excess and overindulgence? The sociocultural influences of one's ethnic group can be particularly important.

> Jews, Italian-Americans, and Chinese-Americans, who specify appropriate ceremonial, nutritional, or festive uses of alcohol but who negatively sanction overindulgence and drunkenness, have lower rates of alcoholism. Conversely, other nationality groups such as Irish-Americans and English-Americans appear to more positively sanction alcohol consumption as a social activity and sign of manhood and also experience higher rates of alcoholism. (Hirschman, 1992: 156)

When the sociocultural influences encourage morality and self-restraint, there is reason to believe that people, even those with significant imbalances, are less likely to become involved with addictive goods. The opposite is true when sociocultural influences encourage intemperance.

Current Life Situation

A fifth determinant of the likelihood of addiction is the advent of a particularly stressful life situation. The arrival of prolonged inescapable stress that people feel unable to control and that exacerbates preexisting imbalances is often the precipitating event leading to addiction (Hirschman, 1992; Peele, 1985; Ruden, 1997). Role transitions and personal crises can be the significant stress creating events; these include the death of a loved one, deterioration of a marriage, starting college or a new job, chronic illness, abusive family situation and dishonor. Larger societal conditions that produce significant stress include wartime, poverty, societal transformations such as those occurring in Eastern Europe, and the acculturation and deculturation stress experienced by Native Americans (Ruden, 1997: 38–46). It is interesting to note that many American soldiers felt inescapable stresses during the Vietnam War, and 20 percent of them became addicted to narcotics. However, when they returned to the US, 'after ten months, only one percent still considered themselves addicts, a startling 95 percent remission rate' (p. 106). For this group, at least, the cessation of their chronic inescapable stress was the critical factor enabling them to give up their addictions.

One other aspect of the individual's current life situation, the availability of alternative rewards, should be noted. Stanton Peele's (1985: 154–6) research, for example, strongly indicates that the appeal of drug use to individuals is substantially diminished when people have available to them sufficient alternative nonaddicting life activities to make life without addiction worthwhile (also see Peele and DeGrandpre, 1994: 3, 8).

The Individual's Perception of the Addictive Good

The five factors above determine a person's degree of imbalance. The individual's personal capital endowment is the most important factor; the other factors serve to moderate or exacerbate the imbalance. Whether the degree of imbalance is above the threshold level and how much so determines the degree of bias that an individual will bring to bear in evaluating the expected benefits and costs of using an addictive good. The expected benefits are the person's estimate of the strength of the pleasure and symptomatic relief provided by the good. The expected costs are the person's estimate of the strength of the difficulties and negative experiences associated with the good's use. An individual with a degree of imbalance above the threshold is expected to be biased in the sense of overvaluing the benefits greatly and undervaluing the costs greatly.

The bias derives from several different kinds of defective mental processing. First, when an individual is in the throes of strong craving, the person has little or no ability to consider relevant information and preferences. This individual cannot say no to the addictive good, nor can the individual think clearly enough to use information in the process of evaluating benefits and costs. If the craving is weaker, the individual's mental processing will be partially defective but still biased toward using the addictive good. Second, as indicated earlier, an individual's mental book-keeping may involve denial (a well known and common psychological process) of certain costs associated with use of an addictive good. This is a bias, and it also involves defective information processing. The third biasing factor is not a matter of defective information processing, but defective mental performance is involved. It is that the addict or would-be addict lacks a stable self with stable preferences, a self that knowing what it wants can determine in a nondependent fashion what the benefits and costs of different goods are, and thus, make an appropriate, that is, rational, decision. The person who is in the process of giving up on one's self or attempting to escape from self through dependency on addictive goods is clearly biased towards these goods and is obviously not making a rational decision in the sense of choosing what is best for oneself.

Someone could argue, in opposition to the above, that there is no bias involved because the person is simply perceiving the addictive good from the perspective of a changed preference pattern, one reflecting the person's recent use of the good and accumulation of consumption capital. Such a preference change is indeed possible, even likely, but, recall, the bias explained above stems from defective mental processing not preference change. One could also argue as I have elsewhere (Tomer, 1996) that the preference change toward an addictive good is a change toward an inferior preference pattern, but for the sake of clarity let's leave that argument aside.

Another possible argument is that an individual would choose addictive behavior because of a very high rate of discount. Such an individual would give near term benefits a very high weight and distant costs a very low weight. Apparently, it is common for addicts to behave this way. While many would consider this behavior to be undesirable, it is not economically irrational behavior. Strictly speaking, there is no biased perception of benefits and costs involved as there is with defective mental processing.

In sum, an individual with a significant imbalance is likely to manifest the kind of defective mental processing that leads to biased perception of the expected benefits and costs of addictive behavior. When this bias is strong, the individual is oriented to perceiving the use of an addictive good favorably and, thus, has a desire for the addictive good, perhaps a great desire and longing. Such an individual may also develop an intention to try it when it becomes available and affordable. Thus, such imbalanced persons are much more likely to become addicted than more balanced persons.

The Reality of the Addictive Good

Another element to consider is the reality regarding the addictive good. The person confronting the possibility of using this good will have to consider its availability, its affordability, and its attractiveness. If a good is very hard to get, very expensive, and does not promise an experience of sufficient quality, even an individual with a great desire for the good may find it prohibitive. Although the addict or would-be addict may have a biased perception of what the good itself offers, this person may be unbiased with respect to these practical reality factors.

Metapreferences and Other Preferences

There is one other element involved in determining whether a person will take the final step toward addiction (or, if already addicted, will remain addicted). Conceivably, a person with both a high desire for an addictive good and sufficient temptation in the form of available, affordable and attractive addictive goods might still resist taking this last step. That would be the case if this choice were in conflict with the individual's metapreferences. Metapreferences are one's preferences about one's preferences; they reflect one's moral values and wisdom, and perhaps, the deep sense of what is really right for us (what I have referred to as true preferences) (see Tomer, 1996: 621–5). Suppose the tempted person's metapreferences about addictive goods were that they are immoral and unwise. This individual would experience considerable intrapsychic stress that might lead the person to resist addictive behavior and to seek a more satisfactory pattern of behavior. Metapreferences, then, are a potential restraining factor, a factor that might tug the individual toward a more balanced, sensible path. Unfortunately, there is one other possibility. It is that a person's strong unrestrained preferences might lessen the resistance to the addictive good. Unrestrained preferences are our desires for pure sensory pleasure unrestrained by considerations of morality or ethics (pp. 625–6). The net resistance to the final step in becoming addicted depends on the relative strength of one's metapreferences and unrestrained preferences.

Overview of the Model

The important elements of the socio-economic model of addictive behavior are shown in Figure 9.1. The model is designed to explain the likelihood of an individual becoming addicted. A key feature of the model is the notion that individuals who become addicted have significant imbalances, imbalances exceeding a certain threshold level. The degree of imbalance along with four other considerations that modify or act in conjunction with the degree of imbalance are determined by five external and internal factors. These are: (a) the individual's endowment of personal capital; (b) the individual's consumption capital accumulation; (c) the individual's

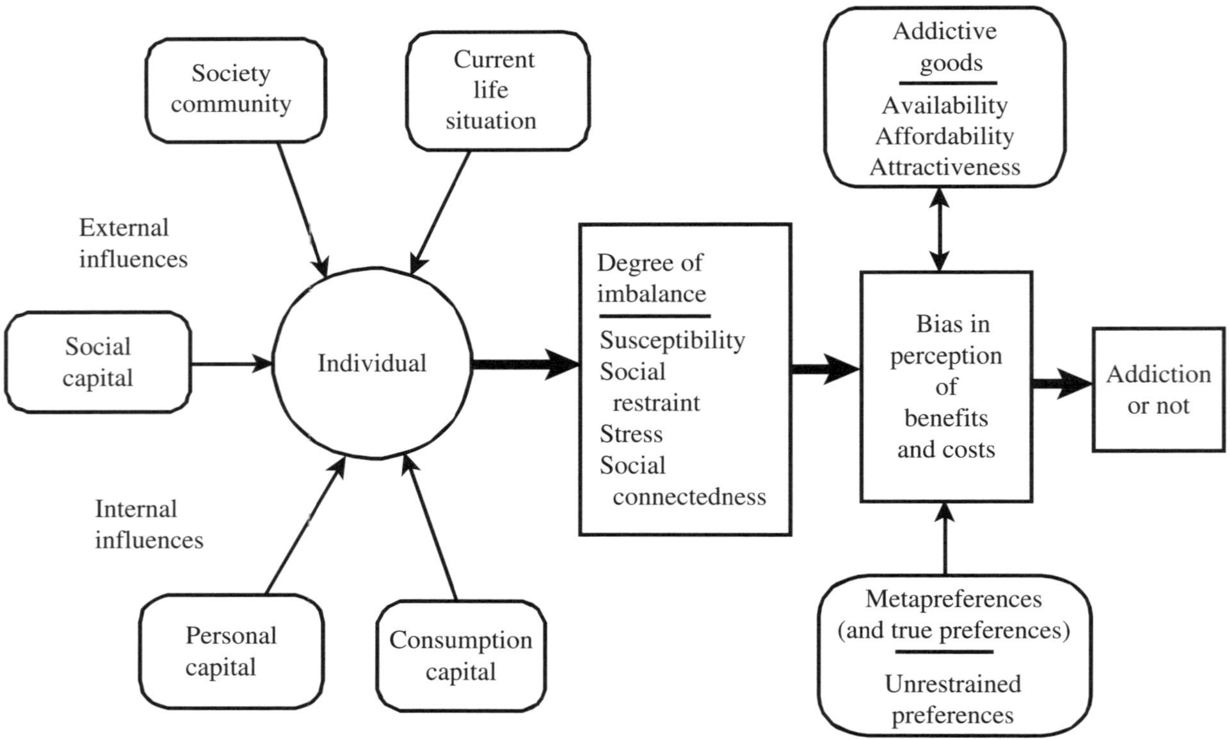

Figure 9.1 Socio-economic model of addictive behavior

investment in social capital; (d) society and community influences; and (e) the individual's current life situation. The personal qualities reflected in personal capital are what essentially determine the level of imbalance. Consumption capital along with society and community influences determine an individual's susceptibility to addictive goods. The social capital endowment determines an individual's social connectedness. Society and community influences may influence the individual toward or away from restraint. And the individual's current life situation explains the level of inescapable stress the individual is exposed to.

If the degree of imbalance as modified by the individual's susceptibility, social restraint, social connectedness, and stress exceeds the threshold, the individual will be biased in their evaluation of the net benefits of addictive goods, that is, biased toward using these goods. If these goods are also reasonably available, affordable, and attractive, this individual would be expected to become addicted through a process involving repeated use of the addictive goods, unless, of course, the strength of the individual's metapreferences leads the person to resist this step. If addiction is the unhappy result, the addict with strong metapreferences against addictive behavior will most certainly experience regret at a later point in time.

IMPLICATIONS OF THE MODEL

Addiction Is Not a Physiological Disease

There is a widespread belief that addiction, such as alcohol or drug addiction, is a physiological disease. Phelps and Nourse (1986: 7–8), for example, state that 'Addictiveness – the capacity to become an addict to anything – is a built-in physiological state, something you are born with. Either you are born addictive or you are born nonaddictive.' Thus, in their view, the capacity for addiction is a genetic flaw related to carbohydrate metabolism. The research of leading authorities on addictive behavior such as Stanton Peele does not support this view; neither does the model developed here.

Avoiding Addiction

The model's main implications for the way people should behave to avoid addiction are not surprising. They read like platitudes. First, people should try to reduce their imbalances by making appropriate investments in personal capital. For example, people can benefit from programs that aim to raise their emotional intelligence. Second, people should attempt to become more socially connected, making appropriate investments in social capital. Third, people should avoid intemperate social influences. Fourth, people should avoid, where possible, stressful life situations. Moreover, people should seek genuinely rewarding life situations.

Ultimately, the best approach to avoiding addiction is to follow Buddha's 2500 year old teachings on how to become enlightened. This path involves, among other things, mindful meditation, moral conduct, mental discipline, and importantly, nonattachment in order to eliminate suffering and find peace (Ruden, 1997). In the absence of attachment to pleasurable things, craving can be avoided. 'If there are no attachments, there can be no loss. No loss, no suffering. No suffering, no inescapable stress' (p. 89). Further, the peacefulness that comes from meditation is associated with higher serotonin levels, and thus, a brain terrain indisposed to develop craving. Thus, as Buddha's teachings indicate, a person can find true peace, and thus, balance by living in accord with one's true self (or true preferences), a self that is not attached to any false way of being.

Healing Addiction

The model is very suggestive regarding a number of important approaches to healing addiction. It is beyond the scope of this chapter to be comprehensive in this respect. First on the list are a great variety of therapies that promise to correct people's imbalances. Among these are 'holistic therapies' which have been gaining much greater acceptance. These include acupuncture, homeopathy, massage therapy, aromatherapy, yoga, nutrition therapy, hypnosis, biofeedback training, and many more (Apostolides, 1996).

> Holistic therapies work to restore balance by connecting mind and body. They take away some of the underlying causes of abuse by helping people become aware of and take responsibility for the way they think, feel, and act. The goal of many holistic therapies is to restore the body to its naturally healthy state. (p. 35)

Holistic therapies are often used along with more conventional psychotherapy. According to Khantzian (1987: 232–3), carefully targeted psychotherapy that results in symptomatic relief also reduces or eliminates addictive involvements.

The second type of approach suggested by the model is to reduce or eliminate stressful life conditions. According to Ruden (1997: 110), an individual has a responsibility 'to be actively engaged in the process of correcting and preventing the stress-induced changes that predispose him to a craving brain.' Families, communities, and governments have similar responsibilities to help make living conditions less stressful. The Community Reinforcement Approach which has produced unusually strong results includes 'a broad-based behavioral package of stress management, family counseling, job preparation, social skills training, recreational planning, and a buddy system' (Peele and DeGrandpre, 1994: 13).

The third approach overlaps with the second; it involves making the addicts life situation more rewarding.

> Whether in therapy or not, addicts improve when their relationships to work, family, and other aspects of their environment improve. Addicts have come to count on the regular rewards they get from their addictive involvement. They can give up these rewards when they believe they will find superior gratifications from other activities in the regular fiber of their lives. (Peele, 1985: 154)

The fourth approach suggested by the model is for the addict to face squarely the full reality of the addiction. This represents a direct attempt to overcome the biased perception of the benefits and costs of the addiction. According to Ruden (1997: 109–10), a key to beginning the healing process is the removal of denial. The addict must admit to and confront the entire extent of the problems caused by the addiction. This step should avoid stigmatizing the addict. According to Peele (1985: 156), the addict must understand the hurt, desire to overcome it, and feel sufficient self-efficacy to manage the recovery process. There are different ways that the addict's needed self appraisal can occur. Sometimes the addict must 'hit rock bottom' before denial is given up.

Healing an addiction is not easy. Ultimately, to become healed, an addict must at least become highly motivated, wise, and skillful. It may also be necessary to gain the support of family, friends, and community and to enlist the aid of a number of skilled therapists.

CONCLUSIONS

Drawing on important insights from psychological and other noneconomic literature and combining these with economic insights, this chapter has provided a careful explanation of why addictive behavior is not rational and has developed a socio-economic model to explain addictive behavior. This model, an alternative to mainstream economists' rational addiction theory, enables us to understand why addiction is not rational either in the sense that economists use this word or in other senses. The model incorporates a much broader conception of human behavior than does mainstream economics, and thus, a broader recognition of the variety of factors that influence human behavior, most notably a person's endowment of intangible capital. The model is important in that it indicates specifically why an individual who is ordinarily rational might behave irrationally where addictive goods are involved. The model is also important because, in contrast to rational addiction theory, it is consistent with both our intuitive wisdom and the wisdom of religious and spiritual traditions. There is much scope for further research: (a) to apply this model to specific types of addiction; (b) to test the hypotheses of the model; (c) to develop further its implications, particularly its implications for the behavior of the markets for addictive goods and its implications for government policy; and (d) to develop similar models explaining other behavior that is not rational.

NOTES

1. In Gary Becker's (1996: 4–10) use, the term personal capital 'includes the relevant past consumption and other personal experiences that affect current and future utilities.' Thus, his personal capital concept is in part what he has previously called consumption capital and in part the personal qualities (shaped by life experiences) that affect preferences (the (sub)utility function).
2. Michaels' (1988: 76–7) model of addiction and compulsion uses a self-esteem threshold. When an individual's self-esteem falls short of the threshold, addictive and compulsive behavior is likely to follow.
3. It is certainly possible that an addiction could occur to a 'normal' person, that is, a person without a significant imbalance or pathology. However, the model developed here implies that this would be a rare event.
4. The concept of consumption capital used here is different in some respects to the one used by Gary Becker and his coauthors. For example, according to Becker *et al.* (1991: 237), current consumption of addictive goods raises consumption capital and reinforces future use by increasing the desire for present consumption, thereby increasing the addiction. James Gamble, a Maryland physician and writer, in his communication to me said that what Becker is referring to is really what psychologists call conditioning. Conditioning occurs as positive experience reinforces use of a good, thereby developing a conditioned reflex. Conditioning does not necessarily imply dependency or craving or even that the good is harmful, the hallmarks of addiction.

REFERENCES

Adler, Mortimer J. (1978), *Aristotle for Everybody: Difficult Thought Made Easy*, New York: Macmillan.

Akerlof, George A. (1991), 'Procrastination and obedience,' *American Economic Review*, **81**(2), 1–19.

Apostolides, Marianne (1996), 'How to quit the holistic way,' *Psychology Today*, **September/October**, 33–76.

Becker, Gary S. (1996), *Accounting for Tastes*, Cambridge, MA: Harvard University Press.

Becker, Gary S. and George J. Stigler (1977), 'De gustibus non est disputandum,' *American Economic Review*, **67**(2), 76–90.

Becker, Gary S. and Kevin M. Murphy (1988), 'A theory of rational addiction,' *Journal of Political Economy*, **96**(4), 675–99.

Becker, Gary S., Michael Grossman and Kevin M. Murphy (1991), 'Rational addiction and the effect of price on consumption,' *American Economic Review*, **81**(2), 237–41.
Frankl, Victor E. (1984), *Man's Search for Meaning*, New York: Washington Square Press.
Fukuyama, Francis (1997), 'Social capital: lecture I, the great disruption,' The 1997 Tanner Lectures at Brasenose College, Oxford, unpublished manuscript.
Goleman, Daniel (1994), *Emotional Intelligence*, New York: Bantam Books.
Herrnstein, Richard J. and Drazen Prelec (1992), 'A theory of addiction,' in George Loewenstein and John Elster (eds) *Choice Over Time*, New York: Russell Sage Foundation, pp. 331–60.
Hirschman, Elizabeth C. (1992), 'The consciousness of addiction: toward a general theory of compulsive consumption,' *Journal of Consumer Research*, **19(September)**, 155–79.
Hoch, Stephen J. and George F. Loewenstein (1991), 'Time-inconsistent preferences and consumer self-control,' *Journal of Consumer Research*, **17**, 492–507.
Hoffman, Edward (1994), *The Drive for Self: Alfred Adler and the Founding of Individual Psychology*, Reading, MA: Addison-Wesley.
Kahneman, Daniel (1994), 'New challenges to the rationality assumption,' *Journal of Institutional and Theoretical Economics*, **150**(1), 18–36.
Khantzian, E.J. (1987), 'Psychiatric and psychodynamic factors in cocaine dependence,' in Arnold M. Washton and Mark S. Gold *Cocaine: A Clinician's Handbook*, New York: Guilford Press.
Michaels, Robert J. (1988), 'Addiction, compulsion, and the technology of consumption,' *Economic Inquiry*, **26**(January), 75–88.
Orphanides, Athanasios and David Zervos (1995), 'Rational addiction with learning and regret,' *Journal of Political Economy*, **103**(4), 739–58.
Peele, Stanton (1985), *The Meaning of Addiction: Compulsive Experience and Its Interpretation*, Lexington, MA: Lexington.
Peele, Stanton and Richard J. DeGrandpre (1994), 'Cocaine and the concept of addiction: environmental factors in drug compulsions,' The Stanton Peele Addiction Web Site, January, 1–20.
Phelps, Janice K. and Alan E. Nourse (1986), *The Hidden Addiction and How to Get Free*, Boston, MA: Little Brown.
Ruden, Ronald A. (1997), *The Craving Brain: The Biobalance Approach to Controlling Addictions*, New York: HarperCollins.
Schelling, Thomas C. (1996), 'Coping Rationally with Lapses from Rationality,' *Eastern Economic Journal*, **22**(3), 251–69.
Schwartz, Tony (1995), *What Really Matters: Searching for Wisdom in America*, New York: Bantam Books.
Thomson, J.A.K. (1953), *The Ethics of Aristotle: The Nicomachean Ethics Translated*, London: George Allen and Unwin.
Tomer, John F. (1996), 'Good habits and bad habits: a new age socio-economic model of preference formation,' *Journal of Socio-Economics*, **25**(6), 619–38.
Winston, Gordon C. (1980), 'Addiction and backsliding: a theory of compulsive consumption,' *Journal of Economic Behavior and Organization*, **1**, 295–324.
Yuengert, Andrew M. (1997), 'Rational choice with passion: virtue in a model of rational addiction,' Unpublished paper, Pepperdine University, Malibu, California.

10. True preferences, metapreferences and actual preferences: a socio-economic model of preference formation

Desire and aversion, though powerful, are but habits. And we can train ourselves to have better habits.

Epictetus, Manual for Living: A New Interpretation by Sharon Lebell

INTRODUCTION

Should government discourage cigarette smoking? What about advertising aimed at women and promoting dieting to become super slim? Mainstream economists have, with few exceptions, taken the position that governments ought not to intervene in matters relating to people's subjective preferences. After all, in these economists' view, the essence of rationality is choosing in line with one's well-defined, stable wants (McPherson 1984: 237). Many would presumably agree with Tollison and Wagner (1992: 158) who argue that 'individuals who are observed to make particular choices are necessarily maximizing their individual welfare.' Further, these authors contend that cigarette smokers are entirely rational and not addicted, the cigarette smoking being entirely under their control (pp. 158–60). Accordingly, Tollison and Wagner argue strongly against any attempt to change smokers' preferences and against the idea that there is anything 'wrong' about smoking.

The socio-economic model of preference formation developed here is based on some radically different ideas concerning preferences and rationality, and thus leads to very different conclusions concerning the desirability and inviolability of people's preferences. The model is a multiple utility or multiple self model that integrates economic insights with many noneconomic ones. It might legitimately be called a 'New Age' model because it brings to bear perspectives from humanistic psychology, from psychics, and from spiritual and religious teachings in both eastern and western traditions. The construction of this model represents an attempt in at least a small way to transcend the materialistic tradition of economics and other social sciences, a tradition that denies the existence of spiritual or soul-like elements within people.

The second (next) section develops in step by step fashion, the main elements of the model: actual preferences, metapreferences, true preferences, unrestrained preferences, individual predispositions and personal capital, and external influences on preference formation. The third section provides perspectives on the model by comparing the model's multiple self-conception to those of a number of prominent socio-economic authors. The fourth section analyzes how the economic concept of externalities applies to the model but in a way that differs from standard usage. In the fifth section, the implications of the model for the concepts of altruism and merit goods and also for government policy are examined. The last section provides conclusions.

THE MODEL OF PREFERENCE FORMATION

The model developed below is a four self model. The four selves correspond to four types of preferences: actual preferences, metapreferences, true preferences and unrestrained preferences. Also included in the model is the ego, that part of the psyche which considers the different selves along with the external world and decides what action to take. First consider actual preferences.

Actual Preferences

In general, the ego's choices among alternative goods are governed by one's actual preferences. On occasion, however, an individual's choices will not reflect his or her actual self but will reflect the influence of two other selves, the selves associated with either metapreferences or unrestrained preferences. These preferences will be considered later.

One's actual preferences could be innately determined, but for the most part they are determined by the degree to which one has developed the capacity to use and appreciate goods. Economists such as Gary Becker have formalized this insight (see, for example, Stigler and Becker, 1977) and named this human capacity consumption capital, a kind of human capital. But the insight itself is much older. For example, John Stuart Mill recognized that it is possible to improve oneself by developing one's capacity to appreciate and obtain satisfaction from the 'higher pleasures' (McPherson, 1982: 261). Similarly, John Ruskin recognized that for consumers to realize the full potential value of their goods, they would have to produce the capacity to use and appreciate these goods (Lutz and Lux, 1979: 39–40).

Consumption capital is a lasting attribute embodied in people. A person's endowment of consumption capital determines his or her appreciation for generalized types of goods (general consumption capital) as well as for specific goods (specific consumption capital) and determines how they will use these goods. Consumption capital is developed: (a) through past consumption experience; (b) through formal and informal training; (c) through exposure to external influences that condition attitudes relating to particular types of consumption, and so on. For a tennis player, consumption capital involves all the skill and appreciations necessary to play well at the desired level of competition. For a drug addict, consumption capital involves knowledge and appreciation about how to use and obtain the substances through which one can experience highs. In sum, a person's accumulation of consumption capital determines his or her actual preferences whether or not these preferences are judged desirable.[1]

The concept of consumption capital used here differs from that of Becker. In his view (for example, Stigler and Becker, 1977), preferences are unchanging over time, but owing to accumulation of consumption capital, say, for music appreciation, the individual will acquire skill and appreciation of music that allows the household production of music appreciation to be more efficient. In the present model, the accumulated consumption capital changes the individual's actual preference for music. As Tyler Cowen (1989: 129) points out, the difference between the two views is somewhat arbitrary; the Becker view is just an alternative theoretical way of representing the situation.[2]

Metapreferences

Metapreferences are one's preferences about one's actual preferences and reflect the normative judgments of a higher order self, the *meta-self*. Harry Frankfurt (1971), a philosopher, is generally credited with being the first to write in depth about metapreferences, and the idea has been subsequently explored by economists such as Amartya Sen (for example, 1977). Metapreferences derive from the human capacity for reflectiveness, the capacity to stand in judgment of our preferences and to contemplate more or less consciously their worth (McPherson, 1984: 241).

Metapreferences often conflict with actual preferences. For example, a person may have actual preferences (and accumulated consumption capital) relating to smoking cigarettes but be unhappy with this habit. Similarly, with respect to tennis, one may have developed a pattern of cheating on certain line calls or throwing one's racquet in frustration but not be happy with this pattern. In both situations, one's metapreferences are for a different pattern of preferences than one's actual preferences. Because of l power, time, energy, attention and resources (including special ıssistance). Obviously, certain addictions or cravings are much ult than others to give up.

off to these activities is increased well-being. Because our actual s usually diverge greatly from our true preferences, we fail to potential well-being. This well-being failure is a failure of people heir true humanity, to become all that they are capable of becom- extent that we either do not attempt to change our actual prefer- e direction of our true preferences or are prevented from doing so, nce this well-being failure.[5] Such 'failures' could range from ordi- nal shortcomings to life-threatening addictions. In some cases, the y reflect systematic societal or cultural influences that condition s or inculcate beliefs consistent with certain preferences. These range from beer and soda advertising to the widespread belief that is the spread of preference for health reasons to the subtle societal oncerning what is considered feminine beauty. Societies may also ove well-being by countering undesirable actual preferences, for rough anti-drug and anti-cigarette proselytizing.

ortant implication of the above is that consumer sovereignty in of 'false preferences,' as opposed to true preferences, is not a .

not make a person better off by satisfying a preference for a glass of ised on the false beliefs that it is water or that it will make one immor- t philosophers who associate well-being with preference satisfaction ntly require that the preferences be suitably 'corrected.' This introduces tive element of well-grounded or true belief into a preference-based (Hausman and McPherson, 1993: 690; see also the introduction to Sen ams, 1982).

important implication concerns the meaning of rationality. As economists view it, rationality refers to the optimal choice rnatives given one's actual preferences or wants. But consider- lysis above, rationality requires much more. Rational behavior overing what is really in one's best interests and making efforts n one's preferences in that direction. That is, your behavior can sidered rational if you are choosing what is really good for you 993: 4–5).[6] Choice in accord with false preferences is irrational s cognitive processes are extremely efficient.

d Preferences

d preferences are our preferences for goods that satisfy rally a person's lower or physical needs) unrestrained by any

this conflict, one may experience intrapsychic stress in the form of regret, shame, guilt, or ambivalence concerning one's consumption behavior (Etzioni, 1986: 177).

Metapreferences have several origins. First, they derive from the moral strictures (concerning self and community) that we all learn from our families, society, and our group memberships. These moral values, along with ancient wisdom, become internalized, and thus, become part of our preferences (Gintis, 1974: 419; Etzioni, 1988: 45–6; van der Veen, 1981: 346), though not necessarily our actual preferences. Second, metapreferences derive from the conclusions we draw from observing other's satisfactions (Gintis, 1974: 419). We may want, for example, to experience the types of satisfaction that we see others, but not ourselves, obtaining. Third, metapreferences derive from our wise, rational, long-term oriented contemplation and thinking. And fourth, they derive from personal introspection and intuition regarding a third set of preferences, our true preferences. The last will be explained later.

As indicated above when metapreferences conflict with actual preferences, one is likely to experience some form of intrapsychic stress. It is expected that the individual experiencing this discomfort will attempt to find a pattern of behavior that is more satisfactory (or more metapreferred) than simply behaving in line with actual preferences. Jon Elster (1985: 256–7) suggests three strategies for doing this. First, one can 'exploit extrapsychic mechanisms of precommitment by making it physically impossible for oneself to choose' in accordance with actual preferences. In some cases, this may mean arranging to limit one's freedom of movement with respect to certain options. Second, one can 'exploit intrapsychic mechanisms of mental bookkeeping or "framing."' This may involve avoiding exposure to information or conditions that would trigger the desire to behave in line with actual preferences. Third, one can take actions to bring about a change in actual preferences in order that one no longer wants to choose the behaviors that were formerly preferred (see also Ainslie, 1992: 130ff). The third strategy would seem to be superior to the others because it represents a lasting resolution of the conflict. No doubt, the first two can help a person improve their behavior, but the underlying conflict remains. Thus, there is always a danger that the adopted mechanisms for 'self-control' may fail, that the person may fail to be on guard, thereby allowing the actual self/preferences to reassert themselves (see Elster, 1977; Schelling, 1980).

True Preferences

An individual's true preferences are that person's unique set of preferences that represent what is really and truly the best for that person. The term, true preferences, as used here has several levels of meaning: economic, biological/psychological and religious/spiritual. On the first (economic) level, following John Harsanyi (1982: 55), 'a person's true preferences are the preferences he *would* have if he had all the relevant factual information, always reasoned with the greatest possible care, and were in a state of mind most conducive to rational choice.'[3] True preferences would differ from actual preferences to the extent that actual preferences 'are based on erroneous factual beliefs, or on careless logical analysis, or on strong emotions that at the moment greatly hinder rational choice.'

On the second level, true preferences correspond to the true biological/psychological nature of an individual. Abraham Maslow (Hoffman 1988: 215) 'emphasized that each of us has an intrinsic core of personality – what he called a "real self" – unique and yet possessing traits in common with all humans.' In this view, a person's true self is inherently good or neutral, not evil, and reflects the biological essence of the person, not superficial cultural characteristics. Further, Maslow observed that people with the highest mental health are those who have acted in accord with their true preferences, thereby achieving self-realization involving full use of their talents and potentialities (p. 187).

On the third level, true preferences correspond to an individual's ultimate inner spiritual or religious truth. For example, Edgar Cayce, the famous psychic and source of spiritual inspiration, urges everyone to know one's true self and to seek attunement with the Divine within, thereby coming to know one's true destiny (Puryear, 1982: 9, 237). In Williamson's (1993: 42, 117, 258) view, discovering one's true self is the path to enlightenment and a return to God. Following this spiritual path is like a detoxification in which one actualizes the Christ within and becomes purified of fearful thoughts. Although the latter authors emphasize the religious or spiritual side, their ideas have much in common with those of humanistic psychologists such as Maslow.

In sum, true preferences are the preferences that a person would have if he or she were perfectly informed and on the path toward becoming a full self-realized and spiritually enlightened human. Because a person's true preferences are objectively true or right for that person, when this person chooses in accord with these preferences, it will lead him or her to the highest health and vitality possible.

True preferences are unique to the individual and are unchanging insofar as they reflect the true essence of the person's life, their core values, life mission, and so on.[4] Moreover, it is difficult to know fully one's true preferences. Of course, life experience and one's reactions to it provide many clues, but a person would need perfect intuitive ability to know fully one's true preferences. Therefore, most of us have a limited consciousness of our

true preferences. The part of true prefer
part present in our metapreferences.

With the exception of a handful of n
ized and enlightened beings, a person's
from his or her true preferences. Thus,
sonal development is preference transfo
preferences closer to one's true prefere
John Stuart Mill's 'general view that s
living could be judged objectively bett
others' (McPherson, 1982: 254). Mill be
dency to develop their capacities along t
'higher pleasures' and that this 'interes
role in their lives' (pp. 262–3). Accordir
theory to rest ultimately on people's dee
wants to be able to criticize existing pr
erences [are] less legitimate or less genu

Other leading economic thinkers
Knight suggested that 'what the comr
isfaction for the wants he has, but n
1984: 237). What Albert Hirschman
changing your preferences to conforr
moral aspiration' (p. 244). Also, in K
of labor in the *Economico-Philosophic*
a view of the free, unalienated indivic
idea of a person acting in accord wit
view, a worker under typical capitalist
to be himself, to develop himself' (p.
'self-determined, i.e., . . . determined
and constitution' (p. 77).

How does one transform one's a
answer. However, as suggested above,
recognize a purification process or pa
to reach toward these ends. In order
give up or let go of many of one's
gradually adopt preference patterns
of transforming one's consumptio
Buddhism emphasize a process in wh
for goods is reduced. According to
potency of these cravings and looser
work of spiritual life.' To do this, Bu
consumption but meditation, reflec
on (Kolm, 1985: 240). More general

ability, w
types of
more diff

The pa
preferenc
realize ou
to realize
ing. To th
ences in t
we experi
nary pers
failures n
preference
influences
margarine
influence
try to imp
example t

One im
the servic
good thin

One do
poison
tal. Mo
consequ
an obje
standar
and Wil

A secon
mainstrea
among alt
ing the an
implies dis
to transfo
only be co
(see Lutz,
even if one

Unrestrain

Unrestrain
needs (gen

consideration of the needs of other people. These are our desires or passions for pure sensory pleasure, for satisfaction, for us only. Our unrestrained self is essentially Freud's id. Considerations of morality or ethics do not enter here.

To the extent that one's actual preferences do reflect a consideration of others and incorporate a sense of fair play, and so on, one's actual preferences will diverge from one's unrestrained preferences. When this divergence exists, there is the possibility of temptation. That is, one may encounter situations or impulses that lead us to choose the temptation, a choice that is in accord with our unrestrained preferences but not with our actual preferences and certainly not with our metapreferences or true preferences.[7] Once having yielded to the temptation, the experience may lead to a change, presumably a deterioration, in one's actual preferences.[8] For example, consider a man who prefers to have sex solely with his wife for both love and security reasons. Suppose this man visits a strange city without the accompaniment of friends and associates, and at a moment of weakness, he encounters an attractive and affordable prostitute. It is not inconceivable that he will yield to the temptation. The implication is that even as one's personal development progresses and one adopts improved preferences, 'lower activities remain temptations that threaten higher ones' (Ainslie, 1992: 116), raising the possibility that deterioration of actual preferences could occur.

Individual Predispositions and Personal Capital

Individuals generally are predisposed toward certain types of actual preferences for consumer goods. Individual predispositions are determined by a person's basic behavioral functioning that derives from one's inherited and acquired physical and psychological makeup. These predispositions whether determined by genetic inheritance or one's life shaping experiences at home or school or work relate to one's internal biochemical balance, one's physical health and conditioning, and one's psychological tendencies.

These predispositions for most people often have a problematic aspect in the sense that individuals are frequently predisposed to preferences that are antagonistic to their true preferences. In other words, many of us are predisposed to crave and overuse certain types of goods and to underconsume others. This could occur when a person has a tendency to adopt certain types of consumption patterns in order to satisfy his or her unfulfilled psychological needs such as for love or emotional security instead of to satisfy the needs ostensibly being satisfied. Two examples of this are eating to excess or jogging to excess which are both not only harmful but largely not directed toward acquiring nutrition or improving physical conditioning.

'Food is not taken simply to nourish the body but as a substitute for deeper nurturings unreceived' (Levine, 1991: 138). People with such predispositions have in effect latent addictions, addictions waiting to happen, that is, waiting for the exposure to particular goods and the habituation/appreciation process that connects use of the good to their underlying psychological needs.

There are many other psychological patterns that are related to predispositions. Some people use consumer goods, especially physically addictive substances, to allow them to avoid facing problems, to avoid having to relax naturally, to avoid facing uncomfortable responsibilities, to avoid unpleasant thoughts and bodily sensations, to escape psychological pain, and so on. People with these tendencies or predispositions are more easily tempted and more easily acquire the consumption capital associated with addiction or unhealthy habits than others do.

Individual predispositions, because they are embodied in people and because they are often a very important determinant of the amount of satisfaction people can obtain from goods, are a kind of human capital, namely personal capital. Personal capital is an antecedent to, and closely related to, general and specific consumption capital because one's actual preferences for general types of or specific consumer goods are built upon one's predispositions. Personal capital is distinguished from other types of human capital in that it is related to an individual's personal qualities, the qualities that enable one to have or develop the capacity to obtain satisfaction from one's life activities.[9] One's endowment of personal capital reflects one's genetic inheritance and the events that have shaped one's life, but it also reflects one's self-improvement efforts. Increasingly, people are investing in their own personal capital through self-improvement activities including psychotherapy/counseling, reading books, listening to or viewing audio and video tapes, attending seminars, seeking advice and wisdom from gurus or other religious/spiritual people, engaging in practices such as meditation and yoga, and undertaking a variety of other therapies and experiences.

In some cases, the investments in personal capital are for the purpose of overcoming one's particular problematic predisposition. For example, one might engage a psychotherapist in order to become less controlled by unfulfilled psychological needs, and thus become less inclined to abuse alcohol or drugs. Investments in personal capital may also be oriented towards: (a) helping individuals gain a greater awareness of their true preferences, that is, moving their metapreferences toward their true preferences; and (b) acquiring greater knowledge and experience concerning how to transform one's actual preferences toward one's metapreferences. Thus, an individual's stock of personal capital indicates the healthful quality of one's predispositions.[10]

External Influences on Preference Formation

In addition to individual predispositions, external influences ordinarily are important in shaping a consumer's actual preference patterns. As indicated earlier, systematic societal or cultural influences can improve or retard well-being depending on whether they influence actual preferences in the direction of true preferences or not. When people have available to them healthy outlets for satisfying their needs and largely receive messages supportive of healthy consumption patterns, people's actual preferences will tend to be healthy ones; and when the reverse is true, their preferences will tend to be of an addictive or unhealthy nature. In the case of anorexia nervosa, the eating disorder involving excessive preoccupation with becoming slim through dieting, the fact that women in American culture receive many messages encouraging them to be very slim seems to be a decisive factor. More generally, it is widely acknowledged that advertising and marketing efforts have fostered many consumption patterns that are less than totally healthy and far removed from people's true preferences.

Consider how in terms of our model an external influence such as advertising can influence preference formation. First, advertising could provide information about and draw our attention to tempting goods and experiences, instigating our unrestrained self to act against the interests of our actual self. For example, ads can tempt us to try extremely sweet desserts or enticing alcoholic beverages currently excluded from our diet. Second, advertising can influence the evolution of our actual preferences by conditioning our attitudes, developing new sensitivities, reinforcing existing patterns, providing knowledge about new goods, and developing new appreciations and lifestyles. Third, advertising can influence our metapreferences to the extent it influences our moral values and wisdom and raises our consciousness of our true preferences. It should be noted that there are many other external influences besides advertising and many other institutions besides business that can exert these influences.

Summary of the Main Features of the Model

The most salient features of the socio-economic model of preference formation developed above are indicated in Figure 10.1. An individual's initial actual preferences which reflect his or her investment in general and specific consumption capital are likely to change to the extent that they differ either from one's metapreferences or one's unrestrained preferences. Temptations from the latter could lead to a deterioration of actual preferences. Or the intrapsychic stress that occurs when higher order preferences are significantly out of synch with actual preferences could lead to improved

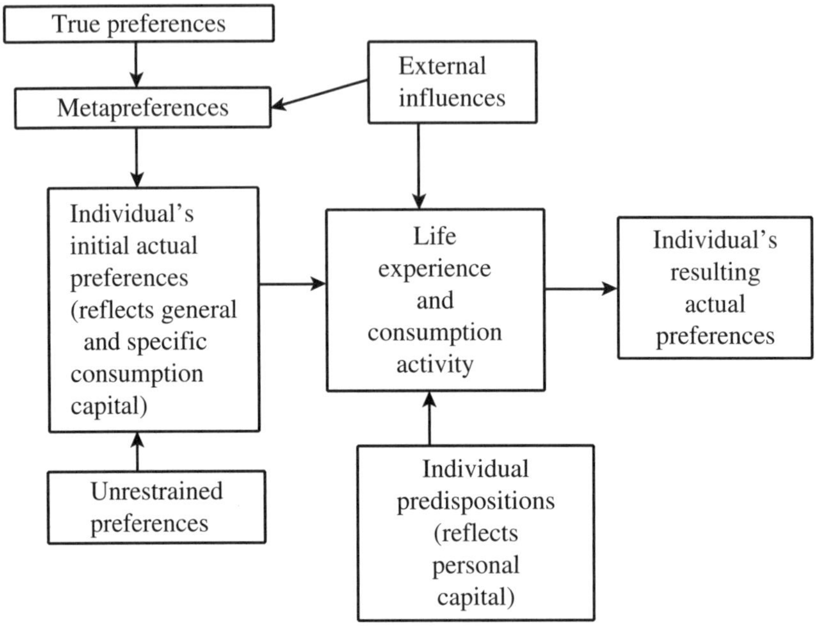

Figure 10.1 Main features of model of preference formation

actual preferences. On the one hand, metapreferences reflect acquired wisdom and moral values that generally derive from external influences. On the other hand, they reflect, albeit imperfectly, one's true preferences, one's unique preferences corresponding with one's deep inner truth. Metapreferences will change over time as an individual gains greater consciousness of and knowledge of his or her true preferences. When one's actual preferences move closer to one's true preferences, that is, when a person comes closer to realizing his or her unique potential, a person's well-being is considered to have improved.

Depending on the path of one's life experiences and consumption activities, one's actual preferences will evolve. This evolution is conditioned by many external socio-economic influences and affected by an individual's physical and psychological predispositions to use consumer goods in healthy or unhealthy ways. Because these predispositions have much to do with one's capacity to gain well-being from consumer goods, they are usefully viewed as a kind of capital, personal capital. As a result of the variety of these influences, an individual's actual preferences will evolve bringing into existence a new stock of general and specific consumption capital as shown in Figure 10.1.

COMPARISONS TO OTHER SOCIO-ECONOMIC MULTIPLE SELF CONCEPTIONS

There is a growing literature concerning individual choice and preference formation that incorporates the idea that persons have two or more contradictory selves or preferences vying for control (see Aaron, 1994).[11] Most commonly, there are two selves contending, one of which rationally focuses on the person's long-term best interests, while the other focuses, perhaps irrationally, on short-term interests, that is, obtaining immediate satisfaction (see, for example, Elster, 1977; Schelling, 1980; Winston, 1980; Ainslie, 1992). In Thaler and Shefrin's (1981) version, there is the completely selfish myopic doer versus the farsighted planner. In Cowen's (1991) version, there is the rule-oriented self, which imposes regularities and controls on behavior, versus the impulsive self, which favors spontaneity and unpredictability. Neither of these two selves is necessarily the rational one. If the rule-oriented self is too strong, leaving little room for spontaneity, it would be irrational, and injurious to mental health, for it to dominate the impulsive self.

In Harvey Leibenstein's writings on X-efficiency, there is a two self conception. According to Leibenstein (see, for example, 1976: 76–82), the employee who is deciding how much effort to expend is torn between his or her desire to be responsible, conscientious, and adhere to high standards (responsible self) and the desire to avoid responsibility and to be unconstrained (unrestrained self). These two selves correspond closely with Freud's superego and id. Leibenstein's responsible self is similar in some ways to my meta-self, but there is nothing corresponding to the true self or the influence of the true self on the meta-self.

In Mark Lutz and Kenneth Lux's (1988: 105–16) two self conception, there is a higher self and an ego-self. The ego-self is concerned only with his or her self-interests; it is concerned with maximizing these interests unrestrained by moral considerations. Lutz and Lux's concept of the higher self is akin to the true self concept. It is the self concerned with truth seeking, principled behavior, and moral values and aspirations; it is the self that 'yearns to be realized.' Moreover, this higher self is only the part of the true self that one is conscious of, and one's intuitive knowledge of the true self may be fallible. Also, note that Lutz and Lux's higher self is not like the superego in the sense of being an externally imposed parental authority.

In Amitai Etzioni's (1986) view, there are two selves, corresponding to 'two irreducible sources of value or "utility," pleasure and morality' (p. 159). Pleasure or satisfaction is 'derived from doing what one likes, enjoys, and finds pleasurable'; morality refers to 'the sense of *affirmation* that accompanies living up to one's moral commitments that are often in themselves taxing rather than pleasurable' (p. 160). Morality derives from the duties and obligations to parents, culture, and peer or reference groups that have been internalized through a socialization process (pp. 169–70). Morality is not seen as stemming from an internal source such as true preferences. Etzioni emphasizes moral considerations as distinctly different from those related to pleasure or satisfaction, which is in contrast to the blending of these considerations in the model developed here. For example, in my model, one's actual preferences regarding the use of wine are likely to include a combination of moral and pleasurable considerations. Also, in my model, one's metapreferences regarding wine are likely to differ from one's actual preferences in that higher moral values and obligations as well as elements of one's true preference (pleasure included) are reflected there. It should also be noted that because Etzioni's two utility conception does not use the concept of true preferences, it offers limited insight regarding the question of how a person can develop and raise his or her well-being, say, through a process leading to self-realization or even enlightenment.

EXTERNALITIES

The present model includes two important external effects or externalities. According to the usual definition, negative (or positive) externalities involve costs imposed upon (or benefits received) by third persons who did not consent to these impacts nor receive compensation (or pay) for them. Where externalities exist, market activity by itself is expected to fail to produce an efficient or welfare maximizing result, that is, it will ordinarily lead to too much or too little production of the goods involved. In the model here, the nature of the externalities is slightly different in that the external effect on the third party is either a detrimental or beneficial preference change.

David George's (1993: 330–43) analysis of externalities focuses on a situation in which the external effect is a firm's advertising or marketing influence on prospective customers' actual preferences but not on their metapreferences. When the influence is detrimental, this leads the would-be customer to choose in accord with a less preferred preference pattern, which, George's analysis shows, lowers this individual's welfare (pp. 334–9). For example, a cigarette manufacturer's advertising might influence many people to prefer to smoke despite their metapreference not to smoke. This results in too many actual preferences for smoking, an outcome which is inferior compared to people's pre-advertising preferences. This is inefficient because profit maximizing firms will use too much advertising on account of not considering the third party costs, the deterioration of people's preferences, in their decision making. In the case of a positive external effect on actual preferences, the opposite is true.

In the present model, the externalities are similar to the ones George analyzes in that they involve significant external positive and negative influences on actual preferences. An important difference is that in the model here what is crucial to an individual's well-being is whether the externally influenced preference change is toward or away from the person's true preferences (metapreferences, which may change due to the external influence, are not important in this respect). If, for example, cigarette advertising is persuasive, resulting in more people preferring to smoke, and cigarette smoking is truly inferior to not smoking, then the persuaded individuals will be worse off, and society will wind up with an overall deterioration of preferences. This movement of actual preferences away from true preferences worsens the well-being failure. As in the analysis above, there is an inefficiency because businesses are not forced to consider the cost associated with the preference deterioration in their decision making. An opposite example is the case of anti-cigarette proselytizing that influences people's preferences toward their true preferences, thereby lessening the well-being failure.

The second type of externality in the model does not stem from someone's attempt to influence the preferences of another. Rather, the external effect occurs because of changes in actual preferences produced by the intrinsic nature of certain goods. Consider two goods, A and B, which are equally unpreferred from the standpoint of true preferences: A has a greater addictive quality for people with certain predispositions. Thus A produces a much more rapid growth in consumer appreciation of its qualities and in habituation, that is, more rapid formation of actual preferences and accumulation of consumption capital. The hypothesis is that goods resembling A are the ones to which people are much more likely to develop addictions or other attachments that are particularly hard to give up. For example, let us compare two goods, peca cola (good A – a soda spiked with a stimulating drug) and coffee (good B). Because peca cola resembles good A, it is expected that for consumers the cola will become more quickly preferred and habitual relative to coffee and the habitual use of the cola will be harder to overcome. Therefore, its consumption will contribute more to well-being failure than coffee. This is inefficient because firms will produce and sell too much peca cola on account of not considering the full cost to consumers, and society, stemming from its especially addictive quality.[12]

IMPLICATIONS

Altruism

The concept of true preferences and its relationship to well-being helps to understand what altruism really means. Altruism is not simply the pleasure you receive from someone else's pleasure, that is, your vicarious experience of another's pleasure, as many mainstream economists have analyzed it. The essence of altruism, following Auguste Comte, is a 'life devoted to the good of others' (Lutz and Lux, 1988: 109). The good of others means what is really and truly good for them, what is in accord with their true preferences. It is not altruism to take pleasure in the pleasure a person receives from eating the chocolate you have given them if that person is overweight and addicted to chocolate. 'A real altruist would urge you to stop eating chocolates, because although you may like the taste of chocolates, it is not in your best interest to eat them' (p. 109). Ultimately, the real altruist is interested in others' realization of their true selves.

Merit Goods

Merit goods, according to Musgrave and Musgrave (1989: 57–8), are the kind of goods that the community has decided should be provided in greater quantity because the private demands or wants for them are insufficient. The Musgraves consider food and decent low-cost housing for the poor to be merit goods. But the basis for determining what is and what is not a merit good seems nebulous even in theory. Perhaps what the Musgraves really mean is that merit goods are ones provided through the government's altruistic efforts to make available goods that are more in line with a recipients' true preferences than are their current choices based on their actual preferences.

Government Policy

Generally, economists' view has been that societal welfare is best achieved by letting individuals' subjective preferences dictate the use of societal resources. Thus, economists have been slow to condemn even the most revolting of tastes and have shown 'little interest in finding ways to enhance and promote tastes that clearly yield beneficial externalities' (Rhoads, 1990: 93).

> The treatment of tastes and preferences in modern mainstream economics is glaringly inadequate . . . The unwillingness to focus on changing tastes leaves unexplored those policies that seek to encourage meritorious tastes and discourage bad ones. (p. 102)

One way to think about the policy implications of the model of preference formation developed here is by analogy with industrial policy. Whereas industrial policy is concerned with government actions that foster the development of firms' productive capacity, especially firms' technological and managerial capacities, the policies implied by our model are ones that foster people's capacities for attaining well-being from their consumption activities. Such policies should encourage appropriate investments in consumption capital and personal capital. They should encourage individuals' self-development activities and remove societal obstacles standing in the way of people discovering and developing their true selves. This seems broadly consistent with John Stuart Mill's concern 'to reform the major institutions of society so that people would come to want things that were more valuable, both to themselves and society' (McPherson, 1982: 268).

What the model specifically implies is that there is a strong case for government action whenever there are clear and glaring well-being failures, and especially when these are produced by systematic societal externalities. Because well-being failures are ubiquitous, the smaller, more ordinary failures, presumably, would not provide sufficient justification for government action. It is also important to note that issues related to encouraging and discouraging certain types of consumption are not new, and many societies, especially the US, are continuing to confront and struggle with issues such as the degree to which cigarette smoking and drug use should be regulated. Unfortunately, economists' thinking on this subject has been as much an obstacle as a help to dealing with these issues and making public policy concerning them.

The growing trend to obesity is one specific area where there is apparently a need for this kind of government action. A recent study conducted by the National Center for Health Statistics in the Centers for Disease Control and Prevention finds that the 'proportion of seriously overweight Americans had increased to more than 30 percent between 1980 and 1991, up from about a fourth of the adult population from 1960 through 1980' (Burros, 1994). In response to this finding, Dr Philip R. Lee, the assistant secretary for health in the Department of Health and Human Services, said: 'The government is not doing enough.' The study provides strong support for those arguing for a national campaign to reduce obesity. Such government efforts would be designed to counteract the root causes of obesity, sedentary lifestyles and an abundance of food, as well as the constant bombardment by food messages encouraging people to eat more than they need.

It is important to sound a note of caution with respect to such government policies. The danger, some will say, is that certain people will claim to know others' true preferences better than they do, and therefore, seek to force changes on them without democratic process or respect for their individual autonomy. While there may be people whose actions justify such fears, neither the model developed here nor the policy recommendation above should give rise to them. First, in the model, individuals (the author included) have a limited consciousness of their own true preferences, not to mention the true preferences of others. Despite this lack of knowledge or consciousness, there presumably is some commonality of true preferences among people, and there is a need to inquire into these common true preferences through a public dialogue. Out of this public discussion and debate should come a consensus on the types of preferences that should be encouraged and discouraged in a way that is respectful of individual liberty. This view seems generally consistent with the views of John Stuart Mill regarding the appropriate role of government in shaping preferences (McPherson, 1982: 267–71). In Mill's view, the essence of the job 'concerns the problem of motivating and educating people to be moral' (p. 270).

CONCLUSIONS

The present model which is a synthesis of a variety of old and new elements provides an explanation for preference change that is a radical departure from that of mainstream economics. Probably the most novel, and presumably most controversial, element in the model is the idea that everyone has a true self with true preferences and that one's well-being is inversely related to the gap between one's actual and true preferences. Another noteworthy element is that one's metapreferences are an imperfect reflection of both external social (often moral) influences and the internal influence from one's true self. The model is particularly important in that it indicates how people might improve themselves through a process involving the formation of new preferences along with investment in personal capital and consumption capital. But it also indicates that other internal and external influences could lead to personal decline as one might develop new, but inferior, preferences. The model has very important government policy implications which have not been developed in much detail, and thus will require future research.

The central ideas of the model are very similar to some of the important ideas of John Stuart Mill. First, Mill criticized the classical utilitarians (the relatively direct ancestors of today's mainstream economists) insofar as they evaluated 'social policies and institutions solely from the standpoint of their effectiveness in satisfying existing wants' (McPherson, 1982: 252). Second, Mill was very much concerned with human improvement, the development of ideal human character, and particularly with the generation of improved wants (p. 252). Now more than ever, it seems appropriate to return to the insights of Mill. Doing so requires the development of socio-economic models that both explain preference change and explain why preference change is desirable and at the heart of self-improvement.

NOTES

1. The consumption capital concept used here is akin to Roger McCain's (1993) 'parameters of sensitivity.'
2. According to Tyler Cowen (1989: 129), 'Postulating that music listening changes the ability of music to produce relaxation does not appear radically different from postulating that music listening changes the taste for music. In both cases the result is already implicit in the functions the theorist has written down, and the only difference is whether this result is contained in the utility function or the household production function.' It should be noted that Gary Becker's (1992: 340) new view is that while preferences (actual) may change, 'metapreferences' are stable.
3. Tyler Cowen (1993: 262) refers to this as perfectly informed or cleansed preferences.
4. It should be noted that there are differences in preferences between younger and older people, differences relating to the inherent nature of physical and emotional maturation processes. The basic argument of this chapter abstracts from these age differences.
5. This implies a conception of well-being different from the subjective preference satisfaction formulation. For a review of other alternatives to the subjective preference satisfaction view of well-being, see Hausman and McPherson (1993: 691–3). Well-being, according to the view taken here, is realized by people to the extent that they are able to live full lives (see Streeten's (1994) discussion of human development). To achieve high well-being requires two things. First, the economy must have developed its ability to use its resources productively. Second, people must have developed themselves and society must have provided opportunities such that people can obtain real or true satisfaction from the goods and services that the economy can make available. It is this second aspect that is left out of mainstream conceptions of well-being.
6. Sen (1987: 13–14) refers to this kind of rationality as 'reflection rationality.'
7. The concept of unrestrained preferences has a similarity to but is not the same as the broader concept of self-regarding preferences cited by Hausman and McPherson (1993: 687) and Lutz (1993: 6). It also has some similarity to the preferences of the impulsive self (Cowen, 1991: 362) but unlike them spontaneity and unpredictability are not the essence of unrestrained preferences.
8. Because consumption capital is a neutral term, a deterioration of actual preferences does not imply a lowering of the quantity of a person's stock of consumption capital. It does, obviously, imply a change in the qualitative nature of this person's stock of consumption capital. No definite statement about the change of the magnitude of this capital stock is possible.
9. The distinction between the nature of the human attributes that constitute personal capital as opposed to the attributes that constitute other types of human capital, especially job-related human capital, is not a sharp one. Clearly, the knowledge that one acquires when one learns about accounting, management or a particular technology is the ordinary job-related human capital. On the other hand, when, for example, one acquires more self-understanding and self-esteem, this would seem to be personal capital in that it is likely to improve one's capacity to obtain satisfaction from life activities especially consumption activities. But this change in personal qualities might have job-related consequences insofar as the individual was enabled to gain improved interpersonal competence in the workplace, and thereby, greater individual productivity and compensation. Thus, personal capital is properly viewed as an antecedent to job-related human

capital as well as consumption capital because not only one's consumption capabilities but one's job capabilities are built upon one's personal qualities or predispositions.

10. John Ruskin believed that too often workplaces involve uncreative labor that 'blinds the thoughts and the eyes, blunts the hopes, steals the joys, and blasts the souls of workers' (Lutz and Lux, 1979: 40). He thought that this would reduce workers' human capacity to use and appreciate consumer goods. Thus, uncreative labor can be interpreted as causing a destruction of workers' stocks of personal capital, thereby making it more difficult for them to find satisfying patterns of consumer good use.
11. Henry Aaron (1994: 14–17) suggests that a person's different types of utility correspond to various locations of the brain where different functions take place and that there is no central processing unit (no grand headquarters) maximizing the weighted sum of these utilities.
12. The original idea for this type of analysis came from James Gamble (1993). His explanation emphasized that the different 'reinforcement schedules' associated with different goods were the key to understanding why people's choice of goods might be inoptimal.

REFERENCES

Aaron, Henry J. (1994), 'Distinguished lecture on economics in government: public policy, values, and consciousness,' *Journal of Economic Perspectives*, **8**(2), 3–21.

Ainslie, George (1992), *Picoeconomics: The Strategic Interaction of Successive Motivational States Within the Person*, Cambridge: Cambridge University Press.

Becker, Gary S. (1992), 'Habits, addictions, and traditions,' *Kyklos*, **45**(3), 327–46.

Brennan, Timothy J. (1989), 'A methodological assessment of multiple utility frameworks,' *Economics and Philosophy*, **5**, 189–208.

Burros, Marian (1994), 'A growing trend: the fat American', *International Herald Tribune*, 14 July.

Cowen, Tyler (1989), 'Are all tastes constant and identical?: a critique of Stigler and Becker,' *Journal of Economic Behavior and Organization*, **11**, 127–35.

Cowen, Tyler (1991), 'Self-constraint versus self-liberation,' *Ethics*, **101**(January), 360–73.

Cowen, Tyler (1993), 'The scope and limits of preference sovereignty,' *Economics and Philosophy*, **9**, 253–69.

Elster, Jon (1977), 'Ulysses and the Sirens: a theory of imperfect rationality,' *Social Science Information*, **16**(5), 469–526.

Elster, Jon (1985), 'Weakness of will and the free-rider problem,' *Economics and Philosophy*, **1**, 231–65.

Epictetus (1994), *A Manual for Living: A New Interpretation by Sharon Lebell*, New York: Harper Collins.

Etzioni, Amitai (1986), 'The case for a multiple-utility conception,' *Economics and Philosophy*, **2**, 159–83.

Etzioni, Amitai (1988), *The Moral Dimension: Toward a New Economics*, New York: Free Press.

Frankfurt, Harry G. (1971), 'The freedom of the will and the concept of a person,' *Journal of Philosophy*, **68**(1), 5–20.

Gamble, James L. (1993), 'Keys to the Kingdom: criteria for consumer psychological market failure,' Unpublished manuscript.

George, David (1993), 'Does the market create preferred preferences,' *Review of Social Economy*, **51**(Fall), 323–46.

Gintis, Herbert (1974), 'Welfare criteria with endogenous preferences: the economics of education,' *International Economic Review*, **15**(2), 415–30.
Harsanyi, John C. (1982), 'Morality and the theory of rational behavior,' in Amartya Sen and Bernard Williams (eds) *Utilitarianism and Beyond*, Cambridge: Cambridge University Press, pp. 39–62.
Hausman, Daniel M. and Michael S. McPherson (1993), 'Taking ethics seriously: economics and contemporary moral philosophy,' *Journal of Economic Literature*, **31**(June), 671–731.
Hoffman, Edward (1988), *Right to Be Human: A Biography of Abraham Maslow*, Los Angeles, CA: Tarcher.
Kolm, Serge-Christophe (1985), 'The Buddhist theory of "no-self," ' in Jon Elster (ed.) *The Multiple Self*, Cambridge: Cambridge University Press, pp. 233–65.
Leibenstein, Harvey (1976), *Beyond Economic Man: A New Foundation for Microeconomics*, Cambridge, MA: Harvard University Press.
Levine, Stephen (1991), *Guided Meditations, Explorations and Healings*, New York: Doubleday Anchor.
Lutz, Mark A. (1993), 'Social economics and economics imperialism,' *Forum for Social Economics*, **23**(1), 1–12.
Lutz, Mark A. and Kenneth Lux (1979), *The Challenge of Humanistic Economics*. Reading, MA: Benjamin/Cummings.
Lutz, Mark A. and Kenneth Lux (1988), *Humanistic Economics: The New Challenge*, New York: Bootstrap Press.
Marx, Karl (1983), *The Portable Karl Marx*, New York: Viking.
McCain, Roger A. (1993), 'The hierarchy of need and moral economics,' *Forum for Social Economics*, **22** (Spring), 1–21.
McPherson, Michael S. (1982), 'Mill's moral theory and the problem of preference change,' *Ethics*, **92**(January), 252–73.
McPherson, Michael S. (1984), 'On Schelling, Hirschman, and Sen: revising the concept of the self,' *Partisan Review*, **51**(2), 236–47.
Musgrave, Richard A. and Musgrave, Peggy B. (1989), *Public Finance in Theory and Practice*, New York: McGraw-Hill.
Puryear, Herbert B. (1982), *The Edgar Cayce Primer*, New York: Bantam Skylark.
Rhoads, Steven E. (1990), 'Economists on tastes and preferences,' in J.H. Nichols and C. Wright (eds). *From Political Economy to Economics and Back?* San Francisco, CA: Institute for Contemporary Studies.
Schelling, Thomas C. (1980), 'The intimate contest for self-command,' *Public Interest*, **60**, 94–118.
Sen, Amartya K. (1977), 'Rational fools: a critique of the behavioral foundations of economic theory,' *Philosophy and Public Affairs*, **6**, 317–44.
Sen, Amartya (1987), *On Ethics and Economics*, New York: Basil Blackwell.
Sen, Amartya and Bernard Williams (eds) (1982), *Utilitarianism and Beyond*, Cambridge: Cambridge University Press.
Sovik, Rolf (1993), 'The pursuit of pleasure,' *Yoga International*, July/August, 32–7.
Stigler, George and Becker, Gary S. (1977), 'De gustibus non est disputandum,' *American Economic Review*, **67**(March), 76–90.
Streeten, Paul (1994), 'Human development: means and ends,' *American Economic Review*, **84**(2), 232–7.
Thaler, Richard H. and H.M. Shefrin (1981), 'An economic theory of self-control,' *Journal of Political Economy*, **89**(2), 392–406.

Tollison, Robert D. and Richard E. Wagner (1992), *The Economics of Smoking*, Boston,MA: Kluwer.
van der Veen, Robert J. (1981), 'Meta-rankings and collective optimality,' *Social Science Information*, **20**(2), 345–74.
Williamson, Marianne (1993), *A Return to Love: Reflections on the Principles of a Course in Miracles*, New York: Harper Perennial.
Winston, Gordon C. (1980), 'Addiction and backsliding: a theory of compulsive consumption,' *Journal of Economic Behavior and Organization*, **1**, 295–324.

11. Beyond the rationality of economic man, toward the true rationality of human man

INRODUCTION

The concept of rationality used by economists is a central, defining feature of economics today. It is important as both a positive and normative concept. Unfortunately, it is a problematic feature in both senses. A very large number of articles and books have been written about the deficiencies of rationality as a positive or descriptive concept, but relatively few have dealt with the deficiencies of economic rationality as a normative concept. This chapter proposes: (a) to review and synthesize the most cogent and telling of the arguments in the latter literature; and (b) based on these to develop a more appropriate normative conception of rationality. It is anticipated that this alternative conception of rationality, true rationality, will be especially appropriate for a humanistic economics. Hopefully, it will be a concept that can better serve as a guide to resource allocation in order that the socio-economy can attain its true potential of human well-being. This alternative conception should also make more sense from a philosophical, spiritual and religious perspective than the economists' conception.

THE ESSENCE OF RATIONALITY

To begin, let's define rationality in a very general way, a way that all economists, mainstream and heterodox, might be able to agree upon. Accordingly, rationality involves the appropriate use of reason to make the best possible choices considering what is under the circumstances really in the best interests of the choosing agent (see Rescher, 1988: Chapter 1 for similar definitions). Wide agreement on this definition is possible precisely because it does not distinguish between the two main types of rationality. The first type is instrumental rationality (also known as the rationality of means or cognitive rationality); this involves applying appropriate reason to choose the best possible means to attain one's ends. Most economists, but especially mainstream economists, recognize this as the only form of rationality. The second type is the rationality of ends (also known as evaluative rationality or expressive rationality); this means applying appropriate reason to choose ends that serve our best interests, that is, to determine what our objectives ought to be. In what follows, these two types of rationality are examined with special attention to the second type. A major argument of this chapter is that economists need to utilize a conception of rationality, true rationality, that includes both types, not just instrumental rationality.

INSTRUMENTAL RATIONALITY

The instrumental conception of rationality is widely understood to derive from the thinking of the eighteenth century Scottish philosopher, David Hume (Sugden, 1991: 752–3). Hume considered a person's ends, one's motivating passions, to operate outside the rule of reason (Rescher, 1988: 93–4). In other words, people's desires or aversions, their appetites, are whatever they are, and people do not try to apply reason to assess their appropriateness. Reason is only applied to choose the best means to achieve these given ends. 'Reason is thus a "slave of the passions"' (p. 94). And an act is considered 'irrational if it is not the best means of achieving the ends that the actor himself had a view when choosing the act' (Sugden, 1991: 753).

Over the years, economists have interpreted instrumental rationality in several different ways. The predominant mainstream economic interpretation is that rational behavior involves choosing in order to maximize one's satisfaction given one's preferences. The rational person uses reason to find the best means to satisfy these preferences. Although the individual is considered self-interested, this merely means that the person desires to satisfy one's own preferences; it does not indicate the substance of those preferences. The person's preferences could be for altruistic behavior, for behavior harmful to oneself, or for immoral or evil behavior.

RATIONALITY OF ENDS

Over the years, some philosophers and even a few economists (and other social scientists) have questioned the mainstream economics view that rationality is entirely an instrumental conception. Frank H. Knight, a leading economist in the early twentieth century, for example, thought the economists' conception of rationality was too narrow: 'Living intelligently [rationally] includes more than the intelligent use of means in realizing ends; it is fully as important to select the ends intelligently' (as quoted in Raines and Jung, 1992: 118). This section argues that what we consider to be rational behavior ought to include applying reason to select ends, not just means.[1] This is because a decision cannot be truly rational unless a person is doing what is really best for that person. This implies that the rational person will have: (a) reflected on his/her values and ends; (b) sought to determine what is really good for him/herself; (c) considered the long-term consequences of his/her behavior; (d) considered what his/her sense of morality is; and (e) considered what gives him/her real happiness.

As Nicholas Rescher (1988: 5) points out, many of us simply do what we desire or want, but such actions may not be in our best interests or real interests. No doubt, we have a motive and some reasons for our actions, but unless there are good reasons for doing so, it will not be what is really best for us. For example, we may want to spend our money gambling on horse races, and we may have some reasons justifying it, but these reasons are presumably unevaluated ones reflecting our desires, not sufficiently good reasons. When our motivating passions 'impel us toward things bad for us or away from things good for us,' this is not rational as there are no good reasons for doing these things (p. 95). 'Certain preferences are absurd – preferences which wantonly violate our nature, impair our being, or diminish our opportunities' (p. 95). To put it bluntly, 'a voyage to a foolish destination – no matter how efficiently conducted – is a foolish enterprise' (p. 96). When there are good, cogent reasons for pursuing certain ends, then intentionally pursuing them is in our real, legitimate interests, that is, it is rational. 'Reasons may override desires: it may be rational to do what one does not desire to do' (Sugden, 1991: 756).

Furthermore, people have a need to reflect on and find what values and ends are right for them. 'It is not enough for an individual to have a set of preferences; it is important that those desires be his or hers in a more active sense. They should belong to the individual because he/she has come through reflection to hold them as his/her own' (Heap, 1989: 148–9). This aspect of rationality is about people's quest for autonomy, that is, people's need to be self directed, to be one's own master, to be not controlled by outside forces, and to achieve a positive sense of freedom which may be accomplished to a considerable extent using reason and reflection to examine one's purposes. In other words, part of rationality stems from people's need to make sense of their world and to come to know what makes their life worthy (Heap, 1992: 22–4).

McPherson (1984: 241) believes that reflectiveness, our capacity to utilize our ideals to stand in judgment of our own preferences, is a key element of human nature. One's reflections may often lead to changing one's preferences to conform to one's ideals (p. 244).[2] Frank Knight, long ago, recognized that 'what the commonsense individual really wants is not satisfaction for the wants he has but more *and better* wants' (p. 237). At other times, people yield to their preferences, falling short of their ideals.

Are there things that are intrinsically good for all or most humans, things that reflection and good reasoning can help discover? As Hausman and McPherson (1996: 71) point out, this has been a central question of moral philosophy. The question is important because if there are such intrinsically good things, it would be in one's best interests, that is, it would be rational, to try to obtain them. The rub, however, is that even leading thinkers have very different views on what these ultimate goods are.

> In some religious views, the ultimate good lies in a relationship with God, while in others such a relationship with God is good because of the eternal happiness it brings. Many people believe that only mental states are intrinsically good but there is less agreement here than it seems, because there are so many different views of which mental states are intrinsically good. Jeremy Bentham holds that the good is pleasure, while John Stuart Mill holds that it is a diverse set of mental states he calls 'happiness.' Mystics find the good in contemplative states of mind. Henry Sidgwick argued for the hybrid view that the good is any mental state that is intrinsically desirable . . . Friedrich Nietzsche regards great achievements as the ultimate goods. Others endorse as intrinsic good a whole potpourri ranging from health and intimate personal relationships to achievements.' (p. 72)

Despite the legitimate differences of opinion about what is intrinsically good, this does not mean that there is nothing of value to be said about this. John Stuart Mill is notable for his view that 'Some kinds of experience or ways of living could be judged objectively better or [intrinsically] more valuable for people than others' (McPherson, 1982: 254). In Mill's view, there are higher pleasures and lower ones, and people would be better off if they preferred the higher pleasures (Hollis, 1983: 254). Mill associated the higher pleasures with people's efforts at self-development or self-realization or character perfection. The upshot is that it is rational to choose a life path involving the kind of self-development that enables you to experience those higher pleasures which are intrinsically (and really) good for you.

It is also rational to choose what is in our best interests in the long-term. One difficulty with trying to do what is in our long-term best interests is that our preferences and desires tomorrow may be different from those we have today. But, as Hollis (1992: 75–9) suggests, it may be possible to anticipate or foresee the preferences we will have after we choose a certain course of action. Thus, rational behavior, in this sense of doing what is best in the long-term, seems to involve reflectively stepping back from the preferences of the moment in order to consider the lasting core of one's preferences.[3] Rationality, however, does not mean being single-mindedly and rigidly focused on the long-term, it presumably means trying to maintain a flexible balance between responding to the needs of the moment and those of the future.

It is also rational to behave morally. Note, however, that from the standpoint of instrumental rationality, following moral precepts would be irrational if these precepts conflict with choices based on our wants and desires. But from the standpoint of rationality of ends, there would be no conflict between rationality and morality if acting morally means acting on the basis of good reasons, for example, good reasons for not pursuing certain of our wants and desires (Hausman and McPherson, 1996: 64). When we make decisions in line with moral commitments, we are not 'hallucinating or falling into a fit'; we are using good reasoning to examine our purposes and as a consequence we may decide to do some things and not to do other things. Thus, when we reflect on our wants and employ good reasons to make moral choices, we are being rational.

Further, rational behavior contributes to our happiness. According to Aristotle, happiness is the 'sole intrinsic good' (Hausman and McPherson, 1996: 71). If so, it would be rational to behave so as to attain happiness. Aristotle called such behavior virtuous. A virtuous person is one who, because of having acquired good habits, regularly makes right choices, choices that leave one with no regrets and that contribute to one's happiness (Adler, 1978: 101). Further, happiness occurs when a person 'fulfills his deepest nature' and there is a 'flourishing of one's truest self' (Segal, 1991: 289). Thus, the ultimate of rationality is to pursue what really brings us this true happiness.

A FRAMEWORK FOR ANALYZING RATIONAL BEHAVIOR

What economists need is a way to integrate the insights above with economic logic concerning rational decision making. Thus, the purpose of this chapter is a synthetic one, that is, it is to develop a conceptual framework that enables a clear link between the noneconomic insights and economic concepts, thereby helping economists and other social scientists attain a proper understanding of normative rationality. Three types of preferences are at the heart of our analytical framework: actual preferences, metapreferences and true preferences. The concept of true preferences was first used along with the two other types of preferences in a socio-economic model explaining preference formation (Tomer, 1996: 620–5). This chapter further develops the relationship between these three preferences and, most importantly, indicates how they are related to a normative conception of rationality. The concept of true preferences turns out to be a key to the development of an alternative concept of rationality, true rationality.

Actual preferences reflect one's wants and desires and also one's ability to use and appreciate goods. They are the preferences that apply when one makes an ordinary choice among alternatives. Actual preferences change over time with consumption experience, thinking and reflection, social influences, skill acquisition, and so on. Thus, actual preferences reflect a person's endowment of two types of human capital: (a) consumption capital, the individual capacity to use and appreciate goods; and (b) personal capital, the individual capacity related to one's predispositions or general personal qualities that enable one to obtain satisfaction from one's life activities.

Metapreferences are a person's preferences about one's actual preferences. Metapreferences derive from the human capacity for reflectiveness, the capacity to stand in judgment of our preferences and to contemplate more or less consciously their worth. 'Many who regularly indulge themselves with food, alcohol, cigarettes, drugs, gambling, incest, prostitution, or pornography hate themselves for doing so and would love to be able to stop' (Rhoads, 1990: 86). Others have preferences, which although more or less acceptable, they aspire to replace by higher, more ideal preferences. The latter people desire to be more ethical, more harmonious, better parents, better friends, and so on (p. 87). One's metapreferences may originate from the social learning we experience in our families, group memberships, and society, or they may derive from our more deliberate efforts to think and contemplate about what is best for us. Another possibility is that they derive from another set of preferences, our true preferences.

True preferences are an ideal and represent the ultimate, unique truth about what is really right and best for a person. There are several levels of this truth. First, unlike actual preferences, true preferences do not reflect factual errors, careless logic, or bias due to the presence of strong emotion. Second, true preferences correspond to what is true for people who have attained their highest biological and psychological possibilities, that is, their potential for high mental health and self-actualization. Third, true preferences correspond to an individual's ultimate inner spiritual and religious truth, the truth for a person who has attained the highest degree of self-realization, enlightenment according to the Buddhists. In sum, true preferences are the preferences that a person would have if he or she were perfectly informed and on the path toward becoming a fully self-realized and spiritually enlightened human. Because a person's true preferences are objectively true or right for that person, when this person chooses in accord with these preferences, it will lead him or her to the highest health and vitality possible.

The main elements of the relationship between these three types of preferences are depicted in Figure 11.1. The essence is a description of what

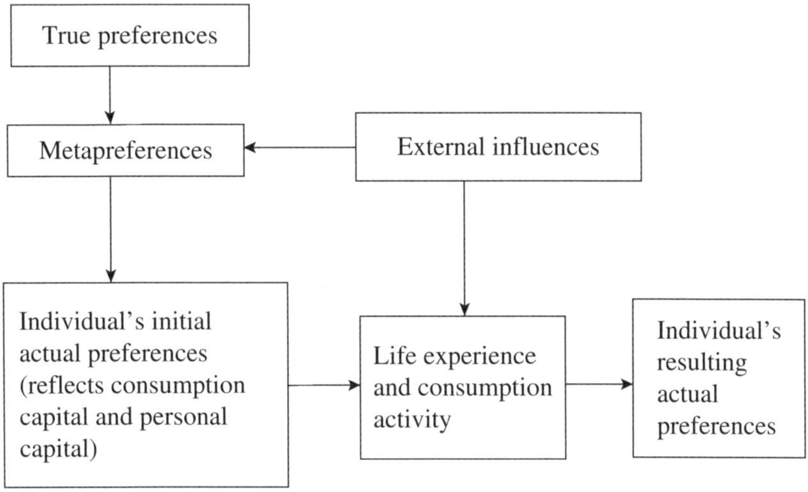

Figure 11.1 Main elements of the relationship between preference types

goes on in the process of preference change. After considering a specific example of this process below, the three preference types are then reconsidered as important elements of the normative conception of rationality. First, an individual chooses among goods based on his actual preferences that reflect his endowments of consumption capital and personal capital. Second, if there is a significant discrepancy between an individual's metapreferences and his actual preferences, this should stimulate change in his actual preferences. Third, the metapreferences, themselves, may change to the extent that one is subject to important external influences such as the wisdom and moral values of one's elders and/or becomes more conscious of one's true preferences. Fourth, actual preferences may change with life and consumption activity or as a direct result of external influences such as cultural values and advertising. Consequently, the net effect of these different influences leads to change in an individual's initial actual preferences, hopefully, but not necessarily, change for the better.

To illustrate, consider two classes of foods, healthy (H) and junky (J), the latter being less healthy and potentially damaging to one's health. Individual A's actual preferences are for J (J preferred over H), and accordingly, J food is normally chosen. However, A's true preferences are for H (H preferred over J) as H food really is better for A's health. The problem is that A does not know about, that is, has not become conscious of, true preferences. But A is somewhat aware of what knowledgeable nutritional authorities say about H and J foods and has absorbed the influences of parents and significant family members, not to mention community and religious influences. A is also affected by external cultural influences including advertising and the styles of youth culture. As a result, A's metapreferences are for a combination of H and J, say 50 percent H and 50 percent J food. In other words, A prefers to prefer much more H food than is currently preferred and is consuming. A, however, does not want to prefer to eat only H food, as would be the case if A's metapreferences were the same as the true preferences. Because of the tension or intrapsychic stress that results from A's metapreferences being out of sync with any actual preferences, A would be expected over time to 'improve' the actual preferences, coming to prefer a combination of foods with a higher proportion of H food than initially. Moreover, it is quite conceivable that with time as A absorbs the lessons of consumption experience and reflects on what is best as well as on the biases of cultural influences, that A's metapreferences may come to be significantly influenced by true preferences. If these new metapreferences then influence the actual preferences, it is possible that A's actual preferences might come to reflect to a significant degree true preferences, a change which is arguably an improvement, and which makes possible a greater degree of rationality. Of course, it could go the other way if A is overly influenced by certain aspects of popular culture and does not become more conscious of what is really beneficial (true preferences).

So much for this descriptive view. Next let's consider the three preference types in the context of a normative view of rationality. If true preferences represent what is really right and best for a person, not only in the short-term but in the long-term, not only materially and psychologically but morally and spiritually, then the ultimate of rationality, true rationality, means choosing in line with true preferences. The notion of true rationality is consistent with both of the two main concepts of rationality, instrumental rationality and the rationality of ends. First, given one's true preferences, it is rational (instrumentally) to use appropriate reason to choose the best possible means to satisfy these preferences. Second, from the standpoint of rationality of ends, it is rational to use appropriate reason to choose ends that best serve our interests, that is, choose ends reflecting our true preferences. As part of this latter process, an individual would have to examine his or her values and purposes in order to discover what is really best considering the long-term consequences, the individual's sense of morality, and what provides the individual with real happiness. Thus, behaving in a truly rational manner (following this particular normative notion of rationality) means attempting, as best as one can, to discover and then to act in accord with true preferences. This idea of true rationality embodies the recognition that except for a few rare mortals, our true preferences will be at least partially hidden from our knowledge. Nevertheless, it is the essence of true rationality to try to act in line with one's true preferences. One's ends ought to be consistent with one's true preferences. Moreover, it is anticipated that as one experiences personal growth, and thus, one's true preferences become more clearly known to oneself, one's decision-making behavior should become more in line with true rationality. This would be the case if ideally our metapreferences come to reflect our true preferences, and our actual preferences in turn become transformed in the direction of our metapreferences.[4]

MERIT GOODS AND TRUE RATIONALITY

Our analysis of true rationality implies that with respect to certain goods there is a likelihood that people will fail to make decisions that fully reflect what is really in their best interests. This brings to mind the concept of merit goods. According to Richard Musgrave, a merit good is a good 'that the appropriate authorities are justified in judging that the level of consumption as attained through the market is too low and that the authorities are therefore justified in interfering with the wishes of the consumer in order to attain a higher level of consumption of the good' (Ver Eecke, 2007: 3). As defined, a merit good, whether it has a private or public good nature, involves a governmental intervention to provide more of the good without the need for any evidence of consumer preferences supporting the intervention (p. 4). In other words, Musgrave makes the case for government intervention in the absence of any market failure (as conventionally defined) (p. 15). While Musgrave does provide some arguments justifying the idea of merit goods and thus government intervention, he is unable to provide a conceptual framework that supplies a complete and satisfactory justification for intervention (p. 4; for his partial justification, see pp. 5–7). This is where our earlier analysis comes in. Using the framework developed here, it can be argued that merit goods are goods for which there is a large persistent failure of people to consume amounts of these goods that it would be truly rational for them to consume. Thus, it is not a conventional market failure (based on actual preferences) which justifies government intervention, but a failure of people to act in accord with their true preferences which justifies government interference with the market.[5]

TOWARD BETTER UNDERSTANDING OF AND REALIZING TRUE RATIONALITY

To more fully appreciate the concepts of true rationality and true preferences, it is important to consider writings that either have anticipated one or the other of these concepts or that have developed the same or similar ideas in other words. It is hoped that reviewing these writings will produce greater insight into the nature of true rationality and the factors that enhance or retard it. Although there are rich bodies of literature (notably philosophical, spiritual, religious) on this subject, almost none of these sources uses the terms true preferences and true rationality. Nevertheless, these authors are concerned in a variety of ways with the gap between what a person wants and desires and what is best for the individual. Some of this literature is concerned with personal growth and transformation, and thus, how people might come to want what is really best for them. Below, the writings close to economics (but not necessarily written by economists), which are often somewhat philosophical in nature, are considered first, followed by noneconomic writings in philosophical, spiritual and religious veins.

The idea that some preferences are ideal, that is, genuine, real, legitimate, or true, and distinctly different from actual preferences has been articulated by a variety of authors. According to Henry Sidgwick (Rescher, 1988: 96), there is a definite gulf between 'what one wants' and 'what is good for one.' The latter is '*what one would want if* – if one were fully informed, undisturbed by passion, painstaking in visualizing consequences, etc.' In Sidgwick's view, ideal preferences are essentially fully informed preferences. Hausman and McPherson (1993: 690) agree and point out that '[actual] preferences may be based on false belief.' Thus an approximation to the ideal preferences would be preferences suitably corrected so that they are based only on true beliefs. Harsanyi (1982: 55) recognizes that:

> true preferences are the preferences he would have if he had all the relevant factual information, always reasoned with the greatest possible care, and were in a state of mind most conducive to rational choice. Given this distinction, a person's rational wants are those consistent with his true preferences.

In the view of Head (2007: 125), an important writer concerning merit goods, true preferences differ from actual (or ex ante) preferences in that they are ex post preferences, that is, they reflect the satisfactions a person actually experiences. In addition to actual and true preferences, Head distinguishes ethical or welfare-relevant preferences which are an individual's ultimate preferences. The latter preferences are higher than true preferences which in turn are higher than actual preferences in the preference ordering posited by Head.

Still another view is that ideal preferences are those we would have if we were closer to being the person we aspired to be, especially if our aspirations corresponded to universally recognized high ideals. In Rescher's (1988: 100) words, the ideal preferences are 'sufficiently enlightened preferences' for such things as 'health, normal functioning of body and mind, adequate resources, human companionship and affection, and so on.' Rescher recognizes that there may be a gap between one's professed wants or felt wants, on the one hand, and one's 'real' wants or preferences, on the other. The latter are 'what the reasonable (impartial, well-informed, well-intentioned, understanding) bystander would think that I ought to want on the basis of what is "in my best interests" ' (p. 102). Thus, one's true interests or preferences are ' "what we would want if" – if we were all those things that "being intelligent" about the conduct of one's life requires: prudent, sensible, conscientious, well-considered, and the like' (p. 104). Despite this appeal to the universal, Rescher recognizes that one's own ideal preferences will be 'shaped in the light of one's own value structure, will – quite appropriately – be different from that of another' (p. 104). Similarly, Hollis (1983: 258) states that a rational agent has rational (or true) preferences, and this 'makes every choice into a choice . . . of what or who to become.' These true preferences presumably reflect the preferences we would have if we had better qualities (the ones we aspire to), that is, fewer hangups, more wisdom, higher ideals, and so on.

Tibor Scitovsky's *The Joyless Economy* (1976) contains an analysis of preferences and rationality that resembles the argument here. In Scitovsky's view, people are overly influenced by the tastes of society's majority who have a strong actual preference for comfort (Sen, 1996: 483). If, however, these people had carefully scrutinized their options, they would have discovered another better set of preferences related to creative opportunities for stimulation that are more truly satisfying than the comforts they settle for (pp. 483–7). Because of the chasm between what people choose and what is best, or at least better, for them, their choices are not rational.

People sometimes have actual preferences that are obnoxious and antisocial; such preferences might be racist, sadistic, or the result of problematic psychological mechanisms (Hausman and McPherson, 1996: 77–80). Presumably these perverse actual preferences are inferior to nonproblematic preferences, and thus, satisfying the former would, arguably, be irrational. For one's behavior to be truly rational, one's preferences would have to be corrected to 'exclude all antisocial and problematic preferences such as sadism, envy, resentment, and malice' (Harsanyi, 1982: 56; Hausman and McPherson, 1993: 690). Such perverse preferences are far from being true preferences which, you may recall, were defined earlier as the preferences of people who had realized their highest possibilities. Moreover, true preferences are the preferences that are consistent with the kind of flourishing life that Aristotle conceived as the ideal. According to Rescher (1988: 205–7), acting rationally (in line with appropriate ends, and thus, true preferences) is an essential element in what it means to be human. It follows that we have a moral obligation to develop ourselves fully in order to realize our potential for rationality. Eliminating our obnoxious and anti-social preferences would be part of the needed self-development.

Religions generally have some teachings that correspond at least roughly to the concepts of true rationality and true preferences. After all, one purpose of religion is to persuade people to give up their actual sinful ways and to take up virtuous ways. Thus, religions generally make a distinction between what we currently want or desire and, on the other hand, what is really good for us, and therefore what we should want. Besides offering insight, religions might help its adherents realize true rationality.

First consider Buddhism. The heart of Buddha's teaching is contained in the Four Noble Truths. They are the truth of suffering (unsatisfactoriness or lack of happiness, harmony, and comfort in life); the origin of suffering, the cessation of suffering; and the path that leads to the cessation of suffering (see, for example, Karthar, 1992: 39–48; Nairn, 2000: 17–32; and Rahula, 1959: 16–50). The origin or cause of suffering is our negative emotions (aggression, greed, ignorance, attachment, jealousy and pride) that lead us to craving and grasping. These negative emotions have much to do with what we want, that is, with our actual preferences. Buddhism teaches us that if we learn about the origin of suffering and then apply the methods of the path which allow us to gain wisdom, discipline, and compassion, we can eliminate our negative emotions, and thereby, eliminate our suffering. In effect, we can transform our actual preferences to preferences that will provide us true happiness or enlightenment. At the core of this transformation is giving up attachment to materialistic or gross forms of pleasure for the more refined and superior kinds, learning to appreciate 'temperance and restraint and [to] enjoy the immaterial or spiritual forms of pleasure' (Koller and Koller, 1991: 375–6). Following the ideal Buddhist path can be interpreted as acting in accord with transformed (or true) preferences which arguably is truly rational if it really does lead to what is best for us (p. 376). It should be noted that Hinduism is very similar to Buddhism in these essential respects.[6]

Clive and Cara Beed (1999) provide an interesting Christian perspective (Biblical Christian realism) on the nature of rationality. According to the Beeds, true rationality is manifested by Christian believers who realize the 'supernatural influence of the life of Christ,' and thus, are able 'to achieve God's desired balance between self-interest and altruism in specific decision-making situations' (p. 508). The 'spiritual input of Christ . . . is regarded as crucial' in that it allows the decision maker to consider a 'full range of benefits and costs' without the necessity of 'conscious and deliberate evaluation processes' (p. 510). In effect, it is argued that Christian believers' molded preferences (presumably different from their original actual preferences and from nonChristians' preferences) enable them to manifest true rationality, which is better than what nonChristians can do and better than the rationality depicted in mainstream neoclassical economics. This 'Biblical rationality leans more towards non-instrumental than instrumental rationality' (p. 510).

Islam, although quite different in its particulars, is similar to the other religions in having teachings that correspond to the concepts of true preferences and true rationality. According to the Qur'an (or Koran), there are two opposing motivational tendencies that act to determine how humans behave (Biraima, 1998/1999). On the one hand, people could be 'motivated solely by the desire to maximize worldly pleasures' in which case an individual's 'whims become his God.' Here the 'self is dominated by the motives of debauchery (greed, niggardliness, arrogance, envy, . . . etc.)' (p. 212). On the other hand, people could be 'motivated solely by the desire to accumulate "good deeds" that yield thankfulness.' Here 'the self is completely dominated by the positive motives of piety (patience, humility, contentment, generosity, . . . etc.).' One is acting 'in complete submission to God and . . . consistent with the purposes of God' (p. 213). The latter clearly corresponds to what Muslims would consider to be true preferences. The actual preferences of an individual would depend on the relative strength of the two opposing motivational tendencies. True rationality from the standpoint of the Qur'an would be acting fully in line with the true preferences of one's 'tranquil self', that is, the motivations of one's higher self (p. 213).

In sum, through our brief examination of three major religions, we find that each teaches that certain kinds of all-too-common, but inferior, behavior patterns (actual preferences) should be relinquished in favor of alternative patterns (true preferences) involving more disciplined, altruistic, pious behavior that will lead their adherents along the path to God or enlightenment, and thereby, to long-run happiness. In other words, each of these religions has a distinctly different perspective concerning what true rationality means and how it can be realized. Interestingly, the different religious perspectives on true rationality have more in common with each other than they do with the mainstream economic concept of rationality.

COMPARING ECONOMIC RATIONALITY AND TRUE RATIONALITY

Socio-Economy Wide Comparisons: Efficiency

If all decision-making agents in the socio-economy are economically rational, carefully calculating marginal benefits and costs, then as we know, resource allocation ought to be Pareto efficient (assuming no externalities or other violations of the assumptions of the competitive market ideal). In this case, benefits and costs would be calculated and decisions made taking into account only purely utilitarian considerations based on whatever people's wants and desires are. This is familiar territory.

But what would the socio-economy be like if instead decision-making agents were truly rational? Decisions would not be made on the basis of utilitarian considerations alone; ends, not just means, would now matter. Presumably decision makers would take into account noneconomic as well as economic factors, subtle externalities, moral/ethical considerations, and even religious/spiritual considerations. The truly rational decision maker is one who manifests altruism, not pure self-interest, and wisdom, not simply good logic and cognitive ability. Thus, where negative or positive externalities exist, it could be argued that the truly rational decision maker would not behave in the classic self-interested, short-run, maximizing fashion, either imposing costs on society or failing to provide benefits to society. If so, this would represent a dramatic improvement in the Pareto efficiency of resource allocation. However, overall, the economy with truly rational agents would not be strictly comparable to the one with economically rational agents. Presumably resource allocation in the truly rational case would be ideal, but it is not a strict economic ideal; it is a wise human ideal which would be associated with the highest possible well-being, well-being in a much broader inclusive human sense, not the utilitarian, materialistic well-being that economists tend to focus on (for a broader treatment of well-being, see Tomer, 2002).

The respective resource allocation ideals are useful insofar as they serve to indicate problematic departures from the ideal, problems for which government policy measures might be formulated to remedy. The Pareto efficiency standard has helped to identify economic activities for which resource allocation is inefficiently large, for example, medical care, industries with high levels of pollution, and inefficiently small, for example, public transportation, education. Economically rational allocation, however, must inevitably reflect people's wants and desires which in turn reflect prevailing societal and individual pathologies. So it is limited as a way to make valid social criticisms. The truly rational allocation ideal would be more difficult to know, but, assuming it could be known reasonably well, its usefulness would go far beyond indicating inefficiency in resource allocation. It could be used to understand how societal pathology and bias have distorted resource allocation and to understand how wisdom might be applied to correct the situation in order to make people really better off. Suppose, for example, a society's people were overly attached, even addicted, to a type of food, for example, fast food, with the consequence that this pathology contributed to them being overweight and undernourished. The promise of using the truly rational allocation standard is that it would help to identify this situation and what, if anything, could be done about it. On the other hand, use of the purely utilitarian efficiency standard is unlikely to help one gain insight into these kinds of pathology.

An Important Difficulty with True Rationality

For scholars to provide good explanations regarding rationality concepts, it helps if they have developed their own rational capabilities. So it is typical for economics students who are learning about economically rational behavior to emulate economic rationality and to take pride in the capabilities for rationality that they have developed. For most students of economics, developing their economic rationality is not too difficult. It requires learning certain concepts and developing the ability to be logical and analyze situations using these concepts. Although some students may have to struggle to overcome or control some of their irrational tendencies, becoming economically rational is to a great extent a matter of increasing a certain type of cognitive capability. This is something that standard educational processes are well designed to achieve.

To become truly rational, on the other hand, is a much greater task, a much less cognitive one; it is not an endeavor that standard educational processes are well geared for. Whereas economic rationality involves maximizing the desired outcome given one's actual preferences, true rationality requires behaving in line with true preferences. Thus, part of the process of becoming truly rational is to transform one's actual preferences in the direction of one's true preferences. This would require aspiring to know one's true preferences, becoming aware of them, and reorienting ones actual preferences in line with them. This implies making progress toward overcoming one's emotional difficulties, one's neurotic behavior, and one's egoism, the kinds of things that get in the way of appreciating what is really good for us. It also implies correcting one's erroneous beliefs. Further, as part of this process, one would need to develop greater maturity, emotional balance, wisdom, intuition and other aspects of realizing one's high potential. Obviously, these are not trivial pursuits.

From the above it is very apparent that developing one's capability for true rationality requires much more than an investment in the standard types of human capital utilizing regular educational processes. It would require, for instance, a significant investment in personal capital, particularly raising one's emotional intelligence. For example, suppose that one's lack of patience is the personal quality that in decision making causes one to be biased against choosing the kind of options that would be best for oneself in the long-term. Thus, to increase one's true rationality capability, one must learn, and expend resources, to become more patient, thereby making an appropriate personal capital investment. Similarly, a person could through other types of maturational learning become less angry, more disciplined, more enthusiastic, more focused and committed to one's goals, more generous, more compassionate, less attached to desired outcomes, more ethical, more empathetic, more intuitive, more willing to take risks, more creative, less fearful, less worried, more hopeful, more altruistic, less susceptible to discouragement, more even tempered, more temperate, more joyful, more appreciative of beauty and spiritual aspects of life, and so on. Again, although it is possible to raise one's true rationality capability, it is a very big endeavor.

Perhaps it is already clear that placing true rationality at the heart of economics instead of economic rationality could conceivably cause great difficulties for the economic profession and economic education. Economics is hard enough to learn; introducing an appreciation of true rationality and an expectation that students make some progress toward realizing true rationality into the curriculum would be a great challenge

IMPLICATIONS FOR ECONOMICS AND POLICY

If the idea of true preferences is valid, and if on the average people's actual preferences are not close to their true preferences, and if the highest long-run well-being can only come from satisfying true preferences, it follows that people's actual preferences are on the average inferior, and people's well-being could be improved by helping them change their actual preferences in the direction of their true preferences. While this proposition goes very much against the grain of modern economics, there is a significant intellectual tradition supporting it, most notably the writings of John Stuart Mill. Mill expressed the view that people would be better off if they had different wants, wants for more valuable things, the higher pleasures (McPherson, 1982: 268, 270). Although he was a strong defender of individual liberty, Mill believed that 'society was justified within appropriate limits in encouraging [the] cultivation' of better wants (p. 270). What Mill advocated was 'reform [of] the major institutions of society so that people would come to want things that were more valuable, both to themselves and to society' (p. 268). Besides Mill, economic writers such as 'Jeremy Bentham and Alfred Marshall, were [also] alert to the benefits of encouraging public-regarding tastes' (Rhoads, 1990: 93). In contrast, contemporary economists have been extremely slow to condemn even disgusting tastes and have hardly bothered to encourage tastes yielding positive externalities for society (p. 93). Present day government leaders (regardless of political persuasion), however, for example in the US, seem to have more understanding of this issue than contemporary economists. Several years ago the US federal government announced a program designed to encourage people to get more exercise. Apparently, people's actual preferences for exercise is deficient, and people would be healthier on average, and better off, if they preferred more exercise and acted on those preferences.

A question that arises in this context is how the market performs in helping people have their true preferences. Has the market and the institutions of the market economy helped people improve their preferences? In *Preference Pollution*, David George (2001) provides much evidence that unrestricted commercial persuasion designed to shape tastes has, if anything, caused a lowering of our tastes, not an improvement. Thus, there is a 'market failure' that in some cases would justify government corrective action.

CONCLUSION

Is it rational to choose whatever good or service best satisfies one's existing preferences? If so, when a dog selects one dog food over another, the dog is being rational, even if the food chosen is known to cause sickness and death in dogs. For this and many other reasons outlined in this chapter, the normative concept of economic rationality used in mainstream economics today is deficient. This chapter argues that the appropriate normative concept of rationality is true rationality. To help economists understand the significance of true rationality, this chapter provides a framework involving three types of preferences, a framework that links noneconomic insights with economic concepts. To be truly rational, one must decide among alternatives based on one's true preferences, not simply one's actual preferences. To be truly rational is to make the choices that are really the best for you, all things considered. To become truly rational requires appropriate investment in intangible capital, especially personal capital. True rationality is an ideal that few individuals can attain; nevertheless it is a useful ideal. Utilizing the notion of true rationality, we can examine one's socio-economy in order to learn not only whether resources are being used efficiently but whether resources are being used wisely, that is, to attain the highest possible well-being of the population. In this regard, it is important to utilize a concept of rationality that relates to human being's highest potential, not simply a concept that can apply to any animal. If mankind is to flourish, to reach toward its true potential, it is not enough to strive for economic rationality, mankind must learn how to become more truly rational. We need to move beyond the rationality of economic man and toward the true rationality of human man.

NOTES

1. Hamish Stewart (1995) argues that 'economists should adopt a broader concept of reason, one which recognizes that rationality and irrationality can be characteristic of ends as well as of means, and that agents try to use their reason to distinguish among goals and choose between them.'
2. As David George has pointed out to me, reflective thinking may not be nearly enough to produce desired changes in preferences. It may be a complex matter to shape ourselves.
3. A person might, thus, be able to choose in a more truly rational manner than would be expected based on his or her actual preferences. This presumes that in choosing the person would apply the preferences he or she anticipates and aspires to.
4. From the standpoint of the model involved, true preferences can be considered an exogenous variable while metapreferences and actual preferences are endogenous variables.
5. In a private communication, Wilfried Ver Eecke explained to me that the merit good concept also encompasses types of goods 'where individuals cannot be expected to have the information or the power to do something significant: assigning property rights, antitrust legislation, credit and banking control, etc.'
6. For useful Gandhian perspectives, see Diwan and Lutz (1985).

REFERENCES

Adler, Mortimer J. (1978), *Aristotle for Everybody: Difficult Thought Made Easy*, New York, Macmillan.

Beed, Clive and Cara Beed (1999), 'A Christian perspective on neoclassical rational choice theory,' *International Journal of Social Economics*, **26**(4), 501–20.

Biraima, Muhammad H. (1998/1999). 'From rationality to righteousness: a universal theory of action,' *Humanomics*, **14**(4) and **15**(1), 206–61.

Diwan, Romesh and Mark Lutz (eds) (1985), *Essays in Gandhian Economics*, New Delhi, Gandhi Peace Foundation.

George, David (2001), *Preference Pollution: How Markets Create the Desires We Dislike*, Ann Arbor: The University of Michigan Press.

Harsanyi, John C. (1982), 'Morality and the theory of rational behavior,' in Amartya Sen and Bernard Williams (eds), *Utilitarianism and Beyond*, Cambridge, Cambridge University Press, pp. 39–62.

Hausman, Daniel M. and Michael S. McPherson (1993), 'Taking ethics seriously: economics and contemporary moral philosophy,' *Journal of Economic Literature*, **31**(2), 671–731.

Hausman, Daniel M. and Michael S. McPherson (1996), *Economic Analysis and Moral Philosophy*, Cambridge: Cambridge University Press.

Head, John G. (2007), 'On merit wants: reflections on the evolution, normative status and policy relevance of a controversial public finance concept,' in Wilfried Ver Eecke (ed.), *An Anthology Regarding Merit Goods: The Unfinished Ethical*

Revolution in Economic Theory, West Lafayette, IN: Purdue University Press, pp. 114–51.
Heap, Shaun Hargreaves (1989), *Rationality in Economics*, Oxford: Basil Blackwell.
Heap, Shaun Hargreaves (1992), *The Theory of Choice: A Critical Guide*, Oxford: Blackwell.
Hollis, Martin (1983), 'Rational preferences,' *The Philosophical Forum*, **14**(3–4), 246–62.
Hollis, Martin (1992), 'Autonomy,' in S. H. Heap (ed.), *The Theory of Choice: A Critical Guide*, Oxford: Blackwell, pp. 73–89.
Karthar, Khempo (1992), *Dharma Paths*, Ithaca, NY: Snow Lion.
Koller, John and Patricia Koller (1991), *A Sourcebook in Asian Philosophy*, New York: Macmillan.
McPherson, Michael (1982), 'Mill's moral theory and the problem of preference change,' *Ethics*, **92**, 252–73.
McPherson, Michael (1984), 'On Schelling, Hirschman, and Sen: revising the conception of self,' *Partisan Review*, **51**(2), 236–47.
Nairn, Rob (2000), *What Is Meditation? Buddhism for Everyone*, Boston, MA: Shambhala.
Rahula, Walpola (1959), *What the Buddha Taught*, New York: Grove Press.
Raines, J. Patrick and Clarence R. Jung (1992), 'Schumpeter and Knight on economic and political rationality: a comparative restatement,' *Journal of Socio-Economics*, **21**(2), 109–24.
Rescher, Nicholas (1988), *Rationality: A Philosophical Inquiry into the Nature and the Rationale of Reason*, Oxford: Clarendon Press.
Rhoads, S. (1990), 'Economists on tastes and preferences,' in James H. Nichols and Colin Wright, (eds), *From Political Economy to Economics and Back?* San Francisco, CA: Institute for Contemporary Studies.
Scitovsky, Tibor (1976), *The Joyless Economy*, Oxford, Oxford University Press.
Segal, Jerome M. (1991), 'Alternative conceptions of the economic realm,' in Richard M. Coughlin (ed.), *Morality, Rationality, and Efficiency: New Perspectives on Socio-Economics*, Armonk, NY: M.E. Sharpe.
Sen, Amartya (1996), 'Rationality, joy and freedom,' *Critical Review*, **10**(4), 481–94.
Stewart, Hamish (1995), 'A critique of instrumental reason in economics,' *Economics and Philosophy*, **11**(1), 57–83.
Sugden, Robert (1991), 'Rational choice: a survey of contributions from economics and philosophy,' *Economic Journal*, **101**, 751–85.
Tomer, John F. (1996), 'Good habits and bad habits: a new age socio-economic model of preference formation,' *Journal of Socio-Economics*, **25**(6), 619–38.
Tomer, John F. (2002), 'Human well-being: a new approach based on overall and ordinary functionings,' *Review of Social Economy*, **60**(1), 23–45.
Ver Eecke, Wilfried (2007), *An Anthology Regarding Merit Goods: The Unfinished Ethical Revolution in Economic Theory*, West Lafayette, IN: Purdue University Press.

PART IV

Implications for government policy and the discipline of economics

The three chapters of Part IV are concerned with the implications of the preceding intangible capital analyses for government policy and the discipline of economics. Chapter 12 examines the kinds of intangible capital related government policy that make sense, particularly the kind that encourage needed investment in intangible capital. Chapter 13 provides a detailed analysis of one such policy; it develops a proposal for a new kind of environmental policy, a commitment approach. In this policy, government encouragement of high performance organizations' investment in intangible capital is a key element. Chapter 14 explores the different concepts of human nature in the different schools of economic thought, from the economic man of mainstream economics to the different heterodox men of the different heterodox economic schools. This exploration helps one understand that economic development is not entirely a material process; it is partly a human process, and intangible capital formation is an important part of that process.

12. Government policy and intangible capital

It is widely acknowledged that governments should play an important role in fostering investment in standard human capital through the provision of education and training. Should governments play a similar role with respect to the more intangible forms of human capital? What about noncognitive human capital? Different forms of personal capital? Social capital?

First, it is doubtful that there is much of a need for a standard government regulating role utilizing laws and regulations that correct for the problematic incentives associated with positive or negative externalities. Rather than the government as regulator, what may be needed more is the government as coach in which the government role is the same as or quite similar to the government role in certain kinds of industrial policy (see Tomer, 1993: 216–20). Let's start by considering industrial policy efforts to foster organizational change in firms. Charles Hampden-Turner (1988: 44) has asked: 'Is it possible . . . for capitalist free enterprise to be "coached" to greater humanity and success?' His answer (and my answer as well) is a resounding yes! Firms' socio-economic performance can be raised through appropriate coaching. Coaching makes sense when we conceive of firms as organisms that learn, organisms that not only compete but cooperate, and organisms that are involved in complex social networks. Further, the coaching approach follows when we conceive of firms as fully human, socio-economic entities whose learning (and cooperation) can be nurtured, facilitated, prodded, and otherwise encouraged. It is through such means that the human firm's capacity for competitiveness and responsibility can be raised and, thereby, the economic failure addressed. In contrast to the regulatory approach, the emphasis in coaching is not to get the firm to do the opposite of what it would naturally do but to provide the firm with plenty of opportunity and a conducive environment that will enable it to realize its highest potential in its relationship with society.

The government as coach, *a la* industrial policy, is oriented to developing the economy's capacity, and this generally means developing the capacity of human firms. In essence, the government is assisting in intangible capital formation in firms. Consider some of the specific roles of the government coach. First, an economy suffering from lack of competitiveness might be the result of firms whose organizational learning is deficient. Government might be able to provide the critical help necessary to enable firms to overcome the obstacles to the needed learning (Reich, 1983; Johnson, 1984). If this aid were successful, the targeted firms would have gained competitive advantage, and the nation's productivity would have been raised. Second, poor performance of the economy might be related to firms that lack flexibility and integration, or firms that lack the organizational procedures necessary for rational decision making, or firms that lack the right kind of leadership, and so forth. Conceivably, the government as coach might be able to diagnose these problems and supply the key kinds of assistance enabling them to boost their competitiveness. If the government were to succeed in these efforts, this would develop the nation's intangible collective human capacities, especially its organizational capital and personal capital, and would thereby enable the country to avoid deindustrialization and reach its economic growth goals.

The government coaching role need not be limited to dealing with the problem of competitiveness. Another major role for the government qua coach is developing the firm's, and thus the economy's capacity for responsible behavior. This would address the kinds of economic failure that stem from irresponsible behavior. It is possible for firms to find socially responsible solutions to negative externality situations, thereby obviating the use by government of regulatory incentives. The policy implication is that the government coach can help firms achieve these highly responsible solutions to externality-related failure situations through actions designed either to assist firms in improving their internal capabilities or to improve the external social influences on firms. Other situations may require the government coach to provide critical knowledge or to reduce undesirable and unintended regulatory influences.

In the above situations, the government coach is fostering a type of IC formation in firms which is expected to improve the performance of these firms. In Chapter 6, evidence regarding a long-term decline in children's emotional intelligence (a type of PC) was cited along with the finding that America's stock of SC has declined over the last generation. This suggested that a case could be made for government actions to reverse these unfavorable trends. Perhaps a government coaching role is needed, but presumably a different type of coaching than called for by industrial policy. Also in Chapter 6, 'human factor depravity,' a kind of PC (and perhaps SC) deficiency, was mentioned as a significant obstacle to economic development in some less developed countries. This suggests the need for a government policy akin to industrial policy to foster the kind of IC formation which would eliminate or counteract this obstacle.

Carneiro and Heckman are concerned with certain characteristic noncognitive HC (or PC) deficiencies of young people in the US. Their policy recommendations, however, have a greater resemblance to conventional HC policies than to industrial policy coaching. Carneiro and Heckman's (2003: 137–208) analysis leads them to the conclusion that noncognitive skills and traits (human capital in individuals) involving motivation, self-discipline and social skills are highly valued in the labor market as well as in other aspects of life. Poor levels of these noncognitive qualities are often a consequence of bad family environments with poor parenting. Not surprisingly, these effects show up early in childhood. Moreover, Carneiro and Heckman find that early childhood interventions involving noncognitive HC investments in children from disadvantaged environments have shown remarkable success, producing lasting favorable effects on learning and motivation, even substantially reducing criminal offenses ten years later (pp. 164–5, 170–171). Mentoring and motivational programs oriented to disadvantaged teenagers also have been found to be effective, realizing high payoffs in terms of learning, subsequent employment and earnings (pp. 146, 174, 181). Based on these findings, Carneiro and Heckman recommend that the US government should do more to invest in noncognitive HC, especially that of children from disadvantaged backgrounds who are subject to poor discipline and lack of encouragement at home (p. 147).

The common thread in these different policy recommendations is for government to foster the development of some kind of intangible human capacity that is crucially important for the growth of the economy and is experiencing some kind of blocked growth or development. Presumably because of this blockage, the economy overall is performing substantially below its potential. Clearly in such a situation, it makes sense for the government to facilitate a process by which the critical IC formation takes place, eliminating the blockages. Note that instead of targeting economic growth, the government could act directly to foster the nation's human well-being and rationality by facilitating investment in some other types of intangible human capacity. The following three paragraphs briefly reconsider examples of government policy from earlier chapters in which fostering IC investment is at the heart of the matter.

Chapter 7 deals with the importance of intangible factors for the success of a socio-economic system's transition from socialism to capitalism. A socio-economic system's behavior and performance is determined by both 'hard' and 'soft' elements. Hard elements such as organizational and financial structure and legal and political systems are relatively tangible. Soft elements such as the different types of IC which are characteristic of the system and adapted to it are relatively intangible. To transition successfully to a new system requires not only changes in the hard elements but a lengthy, difficult period in which the economy slowly disinvests itself of old obsolete IC (associated with socialism) and invests in the type of IC adapted to the new system (capitalism). It is important for the country to adopt a transition strategy (akin to an industrial policy) that allows time for and facilitates the necessary IC formation. There is reason to believe that a key factor in the failed transitions in a number of the Eastern European countries was that these nations' rapid radical (neoliberal) reform strategies did not consider the necessity of creating PC and SC adapted to their new market systems. Due to the lack of gradualism, the resultant systemic shock unduly retarded the transition's progress and severely raised the cost of transition in these countries. In sum, well-adapted IC is crucial to the successful functioning of any socio-economic system. A national government's transition strategy cannot ignore this. If it does, the consequences of maladapted IC are likely to be dire for the system's economic performance.

The idea that government should help us achieve well-being is not exactly new. National governments' economic policies have long been targeted at economic problems threatening to the material well-being of its nations' citizens. But Chapter 8 brings a new dimension to this issue insofar as it demonstrates that human well-being is related not just to one's ordinary, lower functionings but also to one's higher functionings. No doubt, each of us is responsible for our own well-being. Each of us must figure out our life's purposes, deal with our hangups, try to improve our interpersonal competencies, and the like. But we must also acknowledge that we live in society, and therefore, share with others not only common social resources but common obstacles to achieving the good, flourishing life (high well-being). Consequently, there is a case to be made that government should help us with some of the more compelling of our common problems, ones related to these common obstacles. If too many of us are getting caught in addictions or becoming obese, perhaps our government ought to help. The government as coach might at least ease the way and help us overcome the worst of these problems, thereby raising our well-being. Fostering appropriate investment in PC and SC is arguably at the heart of most of these problem solutions.

Chapter 10 focuses on preferences and their formation and Chapter 11 focuses on normative rationality in decision making. An important argument common to both chapters is that people's actual preferences might not only be not preferred by them but might be inferior, that is, not what is really best for them. It follows that individuals would be better off choosing in line with their true preferences rather than their actual ones. And it may well be that many people's true preferences have common elements. If so, we could say with good reason, for example, that people generally would be better off giving up their actual preferences for junk food and adopting preferences for more healthy food (say, forming a preference for fresh juice over soda, a preference closer to their true preferences). If the junky food can really be shown to have sufficiently adverse consequences for well-being, there is a case for government measures to encourage such better preferences (and thus, better consumption patterns). In line with this, it could be argued (as it has been in New York State) that school children should not be offered junk food at school cafeterias. The government as regulator and/or coach, according to this rationale, should attempt to improve preferences, habits and choices, leading people to not only better behavior, and resultant improved well-being, but improved IC that supports the higher level of well-being.

The arguments supporting governmental fostering of investment in standard human capital are widely accepted because the role of education and training in contributing to greater income, productivity, and economic growth, not to mention higher well-being, is quite well understood. The role of the more intangible types of IC in contributing to productivity, economic growth, earnings, as well as well-being and rationality, is less well understood and accepted. As a consequence, convincing people that government ought to play an important role in fostering these more intangible types of IC formation is likely to be a harder sell. Building on the more detailed explanations provided in earlier chapters, this chapter has explained why, at least in a number of important cases, a government role encouraging IC formation makes a lot of sense. Consistent with this thinking, Chapter 13, develops a proposal for a new kind of environmental policy. It argues for a 'commitment approach' to environmental policy.

REFERENCES

Carneiro, Pedro and James J. Heckman (2003), 'Human capital policy,' in James J. Heckman and Alan B. Krueger (eds), *Inequality in America: What Role for Human Capital Policies?* Cambridge, MA: MIT Press, pp. 137–239.

Hampden-Turner, Charles (1988), 'Three images of government: the referee, the coach, and the abolitionist,' *New Management*, **6**, 43–9.

Johnson, Chalmers (1984), *The Industrial Policy Debate*, San Francisco, CA: Institute for Contemporary Studies.

Reich, Robert B. (1983), *The Next American Frontier*, New York: New York Times Books.

Tomer, John F. (1993), 'A new rationale for industrial policy: developing the capabilities of the learning firm,' *International Review of Applied Economics*, **7**(2), 208–22.

13. Why we need a commitment approach to environmental policy

with Thomas R. Sadler*

According to Amartya Sen (1977) in his classic 'Rational Fools' article: 'To run an organization entirely on incentives to personal gain is pretty much a hopeless task' (pp. 333–5). This comment regarding employer–employee relations would seem to apply similarly to regulator-regulated relations with regard to environmental protection. Sen might also have said: 'To protect the environment entirely using incentives to business gain is pretty much a hopeless task.' Following Sen, in these situations, a large dose of commitment involving non-egoistic motivation is needed (pp. 327–9).

The principal reason why economists have generally advocated environmental policies based solely on incentives is that their conception of business behavior and motivation derives from the neoclassical model of the firm. While businesses certainly do respond to profit incentives, firms' behavior is also greatly influenced by socio-political considerations and their organizational capabilities. Firms are, more than ever, recognized as socio-economic entities embedded in society. In recent years, a significant group of businesses that are highly innovative, productive, competitive and socially responsible has emerged. These high performing organizations are capable of executing strategies that enable them to be financially successful and environmentally responsible at the same time. These are not the firms that policy makers envisioned when they formulated command and control and market incentive environmental policies. Because of this and other new business realities, there is a need for new types of environmental policies. Thus, the first purpose of this chapter is to propose and formulate a new class of environmental policies, policies based on a commitment approach. The second purpose is to explain why the neoclassical model is deficient as a basis for environmental policy and to explicate the nature of a more appropriate model.

THE NEOCLASSICAL FIRM AND ITS POLICY IMPLICATIONS

The neoclassical firm is the representative firm that produces and sells its output in order to maximize its owners' profit. Its marginal private costs (MPC), the costs borne by the firm, rise with the firm's output. As the firm increases its output, it also generates costs not borne by the firm, that is, its external costs (for example, various types of pollution). These are the costs borne by the firm's neighbors. The marginal external cost (MEC) (or marginal damage) is the increase in the dollar value of harm to neighbors caused by an additional amount of output. The marginal social cost (MSC) is the sum of the firm's MPC and MEC. The model is adapted to the environment by assuming that the firm emits a single, stable, well-defined point-source pollutant. Further, the model contains a variety of unrealistic economic assumptions one of which is that firms, in singlemindedly attempting to maximize profits, never voluntarily internalize costs that they might have been able to impose on others.

Economists typically draw policy implications directly from the neoclassical model. Since inefficiency arises because the firm ignores the external cost it imposes on its neighbors, the policy implication is that government should impose a measure that forces the firm to consider its external costs in its decision making, effectively internalizing these costs. To accomplish this, economists generally prescribe market incentive policies that, by internalizing the external cost, will induce firms to produce the profit maximizing output that coincides exactly with the society's efficient output. Consistent with this, economists generally consider command and control (C&C) regulations to be less desirable than market incentive ones insofar as firms' behavior in response to these C&C regulations is not expected to produce an efficient outcome.

Both market incentive and command and control policies may be considered to be control-oriented policies. Control-oriented policies are designed to control pollution through the use of rewards and penalties administered by the government in order to attain a government's chosen goal. Control-oriented policies are distinguished by the fact that little is expected of the firms whose pollution is being controlled. That is, these firms are not expected to make commitments, take responsibility, be autonomous, be worthy of trust, and so on. These are firms which behave in neoclassical fashion and are merely expected to respond to incentives or comply with regulatory requirements. In this view, firms are the problem, and governments try to limit the damage stemming from their problematic behavior by using policies that control a key aspect of their environmental behavior.

TOWARDS A MORE REALISTIC CONCEPTION OF FIRM ENVIRONMENTAL BEHAVIOR

The Firm as a Socio-Economic Entity

Contrary to the received wisdom of mainstream economics, business firms are not simply neoclassical machines. Even for theoretical purposes, it does not make sense to ignore the human and socio-economic nature of firms (Tomer, 1999: 4–9). From the neoclassical perspective, firms' decision makers acting on behalf of owners choose the course of action leading to maximum profit. In its single-minded pursuit of profit, the neoclassical firm takes into account not only economic incentives coming directly from the markets in which it participates but considers the explicit regulatory incentives imposed by government regulators who are attempting to correct for externalities (especially negative ones). See Figure 13.1. But in its decision making, the neoclassical firm does not consider external social or political influences, does not consider internal relationships or ethical obligations, and is not considered to have a responsibility to society or stakeholders (other than stockholders).

In contrast to the neoclassical firm is the firm as human organism with its socio-politico-economic nature. This socio-economic (SE) firm is part of society; its actions affect society, and it is affected by socio-politico-economic influences. Following Mark Granovetter (1985) and other sociologists, the modern firm is best conceived of as partially embedded in society. While the SE firm responds to perceived profit opportunities, it also acts in accord with moral values, commitments to society and community, and other social bonds and influences depending on the web of socio-politico-economic relationships in which it is involved. The firm's decision makers are often motivated by sociability, approval, status, power, wealth, and even occasionally altruism.

The SE firm's internal organizational capabilities are the key determinants of how the firm responds to the opportunities and incentives it confronts. Among these are the firm's capabilities for: (a) rational organizational decision making; (b) socially responsible behavior; (c) entrepreneurial behavior; and (d) organizational learning. These capabilities derive to a great degree from the firm's investments in intangible capital, particularly organizational capital (Tomer, 1987, 1999) and personal capital (Tomer, 2003).

The SE firm is subject to two main types of external social influences, the macro- and the micro-social forces. The macro-social forces reflect broad community and societal influences, and thus, high level norms and moral values. They also reflect the public's awareness, concerns, goals and demands. Macro-social forces are diffuse and encourage firms to behave in society's

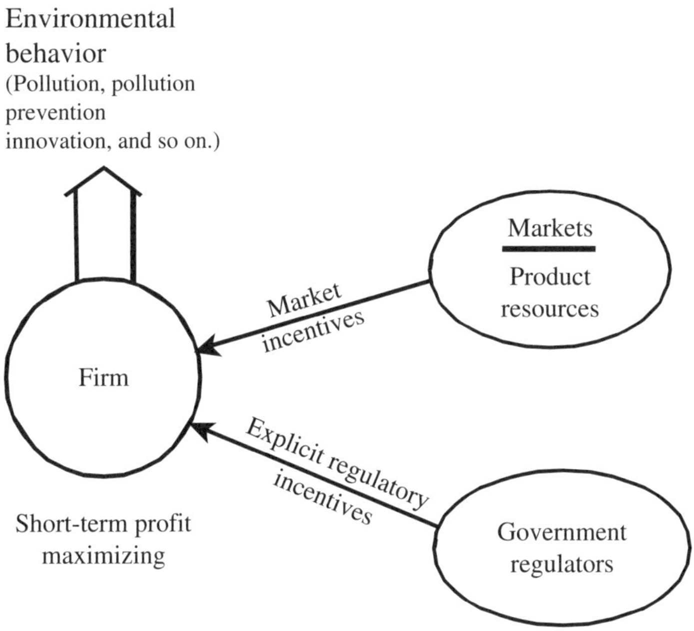

Source: Tomer (1992: 121).

Figure 13.1 Neoclassical model of firm's behavior

overall interest. Public attitudes against environmental degradation and in favor of environmental preservation are an example. Generally, businesses attempt to accommodate to these macro-social forces in order to gain a favorable public image especially in the eyes of its important stakeholders.

The micro social forces are the specific social influences on a firm from extra-firm institutions and infrastructures. Extra-firm institutions include educational institutions, trade associations, suppliers, and consultants, and infrastructures include such things as standard industry and managerial practice. The micro-forces are direct, immediate and salient. They often reflect fears, anxieties, prejudices and social self-interests, and thus, firms' conformance to them tends to block progressive change. On the other hand, the micro-social forces might provide the social encouragement firms need to raise their environmental performance level. Note that macro- and micro-social forces may not be in accord. For example, businesses may experience generalized public pressure to innovatively reduce pollution while at the same time experiencing pressure to conform to traditional practices from some of the institutions (for example, suppliers, consultants) with which they interact regularly.

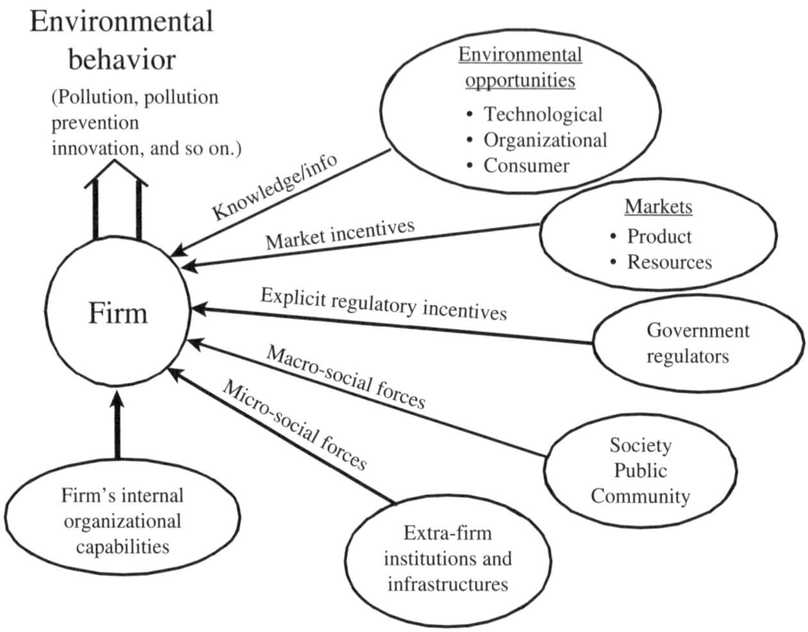

Source: Tomer (1992: 131)

Figure 13.2 Model of the socio-economic firm's environmental behavior

Because of its internal qualities and capabilities and because of the external social forces on it, the SE firm can be expected to behave very differently from the neoclassical firm even though both are subject to the same market and regulatory incentives. Figure 13.2 depicts the firm as an environmental actor and decision maker and the main influences on its behavior. It is useful to conceive of the firm and the other actors with which it interacts to be an environmental system.

The Ideal SE Firm and High Performance Organizations

Actual firms ordinarily manifest some degree of inefficiency and irresponsibility owing either to insufficient investment in intangible capital or discouragement from its external socio-political environment. In contrast, the ideal firm, the Z firm, which is a special case of the SE firm, has developed all its internal organizational capabilities as much as possible, thereby reaching its highest human potential in the sense of being both highly competitive and highly responsible (Tomer, 1999: 9–10). When confronted with a negative externality situation, the Z firm, instead of opportunistically imposing costs on others, can be expected to find a solution that is both acceptable to its community/society and sufficiently profitable in the long run. While no actual firms conform exactly to the Z ideal, there is increasing evidence regarding a group of businesses whose characteristics and behavior have a lot in common with the Z ideal. These businesses are the High Performance Organizations (HPOs), firms that are highly competitive and innovative as well as highly socially responsible. One group of high performing businesses which have gotten a fair amount of attention in the managerial literature and also, but to a lesser extent, the economic literature are businesses with High Performance Work Systems (HPWS). HPWS businesses are sometimes known as high involvement or high commitment organizations; they are organizations based on employee involvement, commitment, and empowerment, not employee control (see, for example, Pfeffer, 1998). HPWSs use an involvement-oriented approach which is very different from the control-oriented approach typical of hierarchical or bureaucratic organizations (Lawler, 1992). An increasing number of studies have documented the financial and economic performance superiority of HPWS organizations (for a short review, see Tomer, 2001: 65–7). The most important reason for this superiority is that workers in HPWS are not agents of principals, are not controlled by structures of incentives, but have become owners or principals in their outlook and motivation (p. 72). One way to think about HPOs is that they are HPWS companies that have not only highly developed their human relations systems but they have highly developed their capability for social responsibility.

HPOs and the Environment

Richard Florida and several coauthors using business survey data find much evidence that environmentally innovative and responsible companies are also high performing organizations in other respects. Among the advanced environmental practices cited in these studies are the use of environmental management systems (EMS), pollution prevention, recycling and green product design. Florida and Davison (2001: 67–8) find that:

> Green companies tend to be more innovative in general and their adoption of advanced environmental practices stems from a deep commitment to finding innovative solutions to reduce waste and improve efficiency. Innovative manufacturing plants also tend to adopt an interrelated bundle of innovative practices such as self-managing work teams, employee input in decision making, quality management, and so on . . . Nearly twice as many high-adopters [of the innovative environmental practices] had total quality management programs and just-in-time systems for inventory control. High-adopters were far more likely to be ISO 14000 certified than other plants.

Reminiscent of their zero defects and zero inventory manufacturing practices, many high performing organizations have set their targets on zero emissions (Florida, 1996: 85). In many of these companies, their total quality management (TQM) practice has been extended to become total quality environmental management (TQEM) (p. 91). In addition, Florida *et al.* (2001) find that firms which have invested in a particular bundle of organizational capabilities including specialized environmental management systems such as environmental performance monitoring systems are the ones most likely to respond to external opportunities by implementing innovative environmental practices. In sum, Florida's (1996: 100) evidence indicates that 'adoption of innovative environmental practices is an element of a more general strategy of productivity-enhancing manufacturing process improvement on the part of [these] firms.' In other words, HPOs seem to have made a strong commitment to high environmental quality that is part of their overall commitment to high quality/performance.

HPOS AND THE NEED FOR AN ALTERNATIVE TO CONTROL-ORIENTED POLICY

Does it make sense to regulate HPOs using the conventional measures of control-oriented environmental policy? The reader by now probably senses that the answer is no. The control-oriented policies were designed for firms that behave like neoclassical firms. On the other hand, HPOs are firms that: (a) have made a commitment to high environmental quality/performance; (b) have invested in the organizational infrastructure necessary for high environmental performance; (c) have demonstrated their ability to take responsibility for their relationship not only to their immediate neighbors but to society as a whole; and (d) have demonstrated their ability to be trusted in the environmental area. For firms with these demonstrated capacities, what is needed is the opposite of control-oriented policy. What is needed is an environmental policy that takes advantage of HPOs commitment, responsibility and trustworthiness. What is needed is a policy that recognizes the socio-economic nature of firms and that SE firms have a high human potential that the right kind of policy can foster. The appropriate policy should take into account that overall environmental performance is a product not just of firm behavior but of the whole environmental system of which firms are a part. The environmental system includes, in addition to firms and government, citizens, environmental groups, extra-firm organizations such as trade associations, consultants, equipment vendors, educational institutions, lawyers and lobbyists, financial institutions as well as managerial and industrial norms of behavior.

RATIONAL POLLUTERS AND POLICY

According to Spence (2001: 1),

> The modern American environmental regulatory system is founded on the assumption that business firms are rational polluters: that the rational pursuit of their self interest guides both their compliance decisions and their participation in the political process. This traditional view of firms implies that environmental regulators must deter pollution through the imposition of fines and penalties.

This control-oriented policy prescription makes some sense for firms which have not developed their capabilities for productivity, innovativeness, and responsibility very highly. Firms such as these with low environmental commitment and capability cannot be expected to be self-regulating; they obviously need external incentives. However, for HPOs, firms approximating the characteristics of the Z firm, control-oriented policy would be a waste of resources as HPOs can achieve high, sustained levels of environmental performance with little or no regulation.

In Spence's (2001: 1) view, there is another reason why control-oriented policy may fail: complexity. He argues that firms typically find it extremely difficult to comply due to the complexity of regulations and their environmental situations. Therefore, 'much noncompliance results from misunderstanding of or ambiguity surrounding environmental rules' (p. 1). Also, in his view most compliance results not from rational polluter behavior but because firms' decision makers desire to adhere to environmental norms and support the system which is generally seen as legitimate and trusted. It follows that conventional (control-oriented) regulation, especially penalty oriented regulation, is counterproductive in that it undermines the legitimacy of the system. For firms which are far from being HPOs, some form of control-oriented policy may be necessary, but more collaborative, voluntary versions may often do better. As Spence (p. 19) concluded, 'the modern American system of environmental regulation . . . has . . . relied too heavily on fear and not heavily enough on duty.' Our view is that we cannot rely entirely on either fear or incentives to business gain (recall the Sen quote in the introduction) to protect the environment. We need a commitment approach.

THE ESSENCE OF A COMMITMENT APPROACH

A commitment approach (CA) to environmental policy is first of all not a control-oriented policy. That is, it does not use rewards and penalties to attain government chosen goals. A CA is a nonregulatory approach in which firms are self-regulated and choose their environmental protection goals and actions. The CA is only for firms that are able to: (a) make a generalized commitment to high environmental performance and (b) develop the capabilities to meet these commitments. The environmental protection (EP) agency that administers the CA would be charged with selecting the particular 'high commitment' (HC) firms that would be subject to the policy. Low and intermediate commitment firms would presumably continue to be regulated under the usual control-oriented environmental policies.

Although the EP agency would not set goals for HC firms nor provide financial incentives, it would engage in certain facilitative actions directed either at HC firms or their environmental systems (ESs). For example, the selected HC firms would be eligible for government technical assistance and information, especially regarding the nature of the pollutants and their deleterious effects. With regard to the ESs, the EP agency could aid the functioning of the systems in which HC firms are embedded by providing education and information to these businesses' stakeholders as well as providing other assistance to stakeholders who have or could have favorable influences on these firms. Also, the EP agency could encourage low and intermediate commitment firms to develop greater environmental commitments and capabilities. This would be consistent with an important long-term goal of the CA, namely developing a larger corps of HC firms subject to the policy. Finally, it would be necessary for the EP agency to accomplish periodic assessments of how ESs' performance departs from the ideal and how these systems' operations require rectification.

A CA to environmental policy arguably would work better if a broad agreement (or consensus) on high level environmental goals and values for the nation/society existed. Such an agreement would provide the all-important context in which firms would make their own general environmental commitments (and make choices on specific environmental goals). As part of the CA, the EP agency ought to facilitate the process by which an agreement is reached. Probably the most important kind of environmental commitment a firm can make is to a general environmental code of conduct indicating broadly what environmentally ethical behavior or social responsibility implies. The CERES principles are a good example of the kind of principles to which a HC firm would be expected to give assent. For firms in industries associated with particular types of environmental degradation, it might be desirable for these firms' commitments to reflect environmental norms and standards geared to these industries' characteristic problems.

In sum, the following are the main elements of a commitment approach:

1. Firms subject to the CA are HC firms selected by the EP agency utilizing criteria related to these firms' demonstrated environmental commitment and capabilities.
2. Other firms, but no selected HC firms, are subject to standard control-oriented policy.
3. HC firms choose their environmental actions in line with their general and specific environmental commitments which in turn are aligned with the nation's/society's environmental goals.
4. The EP agency facilitates the environmental performance of these firms' (along with their ESs) and then monitors and assesses the performance of these firms/systems with an eye toward improving the overall system.

COMPARING THE COMMITMENT APPROACH TO ESTABLISHED SELF-REGULATORY APPROACHES

Increasingly scholars and policymakers are giving strong consideration to and implementing environmental policies involving important elements of self-regulation. The CA advocated here is consistent with this general trend; yet in some respects it represents a significant departure from these other policies. To appreciate this, it is necessary to compare the CA to approaches with non-mandatory elements such as: (a) voluntary agreements/approaches (VAs); (b) management-based policies; and (c) information policies.

A voluntary approach to environmental policy is one where firms voluntarily decide to abate pollution by an amount greater than required under existing regulations, that is, it is voluntary overcompliance (see Khanna, 2001; Carraro and Leveque, 1999; OECD, 1999). To facilitate the comparison between the CA and the VA, consider public voluntary agreements as the prototype of the VA. Its essential features are:

1. The program is designed by the government EP agency which determines its goals, who is eligible, participant obligations and rewards, and so on.
2. The agency invites participation.
3. Accepted participants must agree to meet a specified standard of environmental performance and/or adopt an abatement technology.
4. Participants who are accepted and agree to meet the specified environmental performance sign non-binding letters of agreement (Khanna, 2001: 294).

5. The EP agency generally agrees to provide certain information and technical assistance to participants.
6. The participants are monitored through self-reporting.

In this public VA, the government largely sets the goals and provides for or arranges for the inducements, not all of which are financial in nature (see, for example, Khanna, 2001: 298). The participants in the VA are not selected based on their demonstrated environmental commitment or capability; they are largely self-selected. Because the participants cannot be relied upon to have sufficient commitment or capability, the government must exercise a fair degree of control despite the ostensibly 'voluntary' nature of the program. For example, to induce adequate participation, governments have had to make a credible threat of stiffer regulation in the future for those who do not participate or have had to provide regulatory relief or the promise of it for those who do participate (p. 298). In light of this carrot and stick inducement, it has been observed that this approach 'is not truly voluntary' (Segerson and Miceli, 1998: 110; see also Alberini and Segerson, 2002: 169, 178). The decision by firms regarding whether to participate in the VA has been modeled by economists (see, for example, Segerson and Miceli, 1998; Khanna and Damon, 1999). The decision makers depicted in such models strongly resemble the rational economic man of neoclassical theory, not the decision makers of the socio-economic firm. Firms who participate and commit to a VA generally have been induced into making a quasi-contractual (external) commitment, which is quite different from the 'internal' commitment made by HC firms in a CA. Thus, although the public VA has a voluntary aspect, its essential nature is more akin to that of the control-oriented policies, not to that of the CA.

Another important type of VA is the negotiated (or bilateral) agreement (NA) (see for example, Khanna, 2001; Carraro and Leveque, 1999). In the NA, the environmental performance target is the product of a bargaining process between the government and a firm(s) (or an industry) rather than an objective determined solely by the EP agency. Because the firm(s) are involved in the determination of the performance target, there is arguably a greater element of self-regulation. Typically, at the heart of the negotiation is a firm's offer of improved environmental performance in exchange for less stringent regulation. It should be noted that in these negotiations the government always has the option to threaten tougher regulation if businesses are unwilling to deliver satisfactory environmental performance. Because government can exercise coercive power in the negotiations, the voluntary or self-regulatory aspect of NAs is questionable (OECD, 1999: 17; see also Alberini and Segerson, 2002: 174). Thus, in NAs government behavior *vis-à-vis* firms is likely to lean towards the control-oriented side. This is especially true to the extent that the firms participating as bargainers are not selected on the basis of their demonstrated commitment and capability.

The third type of VA, unilateral initiatives, does not involve a government role, and thus, is not a type of environmental policy. Khanna (2001: 296–7) identifies three types of unilateral initiatives: (a) a firm's own efforts to establish an environmental code of conduct that will lead to improved environmental performance; (b) a firm's efforts to conform to codes/guidelines developed by a trade association; and (c) a firm's efforts to meet the environmental performance standards of a certifying organization such as the International Organization for Standardization. Generally, in these three types of initiatives, there have not been third party efforts to assess the performance outcomes. These unilateral initiatives differ from a CA in that a CA would, while welcoming these individual initiatives, involve a governmental policy aimed at improving the overall environmental outcome.

Management-based regulation (MBR) differs from VAs and also from conventional regulations that require either the use of specific technologies or the achievement of a certain level of environmental performance (Coglianese and Laser, 2003). MBR requires instead that firms engage in a managerial planning process that includes such elements as 'identification of hazards, risk mitigation actions, procedures for monitoring and correcting problems, employee training policies, and measures for evaluating and refining the firm's management with respect to the stated objective' (p. 694). Firms under MBR 'are subjected to reviews by regulators . . . to certify compliance' (p. 694), that is, enforcement actions. While MBR focuses on improving firms' internal management, the ultimate goal, of course, is to improve environmental performance. MBR's advantage compared to conventional regulations is that it allows regulated firms some flexibility, some ability to experiment, and some ability to adopt innovative solutions, but it is not a voluntary, self-regulatory approach. In MBR, all firms are regulated; there is no selection based on demonstrated environmental commitment and capability. And as a result, one of the problematic aspects of MBR is that firms may comply, adopting the prescribed managerial processes, but not be motivated to achieve high environmental performance. In this connection, Coglianese and Nash (2002) have noted that managerial commitment to high environmental performance is far more important than the presence of environmental management systems. So MBR is in one important sense like several of the voluntary types of environmental policies analyzed above, that is, it has a control-oriented nature, and thus, differs from the CA.

Finally, consider information policies. Increasing evidence indicates that information policies involving public disclosure (or labeling or certification) of firms' environmental performance can be effective, particularly as a complement to traditional policies (see, for example, Foulon *et al.*, 2002; Khanna, 2001: 313–17). Further, the evidence indicates that communities (also customers, suppliers and stockholders) concerned about environmental degradation and armed with accurate pollutant data can have a powerful influence on firms' environmental behavior, especially when these groups are organized and knowledgeable. This is true where 'environmental reputation matters for firms whose expected costs or revenues are affected by judgments of environmental performance by customers, suppliers, and stockholders (p. 175). Thus, there is very good reason why our proposed CA to environmental policy should include a public disclosure component, thereby bringing external socio-political-economic forces to bear to reinforce the high internal environmental commitments of high performing organizations.

THE COMMITMENT APPROACH: MANAGING ENVIRONMENTAL QUALITY

It is useful to think of the CA as quality management applied to the whole economy or environment. At the level of the firm or plant, the ideal quality goal has become three zero manufacturing: zero defects, zero inventory and zero waste and emissions (or high product quality, high productivity and high environmental quality). To try to reach this ideal, firms must practice total quality environmental management (TQEM), an extension of the total quality management philosophy to encompass the practices and processes that affect environmental quality. Further, it makes a lot of sense to extend the TQEM approach to the whole economy or environment. Here also the ideal tripartite goal would be high product quality, high productivity and high environmental quality. In firm level TQEM, every worker is responsible for the quality of what s/he produces. Correspondingly, at the economy level under a CA, every firm would be responsible for their contribution to environmental quality. Every firm would need to be committed to high environmental quality and capable of contributing to it. In addition, there would need to be a concern with continuously improving the overall environmental system (including all the individual ESs and more), recognizing that environmental quality is an outcome of how the system as a whole works.

It might be argued that traditional control-oriented environmental policy is to the CA what the 'old' statistical quality control approach is to TQEM. Control-oriented policies are like the old quality approaches that relied on quality inspection without attempting much system improvement. Control-oriented policies, to the extent they use carrot and stick incentives, may push firms to correct their environmental performance without doing much to change the nature of the system that creates the excessive waste and emissions in the first place. Ideally, in the CA, the EP agency would play a role similar to the quality control department in a firm using TQEM. That is, the EP agency's role would be that of facilitator, teacher, and disseminator of information for firms and other organizations in the overall environmental system. The agency's focus would be on continuously improving the overall system, especially raising the environmental capacity of the system through building a larger corps of HC firms that are capable of highly responsible environmental performance.

THE BENEFITS OF THE COMMITMENT APPROACH

The potential of the CA is great. High commitment HPOs which are enrolled in a CA can be expected to make high environmental performance choices that directly benefit themselves as well as their communities and societies. This in turn should make possible vastly reduced regulatory oversight and rule-making for every conceivable type of pollution in every conceivable media. In these situations, the initiative and responsibility for dealing with environmental problems (related to business activity) would be with the firms, not the EP agency, albeit the EP agency's facilitative role may be important. Because of this, the motivation of participating business people would be much higher than if they were operating in a compliance mode. Participating firms would be able to integrate environmental actions flexibly with their other business activities. This should enable these businesses to operate with greater productivity, and it can be argued that economic efficiency would also be increased. Further, in order to successfully undertake these environmental actions, firms would have to develop organizational and other intangible capabilities that will serve them well in other aspects of their business. Finally, we can expect that in the process of improving their environmental performance, these firms would improve their relationships with their stakeholders and eliminate the adversarial aspect of their relationship with the EP agency(ies).

THE EP AGENCY'S RESPONSIBILITIES IN A COMMITMENT APPROACH

If a CA to environmental policy were to be adopted, the EP agency's responsibilities would include the following:

1. selecting the HC firms;
2. identifying environmental problems;
3. researching environmental problems;
4. facilitating the setting of societal environmental values, objectives and priorities;
5. monitoring the environmental performance of ESs and the overall environmental system;
6. providing technical assistance and information to firms and others;
7. fostering the functioning of ESs by helping businesses' stakeholders perform valuable supplemental roles
8. fostering the participation of industries (for example, chemical industry) in the setting of standards for environmental performance;
9. fostering communications and negotiations among relevant parties.

The first of these needs further explanation.

Selecting the HC firms would be one of the most important responsibilities of the EP agency charged with administering an environmental policy based on a CA. Recall that in the CA the selected firms would be self-regulating, and thus, not subject to control-oriented policies. For self-regulation to work, the selected firms must have demonstrated that with respect to the environment they are internally motivated, dedicated to operating in a way that is environmentally harmonious, and dedicated to maintaining and enhancing their necessary environmental capacities. To demonstrate this commitment, firms must do more than state their good intentions. Their commitment must be made credible by a record of environmental actions and accomplishments consistent with the principles by which they claim to be guided (see Smart, 1992 for examples of the kinds of environmental principles that leading companies have claimed to be committed to; see Nakamura *et al.* (2001: 27–8) for a study that identifies three levels of environmental commitment). It would be desirable if these company commitments derived from a dialogue between the company's representatives and the representatives of the governments and communities affected by the company's operations. It would also be desirable if the company commitment reflected the characteristic scientific and technological issues involved in the company's environmental impact.

With respect to the second criterion for selecting HC firms, demonstrated capability, it is important to take note of research that indicates the kinds of capability that are strongly associated with high environmental performance. Florida *et al.* (2001), for example, found that organizational resources (especially plant size and the commitments of top corporate leaders), environmental resources (the number, tenure and experience of environmental staff), company use of environmental performance monitoring systems and processes, and, to a lesser extent, the adoption of advanced manufacturing practices play a key role in the adoption of environmentally conscious manufacturing practices at manufacturing plants. Therefore, it makes sense to use these kinds of capabilities as criteria for accepting HC firms because firms with these capabilities are the ones that can be expected to fulfill their environmental commitments.

THE EPA'S RECENT EFFORTS TO GO BEYOND TRADITIONAL POLICY

With respect to what the US Environmental Protection Agency (EPA) has recently done, there is good news and bad news. The good news is that the EPA is making substantial and interesting efforts to develop programs that go beyond traditional compliance oriented ones. They have developed and are experimenting with approaches that attempt to transform their relationship with regulated businesses. The bad news is that the programs they have so far initiated fall short of embodying a number of the important features of a full-fledged commitment approach.

Judging by what the EPA says in its official pronouncements (see www.epa.gov), it wants to do the right things. That is, it wants to focus on environmental performance, emphasize business responsibility for the environment, emphasize partnership with businesses, emphasize stakeholder collaboration, foster innovation, diversify its EP tools and approaches, and emphasize procedural flexibility, among other things. To move in this direction, the EPA has established a number of flagship innovation programs, most notably the National Environmental Performance Track or simply Performance Track (PT) established in 2000. The PT program selects for recognition and special treatment public and private facilities which apply and are found to have top environmental performance insofar as: (a) their environmental performance exceeds regulatory requirements; (b) they are involved in continuing environmental improvement; and (c) they have a good relationship with their communities. The chosen PT facilities (or members) realize a number of benefits including: (a) being low priority for routine EPA inspections; and (b) experiencing leniency with regard to other procedural requirements. PT members also receive valuable public recognition.

In our analysis, the PT program is a desirable innovation, a further step down the VA path. Certainly it will provide recognition and encouragement to facilities for favorable environmental performance and begin to 'transform' the regulator-regulated relationship. But it is not the same as a CA.

A number of important things need to happen to move from the PT approach to a CA. First, the selected members of a CA ought to be companies, not individual facilities of companies. Second, the two main eligibility criteria ought to be the environmental commitment and the environmental-related organizational capabilities of the firm, not simply their recent environmental performance. The PT program description makes no mention of commitment and capability.[1] If companies truly have high commitment and high capabilities, there is no reason why they should not become self-regulated, rather than just being regulated leniently. Such HC companies should realize high environmental performance at all their facilities. Thus, the real transformation is when firms become self-regulated. Of course, in a CA, the EPA can continue to monitor certain environmental outcomes, to encourage these firms, and to provide certain technical assistance. These do not involve a regulatory role. Finally, the EPA ought to orchestrate a societal or national consensus on environmental goals. This will provide the all important context in which firms make their high level commitments.

THE COMMITMENT APPROACH AND THE PORTER THESIS

The essence of the so-called Porter Thesis is that contrary to conventional wisdom, toughening environmental regulation is likely to stimulate business innovation (thereby raising competitiveness and productivity), not stifle it (Porter and van der Linde, 1995). If that is the case, will introducing a greater degree of self-regulation, *a la* the CA, reduce innovation and competitiveness or raise it? To answer this question, we examine the Porter Thesis more carefully. What is it about introducing regulation that could lead business to step up its innovation? According to Porter and van der Linde (pp. 99–100), 'regulation signals companies about likely resource inefficiencies and potential technological improvements'; regulation focused on information gathering can raise corporate awareness of environmental problems; regulation reduces uncertainty related to environmental investments; 'regulation creates pressure that motivates innovation . . . helping overcome organizational inertia, foster creative thinking and mitigate agency problems'; and 'regulation ensures that one company cannot opportunistically gain position by avoiding environmental investments.' It should be noted that the Porter Thesis is somewhat controversial and is certainly not proven. But assuming for the moment that it is true, is there a basis for believing that a CA would have a similar favorable effect on innovation? In other words, is it reasonable to expect the high commitment HPOs selected for the CA to achieve not only high environmental performance but greater competitiveness through innovation? There is good reason to believe the answer is yes. As Florida's studies have pointed out, these HPOs already have a high capacity for and commitment to innovation and can be expected to continue in that direction. EP agencies can help these companies by signaling what needs doing environmentally without setting regulatory rules and requirements. These companies do not need penalties to prod them to high environmental performance; not only are they already internally motivated and committed, but in the CA their favorable environmental behavior will be reinforced by the concerned members of their society and communities. Therefore, these reasons lead one to believe that introducing a CA to environmental policy is likely to have a favorable effect on innovation similar to what the Porter Thesis posits. It is also possible that another phenomenon similar to the Porter Thesis might manifest with a CA. That is, the CA might lead more companies to choose and become committed to socially responsible behavior especially with respect to the environment. The upshot is that with the CA, we might reasonably expect not only high environmental performance and more innovation but more social responsibility as well.

ANTICIPATING DIFFICULTIES

This chapter has necessarily focused on making the case for a CA to environmental policy, and the emphasis has properly been on how it would function and the benefits it would provide. But the introduction of any new policy, especially one that makes a dramatic break with past policy and thinking, is likely to involve significant difficulties. First, gaining acceptance of the CA through the political process might be difficult. Existing control-oriented policies are strongly associated with the rational economic man/polluter thinking of mainstream economics. Thus, intellectual and ideological resistances to a CA are inevitable. Assuming this obstacle could be overcome, the implementation and operation of the CA would present its own difficulties. Among them are: (a) identifying and selecting a sufficient number, that is, a critical mass, of high commitment HPOs; (b) dealing with selected firms and their environmental systems whose performance is deemed less than satisfactory; (c) making corrections in light of negative feedback about program performance; and (d) making changes to the duties and responsibilities of officers in the EP agency.

CONCLUSION

Increasingly, EP agencies are recognizing the futility of trying to protect all aspects of the environment using control-oriented policies (command and control and market-incentive policies for the most part). In their search for alternative policies, they are developing and experimenting with non-mandatory policies with various degrees of self-regulation. But these policies are not consistent with the predominate economic theory of how firms behave, that is, the rational polluter model. Obviously, this suggests the need for a better theory of firm behavior. Consequently, this chapter presents an alternative model, a socio-economic model of the firm's environmental behavior. This model is utilized to show how human firms are, on the one hand, capable of both ideal socially responsible and highly competitive behavior, and on the other hand, are likely to fall far short of the ideal, depending on the magnitude of their investments in intangible capital. This socio-economic model along with evidence regarding the behavior of High Performance Organizations provides the basis for understanding why a commitment approach is the kind of environmental policy alternative that makes the most sense. With a CA, HPOs which have made credible commitments to high environmental and organizational performance can benefit from a policy environment which brings out the best in these companies through a combination of self-regulation and encouragement. On the other hand, there is reason to believe that traditional control-oriented policies are likely to stifle the innovativeness and idealism of these high performing companies, leading to lower overall environmental performance. Of course, companies which have not made a high environmental commitment nor developed the corresponding organizational capabilities will have to continue to be regulated in traditional ways until they can demonstrate that they have made a strong enough environmental commitment. Hopefully, with the adoption of a commitment approach philosophy by EP agencies at different governmental levels, high commitment firms will become more and more prevalent, leading to a cleaner and cleaner environment without great cost.

NOTES

* Thomas R. Sadler, Department of Economics, Western Illinois University, Illinois, USA.

1. It should be noted that the EPA uses the existence of an environmental management system (EMS) as a criterion for PT membership. The existence of an EMS presumably implies some degree of organizational capability.

REFERENCES

Alberini, Anna and Kathleen Segerson (2002), 'Assessing voluntary programs to improve environmental quality,' *Environmental and Resource Economics*, **22**, 157–84.

Carraro, Carlo and Francois Leveque (1999), *Voluntary Approaches in Environmental Policy*, Boston, MA: Kluwer Academic.
Coglianese, Cary and David Lazer (2003), 'Management-based regulation: prescribing private management to achieve public goals,' *Law and Society Review*, **37**(4), 691–730.
Coglianese, Cary and Jennifer, Nash (2002), 'Policy options for improving environmental management in the private sector,' *Environment*, **44**(9), 10–23.
Florida, Richard (1996), 'Lean and green: the move to environmentally conscious manufacturing,' *California Management Review*, **39**(1), 80–105.
Florida, Richard and Derek Davison (2001), 'Gaining from green management: environmental management systems inside and outside the factory,' *California Management Review*, **43**(3), 64–84.
Florida, Richard, Mark Atlas and Matt Cline (2001), 'What makes companies green? Organizational and geographic factors in the adoption of environmental practices,' *Economic Geography*, **77**(3), 209–24.
Foulon, Jerome, Paul Lanoie and Benoit Laplante (2002), 'Incentives for pollution control: regulation or information?,' *Journal of Environmental Economics and Management*, **44**, 169–87.
Granovetter, Mark (1985), 'Economic action and social structure: the problem of embeddedness,' *American Journal of Sociology*, **91**(November): 481–510.
Khanna, Madhu (2001), 'Non-mandatory approaches to environmental protection,' *Journal of Economic Surveys,* **15**(3), 291–324.
Khanna, Madhu and Lisa A. Damon (1999), 'EPA's voluntary 33/50 program: impact on toxic releases and economic performance of firms,' *Journal of Environmental Economics and Management*, **37**, 1–25.
Lawler, Edward E. (1992), *The Ultimate Advantage: Creating the High Involvement Organizaiion*, San Francisco, CA: Jossey-Bass.
Nakamura, Masao; Takuya Takahashi and Ilan Vertinsky (2001), 'Why Japanese firms choose to certify: a study of managerial responses to environmental issues,' *Journal of Environmental Economics and Management*, **42**, 23–52.
Oak Ridge National Laboratory and Resources for the Future (1994), *Estimating Externalities of Coal Fuel Cycles*, Washington, DC: US Department of Energy.
Organization for Economic Co-operation and Development (1999), *Voluntary Approaches for Environmental Policy: An Assessment*, Paris: OECD.
Pfeffer, Jeffrey (1998), *The Human Equation: Building Profits by Putting People First*, Boston, MA: Harvard Business School Press.
Porter, Michael E. and Claas van der Linde (1995), 'Toward a new conception of the environment-competitiveness relationship,' *Journal of Economic Perspectives*, **9**(4), 97–118.
Segerson, Kathleen and Thomas J. Miceli (1998), 'Voluntary environmental agreements: good or bad news for environmental protection,' *Journal of Environmental Economics and Management*, **36**, 109–30.
Sen, Amartya K. (1977), 'Rational fools: a critique of the behavioral foundations of economic theory,' *Philosophy and Public Affairs*, **6**, 317–44.
Smart, Bruce (ed.) (1992), *Beyond Compliance: A New Industry View of the Environment,* Washington, DC: World Resources Institute.
Spence, David B. (2001), 'The shadow of the rational polluter: rethinking the role of rational actor models in environmental law,' *California Law Review*, **July**, 1–57.
Tomer, John F. (1987), *Organizational Capital: The Path to Higher Productivity and Well-Being*, New York: Praeger.

Tomer, John F. (1992), 'The human firm in the natural environment: a socio-economic analysis of its behavior,' *Ecological Economics*, **6**, 119–38.

Tomer, John F. (1999), *The Human Firm: A Socio-Economic Analysis of its Behavior and Potential in a New Economic Age*, New York: Routledge.

Tomer, John F. (2001), 'Understanding high-performance work systems: the joint contribution of economics and human resource management,' *Journal of Socio-Economics*, **30**(1), 63–73.

Tomer, John F. (2003), 'Personal capital and emotional intelligence: an increasingly important intangible source of economic growth,' *Eastern Economic Journal*, **29**(3), 453–70.

14. Economic man versus heterodox man: the concepts of human nature in schools of economic thought

INTRODUCTION

Economic man, the man who acts on pure economic motives alone, is the concept of man at the heart of mainstream economics.[1] Heterodox economists, while acknowledging that economic man has served usefully for some purposes, know in different ways that economic man is, because it leaves out too much of human nature, a deficient concept of man. They are uncomfortable at best with the idea of characterizing humans in such a reductionist way. This chapter proposes to use the comprehensive view of human nature developed by Ken Wilber to point to the specific deficiencies of economic man. With Wilber's model of human development as the backdrop, it is possible to map the different schools of thought with respect to each other, showing how each of their overlapping conceptions of man include some important elements missing in economic man but fail to include other elements. Finally, the broad conception of human nature allows us to be quite suggestive concerning how economics as a whole, and notably heterodox economics, can improve by using a broader concept of man.

THE ESSENCE OF ECONOMIC MAN

Homo Economicus or economic man is the well-known human actor at the heart of mainstream economics. Economic man (EM) is self-interested, rational, unchanging, separate and unreflective. First, self-interested EM has well-defined preferences for things and experiences that provide satisfaction for the self. EM is oriented to getting more of these to benefit the self. Second, EM is rational in that he has the ability to create mental images of possible goods and the satisfaction they provide as well as the ability to calculate precisely concerning these possible satisfactions. On the basis of these calculations, he acts in a machine-like way to make decisions that lead to his maximum satisfaction. Mainstream economic theory is characterized by reductionism in that everything that EM desires is reducible to a common measure of satisfaction.

Third, economic man is separate and distinct from his physical world and from other humans (individuals, organizations, and other collective entities). He is unaffected by culture/values, society, politics, fads, enthusiasms, and so on unless these enter his preferences. Fourth, EM's character is given and unchanging. This character is assumed; it is not an object of theoretical or empirical study. Thus, within mainstream economics, there is no effort to draw on research from behavioral disciplines such as psychology in order to add realism to his character. Moreover, there is nothing to indicate that EM's character is representative of a valid stage of human development. Finally, EM's consciousness is dominated by his calculating, choosing, and satisfaction obtainment activity. EM is not reflective regarding these activities. He does not stop to consider the appropriateness or rightness of his choices.

While the above is the essence of the economic man concept used by contemporary mainstream economists, it does not necessarily represent the concept of human nature held by these economists. Some mainstream economists regard EM as a construct or abstraction useful for getting definite theoretical results, a construct they use largely because of its consistency with their deductive mathematical models. Or EM may be used because of its purported usefulness in generating successful predictions even if is not realistic. Note that economists may consider the character of EM to be close to human reality in certain spheres of activity such as when dealing with anonymous transactions in competitive markets but not descriptive of human behavior in other spheres (see Viner, 1991: 75–6). While few mainstream economists subscribe to a concept of human nature that is the same as EM, these economists in most cases strongly subscribe to an economic methodology, methodological individualism, at the heart of which is EM. In other words, EM is an inseparable part of their mainstream economic perspective and scholarship, a scholarship which leaves little room for alternative concepts of human nature.[2]

HUMAN NATURE

To properly appreciate economic man and the heterodox men of the different heterodox economic schools of thought, it is necessary to compare them to an accurate and complete view of human nature. No one has taken a more embracing and comprehensive view of human nature than Ken Wilber (see for example, 1996a, b) who has systematically studied the path of human development. Another very important perspective is that of Abraham Maslow, particularly his familiar hierarchy of human need. What follows draws on the ideas of these two writers in order to provide a brief but comprehensive map of human nature.

Wilber's full spectrum model is a map of the entire range of human potential. His view is that human development unfolds in predictable stages. These stages of consciousness include not only those recognized by Western psychologists but those recognized by Eastern spiritual leaders, most notably Buddha. Wilber's distinct contribution is 'integrating and elucidating these disparate thinkers' (Schwartz, 1995: Chapter 9).

In Wilber's (1996a) model, there are ten stages of development which in turn are classified into three main categories: (a) subconscious (the prepersonal stages); (b) self-consciousness (the personal stages); and (c) superconsciousness (the transpersonal stages). At birth, 'there is no real separation whatsoever between inside and outside, subject and object, body and environment' (p. 7). As prepersonal development progresses, the child first begins to recognize that the outer world is different from the self and then begins to interact with the world in an instinctive, impulsive, id-ish manner. Gradually, the sense of self as distinct from the outer world emerges. Development in the personal stages first involves breaking free of the sleep of subconsciousness and gradually acquiring language, beginning to use symbols and concepts, learning to take on roles and follow rules, and developing the capacity for rational understanding, introspective thinking, deductive reasoning, and socially acceptable behavior. In the highest personal stage, a person has developed the capacity for integrated thinking, connecting ideas, relating truths to one another, and integrating mind and body. The transpersonal stages described in the Eastern literature, involve 'processes of consciousness more subtle than everyday, outer-directed experience' (Schwartz, 1995: 356) and a movement toward ultimate unity or nonduality. Through these stages, a person can gain psychic capacities and a sense of higher spirit, can 'touch divinity, even unite with divinity, in an all-encompassing love,' can achieve a union so complete that the sense of self is transcended and radiant bliss is experienced, and can in the final stage reach the 'highest stage nonduality, or the absence of any split between subject and object' (enlightenment according to Buddha) (p. 356). For a list of Wilber's stages, see Box 14.1.

Wilber's (1996a: 4–5) developmental stages are usefully divided into two halves. The first, the Outward Arc, is the movement from subconsciousness to self-consciousness and is characterized by self-assertion, individuation, and conquering outer worlds. The second, the Inward Arc, is the movement from self-consciousness to superconsciousness and is characterized by self-realization, going within, transcending self, and achieving oneness. See Figure 14.1.

According to Wilber (1996a: Chapter 10), human development proceeds from stage to stage, proceeding to successively higher-order wholes

BOX 14.1 KEN WILBER'S STAGES OF HUMAN DEVELOPMENT

1. Subconsciousness (Prepersonal stages)
   a. Pleromatic
   b. Uroboric
   c. Typhonic
2. Self-Consciousness (personal stages)
   a. Egoic
   b. Conceptual
   c. Adjusted, autonomous individual
   d. Mature, evolved
3. Super Consciousness (transpersonal stages)
   a. Subtle
   b. Causal
   c. Ultimate

Source: Adapted from Wilber (1996a).

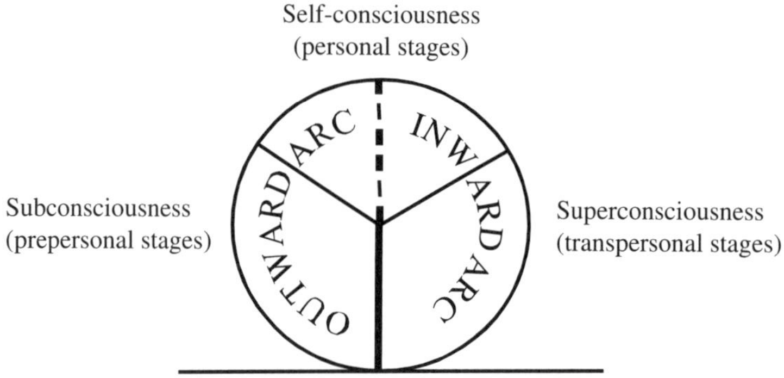

Source: Wilber (1996a)

Figure 14.1 General life cycle

and unities and integrations. Each step to the next stage: (a) involves a transformation in which the elements of the earlier level are included but integrated at a higher level; and (b) involves disidentification with a lower element or structure and identification with a higher-order structure. Each successively higher-order structure is more complex, more organized and more unified. Evolution continues until there is only one Unity, ultimate in

BOX 14.2 CORRESPONDENCE BETWEEN STAGES AND MASLOW'S NEEDS HIERARCHY

1. Subconscious stages	Physiological
	Beginnings of safety
2. Self-consciousness stages	Safety
	Belongingness
	Self-Esteem
	Self-Actualization
3. Super consciousness	Transcendence

4. Higher needs emerge and become prepotent once conducive conditions exist.
5. Needs lower on hierarchy more clearly associated with self-interest; Movement to higher needs involves lessening self-interest/selfishness, broadening interest in others, concern for others, being/living in service to higher truths, values, principles

Source: Adapted from Wilber (1996a).

all directions. It is necessary to successfully complete a given stage before fully inhabiting the next. No stage can be bypassed. Unresolved issues such as repressed material at one stage can block the path to higher development as it consumes attention and energy.

Wilber's model of human development is compatible with Abraham Maslow's view of human nature as reflected in his well-known hierarchy of human needs. The main categories of needs on the hierarchy from lowest to highest are: (a) physiological; (b) safety; (c) belonging (and love); (d) self-esteem; (e) self-actualization; and (f) transcendence. Higher needs generally emerge and become prepotent once lower needs are met and conducive conditions exist. The needs hierarchy is suggestive of a developmental sequence, that is, moving in steps from lower to higher needs, which is quite similar to Wilber's model. Another similarity is the quality of the human wants at different stages of development. At the lowest stages, wants frequently have the quality of desperately craving, striving, or strong needing. At the middle stages, wants are desires, wishes, preferences, and choices. At the highest stages, wants are expressions of a yearning for, a devotion to, an aspiration for, a being drawn to or fascinated by (Maslow, 1971: 324). This reflects a movement away from a sole concern for the needs of self and a movement toward becoming concerned with others and ultimately becoming one with others as development progresses (see Box 14.2).

Economic Man in Light of Human Nature

The limitations and deficiencies of economic man become glaringly exposed when we view EM in light of our broad view of human nature. This section examines one by one the main characteristics of EM in order to understand the shortcomings of EM. First, EM's sole preoccupation with self is deficient. While it is generally true that humans pursue their self-interest, the important question is to what extent is self-interest their main preoccupation. With respect to humans who have reached any of the stages up to the end of the Outward Arc, it is true to a large extent. However, it is true to a much smaller degree the more humans have reached the higher stages on the Inward Arc.

Second, EM's separateness from his physical and human worlds is deficient. On the one hand, young humans in the prepersonal stages have not yet achieved separation from their outer world. On the other hand, humans who have progressed to the transpersonal stages are experiencing various degrees of becoming one with their physical and human outer world. For humans who have reached the personal stages near the end of the Outward Arc, there is some truth to the notion of separateness. However, even here, the variety of influences on human behavior indicates that the notion of separateness is lacking in that humans have many strong connections with their human and physical environment, that is they are partially embedded in society and nature.

Third, EM's machine-like rationality is deficient. It is clear that in the prepersonal stages, young humans do not have the imaging, conceptual, and calculating capacities to be rational. In the transpersonal stages, while humans do possess many of the necessary mental capacities for rational economic behavior, they do not behave in this way because they are oriented to behavior that is much more integrated and holistic. Humans in the middle of the personal stages are those whose behavior might conceivably approximate rational EM behavior. However, even here, there are many reasons why a human's rationality is quite limited. Among these are: (a) the limits to a human's ability to calculate; (b) the psychological pathology and emotional contamination from unresolved issues at lower stages; and (c) the human need to belong and be socially acceptable.

Fourth, EM's unreflective aspect is deficient. This is especially true for humans in the higher personal stages and, of course, the transpersonal stages. Based on their upbringing and socialization, humans, who are beyond the prepersonal level, have internalized moral, ethical, spiritual, religious and other ideals that often lead them to reflect on the rightness and wrongness of their choices. Moreover, humans in the higher personal and transpersonal stages of development have acquired the ability to appreciate universal truths, and thus, they will reflect on their behavior in light of these.

Fifth and finally, the unchanging aspect of EM's character is deficient. From Wilber's model of human development, one can understand that human character transforms significantly from stage to stage as human potential unfolds. In this sense, human character changes significantly. However, one can argue that the typical level of character development for adults in a society is relatively unchanging. Further, it can be argued with some validity that EM's character resembles the typical or 'normal' character of humans in some modern capitalistic societies. This standard level of human development tends to act as a magnet in that it inhibits development above this level, pulling people down to this level, and encourages development to this level, pulling people up. But even this standard character is not unchanging; it evolves over time with societal evolution.

Overall these deficiencies of EM amount to an indictment of economists' use of EM. Maslow, for one, was extremely critical of economists' use of the economic man construct. Maslow (1971: 310) stated that economists have made a 'skilled, exact, technological application of a totally false theory of human needs and values, a theory which recognizes only the existence of lower needs or material needs.' To the extent that EM has value, it fits best as a depiction of mankind for that segment of humanity that has reached close to the half way point in human development, that is, to the end of the Outward Arc. Humans at around this level of development are to a considerable degree self-interested and separate, may have a reasonable capacity for rational behavior, may not be very reflective, and may have reached a level of human development as high as they can expect to reach in their lifetimes. They are not exactly economic men, but they are not terrible approximations. However, for humans at significantly higher or lower stages of human development, the EM depiction fails miserably.

Certainly, EM is far from being a self-actualized human, a mature fully integrated human who has realized a significant degree of his personal potential. And EM is still further from being an enlightened being. EM, as he is ordinarily understood, is not capable of empathy, significant intellectual or intuitive insight, transcendental oneness or other capabilities of a transverbal nature. Nor for that matter does EM have personal problems; he does not have psychological hangups or evil intentions. EM, after all, is simply a machine-like version of a person who has achieved a somewhat typical level of development in a modern capitalistic country. No wonder that at least some economists are disturbed by mainstream economists and their love affair with EM. More than anything else, it is the deficiencies of EM that have given rise to the different stripes of heterodox economics which depict human economic behavior in alternative ways. One way to conceptualize the formation of the different heterodox schools of thought is to think of them as groupings of economists who share common objections to EM and who share a common view regarding what aspects of man should be emphasized to rectify the problems associated with mainstream economists' use of EM.

HETERODOX ECONOMIC SCHOOLS OF THOUGHT

If Wilber's model of human development has provided us with a broad enough view of human nature, one which has helped us expose enough of the deficiencies of EM, it ought to serve well in developing a map of the different heterodox schools of thought in relationship to each other and in relationship to mainstream economics. The idea is to explain how, perhaps in overlapping ways, each heterodox school helps remedy some of the deficiencies of EM, helping us move toward a more fully human conception. It is beyond the scope of this chapter to provide a comprehensive map of all heterodox economic schools of thought.[3] The intention here is to be suggestive of some of the main differences for a number of the important schools of thought and some of their strands. Let's start with the 'old' institutionalists.

Homo Institutional Economicus

Homo institutional economicus or institutional economic man (IEM) is quite different from economic man. Recall that EM is self-interested, rational, unchanging and separate. To begin, IEM does not have a given, unchanging character like EM. IEM behaves in line with habits and rules, is strongly influenced by institutions, and learns from his social and technical experience (Hodgson, 1998). IEM's behavior evolves based on institutional reinforcements and the individual's capability for acquiring new conceptions, frameworks, skills, propensities and modes of cognition (pp. 175–9). Because IEM's character changes with changing societal influences, IEM, unlike EM, is not separate from his human and physical outer world. Further, IEM is not rational in the manner of EM; he is not a lightning calculator of utility, and he does not attempt to maximize utility (pp. 173, 187). Lastly, IEM may be self-interested, but what IEM wants is largely determined by institutions and societal evolution (Whalen, 1996: 92). With respect to the indicated characteristics, IEM remedies some of EM's deficiencies, and thus, represents an improvement. Of course, there are still many important aspects of human nature not included as part of IEM, notably the higher human potential represented by the higher half of Wilber's developmental stages.

Homo Social Economicus

Homo social economicus or social economic man (SEM) is distinctly different from EM. The distinction between SEM and the other heterodox men, however, is not as clear because social economics has within it a number of diverse strands of thought. Among the social economic strands of thought are institutionalism, Marxism/materialism, Post-Keynesianism economics, and humanistic economics (see Samuels, 1990; Elliott and Jensen, 1996). To simplify matters, none of these strands will be considered in this section. Institutionalism was examined above; humanistic economics will be considered below; and it is beyond the scope of this chapter to consider the other strands. The main strand (that is, the remaining strands) of social economics go by a variety of names such as solidarism, theological idealism, secular-normative, moral-scientific, social spiritual (see Samuels, 1990: 274; Nitsch, 1982: 34). For lack of a better term, let us call this main social economic strand 'social idealism' and proceed to compare its character, SEM, to EM.

SEM has two different sides: first, an individual being who is oriented to striving for individual economic betterment like EM, and second a social being who is oriented to belonging to communities and institutions (see O'Boyle, 1994: 292; Waters, 1988: 118). At times, SEM is as rational as EM, but more often SEM behaves non-rationally reflecting both his habits and biases (Waters, 1988: 118). The social part of SEM is other-centered, communal, dependent and culture-bound. SEM, as social being, combines a strong cooperative, collegial, and caring element along with competitiveness. SEM's character has a higher, idealistic side; he has a conscience, and he acts out of a concern for justice, human dignity, duty, loyalty and many other moral and ethical considerations. SEM is a sacred person with inalienable rights. Further, SEM has a need to develop his character in order to realize his higher personal potential. Religiously oriented social economists see SEM as having the capability of achieving perfection in union with God; whereas more secular social economists see the possibility of social perfection through 'a cooperative effort to promote the welfare of the entire community' (Samuels, 1990: 279). SEM, similar to IEM, has characteristics that remedy some of EM's deficiencies with regard to EM's self-interested, rational, separate, and unchanging aspects. SEM's character, more than IEM's, includes the higher aspects of human nature, especially the possibility of character growth, presumably to Wilber's highest personal stage. There is also at least a hint of the possibility of personal growth beyond that, that is, a hint of transcendent possibilities.

Homo Humanistic Economicus

Homo Humanistic Economicus or humanistic economic man (HEM) is the man of humanistic economics which is a strand of social economics. HEM largely shares the characteristics of SEM but, in addition, important elements of HEM's character are drawn explicitly from the writings of humanistic psychologists, notably Abraham Maslow. More than anyone else, Mark Lutz (see, for example, 1985 and with Ken Lux, 1988) has articulated the view that the character of HEM is not only far superior to EM but provides a more relevant and inclusive image of man than the other heterodox men.[4]

HEM is a holistic conception of man whose fundamental needs are represented on Maslow's hierarchy. Lutz emphasizes that HEM has a dual or divided self consisting of the lower self and the higher self. The lower self is the self reflecting the material needs on the low end of the hierarchy, and the higher self reflects the reasonable, ideal, and moral aspects of self. HEM experiences conflict between these two different parts of himself (Lutz and Lux, 1988: 17–18). At the same time, HEM's character has a strong tendency to develop, continually moving toward the higher self or toward self-actualization (or self-realization). As this development occurs, there is a progressive loss of self until with self-realization HEM reaches total selflessness (a transpersonal state) which involves transcendence of one's separateness from the outer world (Lutz, 1985: 105). Note that HEM's higher human nature includes, among other things, the capacity for altruism, self-reflection in line with deeply held values and truths, creativity, spontaneity, commitment and non-power seeking. The existence of this high human potential does not, however, imply its realization; HEM almost always fails to live up to this potential. Although Lutz explains HEM's tendency to develop toward the higher self, the specific stages of development are not indicated as they are in Wilber's model. From the perspective of Wilber, HEM constitutes a more complete view of human nature than does IEM or SEM in that HEM remedies more of EM's deficiencies than do the other heterodox men.

Homo Socio-Economicus

Homo Socio-Economicus or socio-economic man (S-EM), the man in socio-economics, is also distinctly different from EM. S-EM is not a rational decision maker. He chooses

> largely on the basis of emotions and value judgments, and only secondarily on the basis of logical-empirical considerations. Even when he is making decisions

> within the rather limited zone in which he wishes to draw only on logical/empirical considerations, his decisions are still *sub*-rational due to his rather limited intellectual capabilities. (Etzioni, 1988: xi)

S-EM is also different from EM, according to Etzioni (1988; see, for example, Chapter 1 and p. 253), in that his self is divided into two parts, the I and the We. The I side resembles EM in that this part is self-interested and oriented to obtaining pleasure. The We side is oriented to others, to family, community, society and the obligations and commitments, often moral in nature, that membership involves. S-EM's behavior is determined by these two parts which are often in conflict. Because the We side of S-EM is fundamentally different from the I side, these two aspects of self cannot be represented by a single utility measure (see also Coughlin, 1996; Etzioni, 1998). Note that S-EM is reflective in the sense that he reflects on his behavior in light of his moral values. But the socio-economic literature does not emphasize S-EM's development of character nor the possibility of his realizing his highest human potential, the superconsciousness stage of Wilber's Inward Arc.

Among the heterodox schools of thought not covered here are Austrian economics, behavioral economics, feminist economics, Marxist and/or radical political economics, post-Keynesian economics, and ecological economics. Each of these schools presumably embodies a conception of human nature that is at least slightly different from EM and different from the other heterodox schools.

THE HETERODOX SCHOOLS IN RELATION TO THE MAINSTREAM: TOWARD A MORE INTEGRATED HUMAN ECONOMICS

It is important to note that the heterodox schools of thought are for the most part not comprehensive, separate alternatives to mainstream economics. These schools generally accept many mainstream concepts and theories in certain areas and dissent in other areas. Each of the schools has exploited different opportunities (perceived weaknesses in mainstream economics), and thus, they have developed different types or styles of analysis, different philosophies and different views of human nature. Most of the schools, while rejecting pure EM, some types of analysis, and some of the philosophical baggage, are nevertheless eclectic about the rest, utilizing what works. Thus, many heterodox economists are not strictly anti-mainstream; they generally desire to go beyond the mainstream in order to develop an economics with better balance, a better conception of how the economy is integrated with society, and a better ability to understand the complex intangible issues of our day and age. As Fred Foldvary (1996: 20) views it:

> Economic theory is a giant pie, with each school part of the pie. Neoclassical economics is a major slice, but economic reality can be understood only if one takes in the whole pie. And although economists specialize in their research and adhere to various traditions, their basic education should devour the whole pie.

The whole economic pie might be considered as a map of economics on which we can plot mainstream economics and its relationship to the different heterodox schools along different dimensions. In my view, the most fundamental dimension is these schools' concept of human nature. As indicated above, some of these conceptions are complementary to each other and some are substitutes (or competing conceptions). Depending on the research problem, scholars may choose to use different conceptions at different times. Nevertheless, it seems important for economists to aspire to an integrated human economics that incorporates the best of all the different schools of economic thought with a fully human man, not limiting themselves to the conceptions of any of the particular schools. It should also be noted that the economics map has evolved over time. While early economic writers naturally combined their economic analysis with ethical and value judgments, the later attempt to make economics a pure science led to the development of a value free neoclassical economics that eschewed both value judgments and the noneconomic aspects of human nature. This latter development seems to have progressed as far as it is possible to go. Thus, there is now a great need for re-integrating economics with both moral considerations and the left-behind aspects of human nature.

PERSONAL CAPITAL, SOCIAL CAPITAL, HUMAN DEVELOPMENT, AND THE DIFFERENT ECONOMIC MEN

The new concept of personal capital can be used to gain further insight into the different economic men and how they contribute to the whole of economics. Personal capital is a kind of human capital that differs from standard human capital in that the human capacity involved is not the type developed by academic education or by the usual types of job related training. The personal capital capacities are fundamentally different from cognitive intelligence or intellectual knowledge. Personal capital relates to an individual's basic personal qualities and reflects the quality of an individual's psychological, physical, and spiritual functioning (Tomer, 1996: 626–7; Tomer, 1999: 13–14). A very important component of personal capital that has received much recent attention is the human capacity called emotional intelligence which Daniel Goleman (1995, 1998) has written about.

Recall Wilber's model of the entire range of human potential that explains how humans develop through predictable stages. The first half of human development, the Outward Arc, involves development from subconsciousness to self-consciousness, active movement out into the external world; the second half, the Inward Arc, involves development from self-consciousness to superconsciousness, a movement within. As people grow, moving along the human development path, becoming more mature, more capable, more conscious, a good part of this development can be characterized as personal capital formation. Presumably, there are some aspects of standard human capital formation involved, but the basic story is that people are becoming more capable due to psychological or emotional, physical and spiritual growth. Some of this occurs naturally, and some is the result of activities that one intentionally chooses in order to promote certain kinds of growth. As indicated earlier, for each society, there is a 'normal' or typical level of human development. If an adult has not yet reached this stage, social forces will push or nudge the individual to reach the normal level. And if the adult is striving for development beyond this level, many social inhibitions to this growth will be brought to bear.

To a certain extent, the different concepts of human nature in the different schools of economic thought reflect different stages of human development, and thus, differences in personal capital formation. Pure EM, for example, reflects a relatively low stage of development, certainly not all the way up the Outward Arc, as EM is preoccupied entirely with economic or material concerns. In general, the different heterodox men, who, in addition to economic motivation, are motivated in a variety of noneconomic ways, reflect higher stages of human development. Of the different heterodox men, the characteristics of humanistic economic man, in my judgment, are associated with the highest level of development. Naturally, it makes sense to utilize in one's economic research a concept of human nature mirroring a high stage of development.

As Maslow (1971: 315–16) has suggested, human development in the highest stages is somewhat timid. Such development is easily discouraged if societies do not create conducive conditions for it. In other words, the highest kinds of personal capital formation require societal investment in appropriate social capital. Without this, only a few intrepid searchers will reach the highest levels of human development. This perspective is suggestive with respect to the path that economic development should ideally take. Economic development is ordinarily conceived of as a process involving greater and greater tangible capital formation in order to produce more and more goods and services. Perhaps an important part of what economic development should include is personal and social capital formation that enables not only greater material well-being but greater nonmaterial well-being associated with the progress of people to higher stages of human development. When economists only use EM, a man focused only on material concerns, it becomes impossible to conceive of economic development as involving anything more than tangible considerations. Thus, an important argument for using a broader conception of man along with our economic inquiries is that it enables us to conceive of economic development as involving human growth not just material growth.

CONCLUSION

The concept of human nature at the heart of mainstream economics is quite different from the conceptions of the different heterodox economic schools. When viewed in light of a broad model of human development such as that of Ken Wilber, the deficiencies of EM are glaring. Each of the men at the heart of institutional economics, social economics, humanistic economics, and socio-economics are more realistic, that is, closer to true human nature, than EM, partly because each embodies noneconomic motivations and influences. None of the heterodox men, however, are as fully human as Wilber's model.

Carefully comparing the characteristics of each of the economic men is a useful exercise in that it allows us to map the different schools of thought with respect to each other on the most fundamental dimension. Armed with these comparisons, scholars would be able to choose the particular concept of man that best matches their type of inquiry. Further, using a fully human concept of man directs scholars' attention to the idea that economic development is not entirely a material process; it is partly a human process. And intangible capital formation is an important part of that process.

NOTES

1. Although it may violate some people's view of the current standards of political correctness, this chapter will refer to the human in economic thought as a man following a long standing tradition. Thus, the masculine pronoun will be used throughout. It should be remembered that this chapter concerns the nature of mankind (both men and women) and is not concerned with male and female differences.

2. One suspects that the EM concept would find the greatest acceptance in the kind of capitalistic societies in which economic activity had come to be very much separate and differentiated from other kinds of activity.
3. See Foldvary (1996), for comparisons of major heterodox schools of thought and page 1 for a definition of schools of thought.
4. Gerald Alonzo Smith (1996: 115) calls the man of humanistic economics *homo sapiens*, a man who 'strives for that excellence of being which emerges from the deepest and truest part of oneself.'

REFERENCES

Coughlin, Richard M. (1996), 'Whose morality? Which community? What interests?: socio-economic and communitarian perspectives,' *Journal of Socio-Economics*, **25**(2), 135–55.

Elliott, John E. and Hans E. Jensen (1996), 'Can neoclassical economics become social economics,' *Forum for Social Economics*, **26**(1), 15–37.

Etzioni, Amitai (1988), *The Moral Dimension: Toward a New Economics*, New York: Free Press.

Etzioni, Amitai (1998), 'The methodology of socio-economics,' *Journal of Socio-Economics*, **27**(5), 539–49.

Foldvary, Fred E. (ed.) (1996), *Beyond Neoclassical Economics: Heterodox Approaches to Economic Theory*, Cheltenham, UK and Brookfield, US: Edward Elgar.

Goleman, Daniel (1995), *Emotional Intelligence*, New York: Bantam Books.

Goleman, Daniel (1998), *Working with Emotional Intelligence*, New York: Bantam Books.

Hodgson, Geoffrey M. (1998), 'The approach of institutional economics,' *Journal of Economic Literature*, **36**(1), 166–92.

Lutz, Mark A. (1985), 'Beyond Economic Man: humanistic economics,' in Peter Koslowski (ed.) *Economics and Philosophy*, Tubingen: J.C.B. Mohr.

Lutz, Mark A. and Kenneth Lux (1988), *Humanistic Economics: the New Challenge*, New York: Bootstrap Press.

Maslow, Abraham H. (1971), *The Farther Reaches of Human Nature*, New York: Penguin.

Nitsch, Thomas O. (1982), 'Economic man, socio-economic man and *Homo-economicus Humanus*,' *International Journal of Social Economics*, **9**(6–7), 20–49.

O'Boyle, Edward J. (1994), '*Homo Socio-Economicus*: foundational to social economics and the social economy,' *Review of Social Economy*, **52**(3), 286–313.

Samuels, Warren J. (1990), 'Four strands of social economics: a comparative interpretation,' in Mark A. Lutz (ed.) *Social Economics: Retrospect and Prospect*, Boston, MA: Kluwer Academic.

Schwartz, Tony (1995), *What Really Matters: Searching for Wisdom in America*, New York: Bantam.

Smith, Gerald Alonzo (1996), 'Humanist economics: from *Homo Economicus* to *Homo Sapiens*,' in Fred E. Foldvary (ed.) *Beyond Neoclassical Economics: Heterodox Approaches to Economic Theory*, Cheltenham, UK and Brookfield, US: Edward Elgar.

Tomer, John F. (1996), 'Good habits and bad habits: a new age socio-economic model of preference formation,' *Journal of Socio-Economics*, **25**(6), 619–38.

Tomer, John F. (2003), 'Personal capital and emotional intelligence: an increasingly important intangible source of economic growth,' *Eastern Economic Journal*, **29**(3) (Summer), 453–70.
Viner, Jacob (1991), 'The "Economic Man" or the place of economic self-interest in a "good society"' in Douglas A. Irwin (ed.) *Jacob Viner: Essays on the Intellectual History of Economics*, Princeton, NJ: Princeton University Press.
Waters, William R. (1988), 'Social economics: a solidarist perspective,' *Review of Social Economy*, **46**(2), 113–43.
Whalen, Charles J. (1996), 'The institutional approach to political economy,' in Fred E. Foldvary (ed.) *Beyond Neoclassical Economics: Heterodox Approaches to Economic Theory*, Cheltenham, UK and Brookfield, US: Edward Elgar.
Wilber, Ken (1996a), *The Atman Project: A Transpersonal View of Human Development*, Wheaton, IL: Quest Books.
Wilber Ken (1996b), *A Brief History of Everything*, Boston, MA: Shambhala.

PART V

Summing up

15. Conclusion: intangible capital and the human potential of the socio-economy

INTRODUCTION

Intangible capital, you may recall from Chapter 2, includes all the intangible, long-lived human capacities that are embodied in individuals as well as those embodied in human relationships. This includes many capabilities that most economists have excluded from the domain of capital, but it excludes certain intangibles, like most of intellectual capital, which are not embodied in humans. This definition makes sense because it is consistent with the core meaning of the concept of capital as well as with the definitions of different types of IC such as standard human capital and social capital.

This IC definition, the theoretical explanations regarding the contributions of IC, and the relevant empirical findings in this book constitute a broad framework for thinking about IC and its importance. This framework in effect also provides an agenda for further research, indicating what we know about IC as well as the gaps in our knowledge. Many of the preceding chapters have provided examples of the importance of different types of IC, especially personal capital and social capital. But there is much that remains unexplored. In particular, there is a clear need for creative empirical research that would enable much greater understanding of the economic role of these intangible human capacities, especially the more intangible ones.

INTANGIBLE CAPITAL AND THE ECONOMY'S POTENTIAL

In the process of doing research focused on IC, one cannot help but gain an appreciation of the human quality of the economy. As this book has emphasized, the many different types of IC are extremely important for the functioning and growth of any economy. It follows that the potential of a national economy is determined in good part by the investments in individual and collective human qualities that its citizens make. Economists' early focus on the tangible material aspect of economic growth and development along with economists' emphasis on being rigorously scientific in a positivistic fashion have no doubt led to their neglect of the intangible human aspect of the economy. The IC concept is important because it helps remedy this neglect by affording us a way to put the human element back into economics. Research on IC helps us understand that economic progress, movement toward the economy's potential, is closely linked to efforts to improve our human capacities (investment in IC). The different chapters of this book have allowed us a variety of glimpses of the human quality and true potential of our economies. In the following, some of the book's specific topics are viewed through the lens of two questions: How do these different analyses help us understand the economy's potential? What role can government play to help realize that potential?

The explanations and empirical findings summarized in Chapter 3 lend strong support to the thesis that IC, notably its more intangible components, have made an important contribution to long-run productivity growth and growth of national output. There is reason to believe that these intangible factors will be even more important contributors to future economic growth in many nations, not just nations with advanced industrial economies. If this is so, these nations presumably will want to monitor the growth of the important types of intangible human capacity to determine whether the amount and type of investment in IC in their countries is keeping pace with the economic and societal need for it. If investment in IC is found to be deficient, governmental action to deal with this might be warranted. Government policy makers might be concerned, for example, about whether the nation's future workforce will have enough people with the creativeness and motivation necessary to continue the nation's innovativeness and competitiveness in high technology industries. More generally, unless there is sufficient investment in these and similar intangible human capabilities, the nation's socioeconomic potential will not be realized. Alternatively, reflecting Chapters 8, 10 and 11, others may be concerned less about the economy's potential production of goods and services and more about whether the economy's functioning will enable people to experience their genuine well-being potential, including especially their experience of the higher pleasures of life. And along with this, it would be good to know whether we are gaining the capacity to make more truly rational decisions, raising our ability to make choices that will enable us to produce and consume not just what we desire at this moment but what is really best for us.

From the arguments and findings presented in Chapter 4, it is clear why businesses' investments in high performance work systems, involving innovative organizational capital (or organizational social capital) formation, can and often does lead to superior economic and financial performance. Recall that a key reason for these involvement-oriented organizations' high performance relative to control-oriented organizations is that the former are able to elicit deep owner motivation from its members which brings out workers' genuine enthusiasm and inspiration in a way that the agent motivation of control-oriented organizations cannot match. In businesses benefiting from investment in HPWS, productive capacity is higher because of the particular employer-employee relationships that have been developed in these organizations. Besides this higher productivity, there is reason to believe that the workers in these organizations will experience higher well-being (relative to workers in control-oriented organizations) as they are able to realize more of their higher functionings (*a la* Sen), or greater self-actualization (*a la* Maslow). In sum, these investments in organizational capital, along with possibly some complementary investments in individuals in the form of personal capital and hybrid social capital, add to the economy's productive capacity as well as adding to the society's well-being, and presumably its rationality. Such innovative organizational capital investments are clearly a key ingredient if an economy is to reach its potential.

Personal capital, a type of noncognitive human capital in individuals, is an increasingly important intangible source of economic growth as explained in Chapter 6. PC involves human qualities or competencies such as those subsumed under the rubric of emotional intelligence, a topic developed extensively by psychologist Daniel Goleman (see, for example, 1995, 1998; and Goleman *et al.*, 2002). Emotional intelligence consists of a variety of personal and social competencies or 'skills' that some people have 'naturally' but others develop through effort. Goleman's many examples illustrate that unless people have the competencies crucial for their particular work they will not be able to perform successfully. Therefore, if businesses encourage workers' investments in key types of PC, these efforts can be expected to pay off in higher productivity. It should be noted that many of these competencies are very valuable outside the workplace. When people develop empathy and improve their social skills, trustworthiness, self-control, self-confidence, emotional awareness, and so on, these allow life to go easier, thereby improving well-being (and perhaps rationality) on the home front. Because of the importance of these competencies for economic growth and well-being, it is important for a nation to monitor its PC competencies. A significant deficiency in certain key competencies could have serious adverse consequences for a nation. If this were to happen, it would make sense for government to take remedial action, not only to avoid adversity but in order that the economy can realize its potential.

Besides its role with respect to economic growth and productivity, PC, along with social capital, is a key soft factor essential for the functioning of a socio-economic system. As indicated in Chapter 7, a nation making a transition from one type of system to another, for example, from socialism to capitalism, must disinvest in the competencies of the old system and invest in the competencies functional for the new one. These 'investment' decisions may be made in a stressful context, one filled with uncertainty, and thus, the process is likely to be slow and uneven, which may hold back transition progress. Therefore, it makes sense for the national government involved to take the necessary IC investment and disinvestment into account when crafting its transition strategy. In contrast to these dramatic transition situations such as occurred in Eastern Europe during the 1990s, any socio-economic system generally experiences at least slow transformation as its technology, organizations, and industrial structure change and reform over time. This means that its PC and social capital must evolve to accommodate the changing needs of the system. Thus, it might be useful for a nation to anticipate its economic evolution, thereby anticipating the kinds of soft or IC investment that will be required in the years ahead. In the absence of such timely changes in IC investment, the functioning of the system can be expected to suffer, hampering its economic growth and the well-being of its citizens. Ideally, an appropriate amount and type of IC investment can be facilitated allowing the socio-economic system to achieve its potential.

Investment in IC, particularly investment in personal, social and consumption capital, is an important determinant of whether a person is likely to become addicted, that is, fully involved in an addictive pattern of behavior, as Chapter 9 explains. At the heart of the socio-economic model of addictive behavior is the idea that the people who become addicted have significant imbalances impairing their ability to obtain real satisfaction and rewards from life's activities. First, such imbalances are more likely to occur when a person's brain physiology is not functioning well and when the brain's amygdala and prefrontal lobes are not working in a complementary fashion. These are PC factors. Second, if a person's social relationships (social capital) are strong and positive, this has the tendency to lessen a person's imbalances. The third IC factor is the magnitude of a person's consumption capital, a person's capacity to use and appreciate a particular addictive good. The greater a person's consumption capital endowment the greater is his or her likelihood of becoming or remaining addicted. There are other factors in the model such as the stressfulness of the person's current life situation and the availability, affordability and attractiveness of the addictive good. However, the amount and type of a person's IC is a key to explaining addiction. This suggests that encouraging the right types of

IC investment is likely to have a high payoff insofar as it lowers addictive behavior, which in turn leads to more productive workers, higher well-being, and greater rationality. Hopefully, the right type of investment and disinvestment in IC will be forthcoming, and the society can come close to its potential with regard to attaining a very low level of addictive behavior.

As Chapter 9 indicated, an individual's PC deficiency is probably the key underlying causative factor in producing the kind of imbalance that leads to addiction along with its associated irrational decision making. But with respect to rationality, there is a more general problem related to a person's PC deficiency. As explained in Chapters 10 and 11, truly rational decision making occurs when people make decisions in line with their true preferences. That is, truly rational decision making occurs when people choose what is really good for themselves, not merely what they desire at the moment (actual preferences). Generally speaking, people's actual preferences diverge substantially from their true preferences, thus, their decision making frequently diverges from being truly rational. This divergence of actual and true preferences reflects a deficiency of PC. Unless people make the effort to establish better habits, better behavior patterns (investment in PC), ones more in line with their true preference, their PC qualities will be lacking. If people do make these beneficial PC investments, they are likely to pay off handsomely in higher well-being owing to the enhanced true rationality in people's decision making. Ideally, these kind of IC investments will be made, thereby allowing the socio-economy to realize its potential in this respect.

An important implication of this book's analyses is that an economy's potential derives as much from its intangible capital as from its tangible capital and technology. Note that there are very many types of IC, more types certainly than one can readily keep track of. Hopefully, the schema and table in Chapter 2 should enable readers to appreciate the major categories of IC and their relation to each other. With regard to the source of an economy's intangible potential, let's review some of the most important examples. One source of that potential is businesses' investment in creating good employer-employee relationships, for example where high performance work systems have been installed, an investment in organizational capital. A second source is investment in noncognitive human capital, especially personal capital, which can raise business or personal potential by, say, improving the emotional and social competencies of people. A third source is investment in the personal and social capital crucial to the functioning of socio-economic systems, whether these are rapidly transitioning or slowly evolving. Another source is people's investment in personal and social capital that can contribute (inversely) to people's state of imbalance, and thereby to their likelihood of addiction (a negative potential). The upshot is that the economy's positive potential is determined to a great degree by its accumulation of many types of IC.

INTANGIBLE CAPITAL AND MAINSTREAM ECONOMICS

Although there are signs of positive change, it still seems fair to say that the economic mainstream tends to focus on the tangible aspects of the economy to the exclusion of intangible considerations. Given this biased perspective, it would not be surprising for mainstream economists to have a biased view of what economic progress implies and to diagnose problems and recommend solutions in ways that overemphasize the tangible aspects. This, presumably, means that mainstream economic researchers will be insufficiently sensitive to the human quality of the economy, particularly to the subtle intangibles, which can be very important for understanding the performance of the economy. Economists could take a significant step in the direction of overcoming this bias toward the tangible side by incorporating IC into their models and analyses.

THE IDEAL SOCIO-ECONOMY

If the IC concept were a fully accepted part of the thinking and models of economists, their conception of the ideal socio-economy would no doubt be different. The ideal socio-economy presumably would be one with many strong people connections and many strong noncognitive human capacities which would be a complement to the economy's cognitive knowledge/know-how, technology, and tangible capital. The ideal socio-economy arguably would be one in which positive mental attitudes prevailed, along with a great deal of practical and not-so-practical wisdom. In the ideal economy, addictions, and other negative attachments would be extinguished. In the ideal economy, people might be less concerned about accumulating tangible wealth and more concerned about gaining qualities, skills, and capacities that not only enable them to be productive in the usual economic sense but enable them to attain high genuine well-being by virtue of their ability to make truly rational decisions Conceivably, the ideal socio-economy would afford not only opportunities for people to be productive, but opportunities for all to enjoy harmonious, ultimately satisfying lives. In the ideal socio-economy, people would be concerned not just about the growth of their lower functionings but their higher ones. They would aspire to live the flourishing life, the meaningful life, the examined life, the purposeful life, even the spiritual life. Ideally, the structure, or infrastructure, of the ideal socio-economy would be designed to facilitate these aspirations, especially facilitating the necessary IC accumulation.

REFERENCES

Goleman, Daniel (1995), *Emotional Intelligence*, New York: Bantam Books.
Goleman, Daniel (1998), *Working with Emotional Intelligence*, New York: Bantam Books.
Goleman, Daniel, Richard Boyatzis, and Annie McKee (2002), *Primal Leadership: Learning to Lead with Emotional Intelligence*, Boston, MA: Harvard Business School Press.

Index